The
BULB EXPERT

Dr. D.G.Hessayon

CUMBRIA HERITAGE SERVICES
LIBRARIES
This book is due to be returned on or before the last date above. It
may be renewed by personal application, post or telephone, if not in
demand.

C.L.18

COUNTY COUNCIL

EXPERT BOOKS

Contents

		page
CHAPTER 1	**INTRODUCTION**	3–11
	Bulb types	4–5
	History of bulbs	6–7
	Buying & handling	8–9
	Pronouncing dictionary	10–11
CHAPTER 2	**BULBS A–Z**	12–99
	Introduction	12
	Varieties	13–99
CHAPTER 3	**GROWING BULBS**	100–104
	Planting	100–101
	Feeding	102
	After flowering	102
	Watering	102
	Winter protection	102
	Staking	102
	Storage	102
	Increasing your stock	103–104
CHAPTER 4	**USING BULBS**	105–114
	Bulbs in beds & borders	106–107
	Naturalising bulbs	108
	Bulbs in containers	109
	Bulbs in the rockery	110
	Bulbs in the greenhouse	111
	Bulbs in the home	112–113
	Bulbs as cut flowers	114
CHAPTER 5	**FLOWERS ALL YEAR ROUND**	115–116
CHAPTER 6	**BULB TROUBLES**	117–120
CHAPTER 7	**GLOSSARY**	121–124
CHAPTER 8	**INDEX**	125–128
	Acknowledgements	128

Printed and bound in Great Britain by Jarrold & So

ISBN 0 903505 42 8

CHAPTER 1

INTRODUCTION

The close association of human beings with bulbs dates back to prehistoric times, but the story continues to unfold. Not many years ago the main purpose for buying bulbs was to fill flower beds or to edge borders, but nowadays nearly half of the bulbs we buy are planted in containers. These bulbs used to be bought loose from garden shops, High St. stores etc or in bags or sacks from mail order companies and nurseries — now most popular small bulbs are sold in colourful and informative prepacks.

So the Bulb Story continues to evolve, but the basic buying pattern has remained unchanged throughout this century. The main season for purchasing and planting remains the autumn months and three-quarters of all the bulbs we buy are spring-flowering ones. Gladioli, Dahlias and Lilies are bought by many later in the year for summer display, but the bulb scene is dominated by the big four — Narcissus, Tulip, Crocus and Hyacinth.

It seems surprising that such a wide and diverse group of plants should be dominated by just four genera — imagine if half our garden shrubs or half our herbaceous border plants were restricted to just four types! On reflection it is perhaps not so surprising. Crocuses with Snowdrops are the main heralds which tell us that spring is on the way, and no other plants provide such a splash of colour as the many varieties of Tulips and Narcissi on show during April and May.

Spring colour, then, is one of the reasons for this universal popularity, and so is their ease of cultivation — hardly anything can go wrong provided the soil is not waterlogged. All you have to do is dig a hole which is two or three times deeper than the bulb and then replace the soil after planting — there is nothing more to do until the floral display is over. No watering to worry about, no sap-sucking pests to worry about — just a great spring show.

Still, it isn't *quite* as simple as that. The Daffodil or Tulip bulb you have bought will have its flowering quality already determined, and if it is healthy and sufficiently large then the skill of the gardener will have little effect.

What happens in future years, however, does depend on following the rules outlined in Chapter 3. With proper care and cultivation these bulbs will improve and multiply over the years — with poor handling the stock may quite rapidly deteriorate.

The main purpose of this book is to reveal just how many different bulbs are available apart from the big four. Plants to bloom at any season of the year, plants as small as a mouse or as tall as a horse, plants for sandy soils and boggy patches, for beds, borders, grassland, pots, woodland, windowsills, cold greenhouses and heated conservatories. Some bulbs are tricky, but many of the Cinderella varieties are colourful and easy to grow — they are just waiting to be discovered.

The word *bulb* has been used several times on this page and it appears on the cover of this book, but it has no botanical significance. It is used to cover all the *bulbous plants* — those species of the plant world which produce fleshy storage organs. Included here are the true bulbs (see page 4) as well as corms, tubers, rhizomes and tuberous roots which can be purchased in the dormant state for planting. The purpose of this store of moisture and nutrients is to tide the plant over its period of natural dormancy when the soil is dry or cold. This resting period may be in winter or summer, depending on the bulb in question.

On the following pages you will find the background to hundreds of different species and how to care for them, and it is necessary once again to plead for you to be a little more adventurous. A few bulbs are for the specialist and rather more need indoor protection, but even the smallest plot can have Puschkinia, Eranthis, Erythronium, Ipheion, Hardy Cyclamen and Leucojum alongside the Crocuses and Narcissi in the spring garden. Summer offers even more opportunities to try something different. The Lily varieties are rightly popular, but for something different you can try St. Bernard's Lily, Spider Lily or the Delicate Lily. There is no need to stick to bowls of Hyacinth, Daffodil, Crocus and the giant Hippeastrum as your indoor bulbs — Chapter 2 describes scores of varieties which will grow in your conservatory or living room.

Look at the pictures in the A–Z guide, read the descriptions carefully and get to know a little more about this still largely-unexplored region of the plant world.

BULB TYPES

True Bulb

Nearly half the genera listed in the A–Z guide are true bulbs. The Onion represents the basic structure of this type of bulbous plant. The pear-shaped or oval bulb is a complete plant in miniature — at the heart of the bulb is the embryonic flower surrounded by the undeveloped shoot, and the body of the bulb is made up of a series of fleshy scales. These scales are modified leaves held together by the basal plate at the bottom — the scales contain the nutrients which sustain the plant during the dormant period and the first stages of growth. With most true bulbs the scales are closely packed together (e.g Hyacinth) but with some types such as the Lily they are loose and swollen. Most popular bulbs have a papery skin — the purpose of this tunic is to protect the tissues within. Some true bulbs such as the Lily do not have a tunic and are therefore easily damaged by rough handling. Cardiocrinum dies after flowering but other bulbs are perennial — reproduction is by means of offsets (bulblets).

Examples: Muscari, Tulipa, Narcissus, Lilium, Allium.

Corm

Some corms look like true bulbs. Many but not all of these rounded or flattened bulbous plants have a protective smooth or fibrous tunic, and there is the true bulb pattern of a central growing point or two at the top and a basal plate from which the roots arise at the bottom. The stucture of a corm, however, is fundamentally different. The nutrient-holding body is a stem base and not a series of scales, and the tunic is made up of the dry leaf bases from the previous season. Another important difference is that a corm lasts just one year. When active growth is underway the food store is depleted and the corm starts to shrivel. At the same time one or more new corms start to develop on top or at the sides of the old one. These new corms form next year's planting material and will flower during the season. A few corms such as Gladioli form small cormlets around the edge — these tiny corms take 2–3 years before they reach the flowering stage.

Examples: Crocus, Gladiolus, Freesia, Ixia, Acidanthera.

Tuber

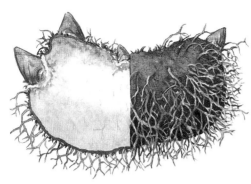

A tuber is a swollen stem which is borne underground like a corm, but there the similarity ends. A tuber does not have a basal plate nor is there a protective fibrous covering. Furthermore there is no neat organisation of the growing points — a Potato has the classic arrangement of a tuber. The buds or eyes are scattered over the surface and so stems appear from the sides as well as the top of the structure. There is no standard shape, but they are usually squat and knobbly. Most types of tuber get bigger as the plant grows but others diminish in size.

Examples: Cyclamen, Gloriosa, Anemone, Eranthis, Begonia.

Rhizome

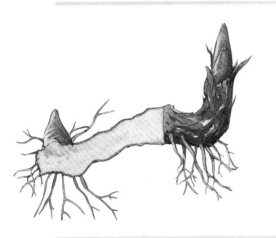

The rhizome, corm and tuber are all bulbous types which are thickened stems filled with nutrients to support the growing plant. Rhizomes differ from the others by growing horizontally and spreading outwards either partly or completely below the soil surface. The main growing point is at the tip of the rhizome, but other buds are formed along the upper surface and along the sides. Roots develop from buds on the underside of the rhizome. Most rhizomes are easy to propagate as the long and branching stem can be cut into segments for planting — make sure each piece has roots and at least one bud.

Examples: Convallaria, Canna, Achimenes, Zantedeschia, Agapanthus.

Tuberous Root

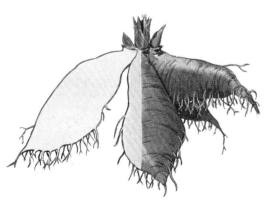

This bulbous type differs from all the others by being a swollen root rather than a swollen stem or a collection of scale leaves. There are several alternative names — root tuber, tuber-like root etc. Dahlia is a typical example and is the best known tuberous root. The swollen storage organs are borne as a cluster from the crown, which is the base of the old stems. These modified roots provide stored nutrients to the plant — during growth fibrous roots are produced to absorb water and nutrients from the soil. These bulbous plants can be propagated by cutting off individual storage roots with a bud- (or eye-) bearing section at the top.

Examples: Dahlia, Eremurus, Clivia, Alstroemeria, Ranunculus.

Pseudobulb

The pseudobulb is a specialised storage organ which is produced by many Orchids. It is a thickened stem base and unlike the other bulbous types on this page the pseudobulb is both green and above ground. It may be oval, cylindrical or globular and from it arise both leaves and flower stalk.

Examples: Bletilla, Pleione.

HISTORY OF BULBS

Articles on the history of bulbs nearly always dwell at length on the Tulipmania which gripped Holland in the 17th century. This chapter is indeed a fascinating one, but it is only one part of a story which began much, much earlier.

The use of bulbous plants is probably as old as mankind itself. From the dawn of human history fleshy roots have been used as food, but we have no idea which types were used. From our more recent past we do know that Potatoes have been cultivated in S. America for thousands of years, the Ancient Egyptians grew Onions and the Cretans exported large quantities of Saffron derived from Crocus sativus.

With the birth of civilisation people began to look on some bulbous plants as objects of religious symbolism and not just as a source of food. Revered beyond all others was the Lily. Lilies were painted on the walls of Cretan palaces over 3,000 years ago and to the Greeks it was the symbol of purity, supposedly arising from the milk which fed the infant Hercules. This association with purity passed into Christianity when the Lily became the flower of the Virgin Mary. The fleur-de-lis symbol was originally based on the flower of the Iris, and appeared in Indian and Egyptian religious paintings before being adopted as the emblem of the French kings from the 5th century onwards.

Bulbs have thus served as food, religious symbols and signs of royal power from early times, but they have also been admired for the beauty of their blooms from the dawn of civilisation. The list of countries which have grown bulbs for decoration from before the Christian era is a long one — Greece, Egypt, India, China, Korea etc. Even longer is the list of bulbs we know to have been used in these countries — Lily, Crocus, Cyclamen, Narcissus, Scilla, Gladiolus, Muscari, Ranunculus, Allium, Iris and Hyacinth.

The Tulip came quite late to the Western World. The Austrian Ambassador to Turkey, Ogier Ghislain de Busbecq, saw these plants in Adrianople and took some bulbs to the Imperial Gardens in Vienna in 1544. He certainly didn't 'discover' the Tulip — these bulbs were highly prized in the Ottoman Empire and there were many named varieties at that time. Busbecq bought his Tulips, which he said "cost me not a little" but this new plant did not at first create a greal deal of interest in Europe. The first Tulips did not arrive in Britain until 1577 and it was not until Carolus Clusius left his job at the Viennese Imperial Gardens in 1593 to become Professor of Botany at Leiden in Holland that the Tulip story really began. He brought with him his stock of bulbs, and these created much excitement.

It was the bizarre or 'broken' Tulip with its feathered, flamed or garishly streaked blooms which created so much interest. Nobody can give the exact date when the Tulip caught the imagination or when the craze to own one of these unusual varieties began. We do know that prices rocketed in France between 1610 and 1620, but it was in Holland in 1634 that Tulipmania broke out.

Possessions of all sorts were sold to buy bulbs — a rare type could cost the price of a farm, house or coach and horses. Of course there were not enough bulbs to go round and so Tulipmania became a paper speculation. Promissory notes were sold from one investor to another and then it happened. In 1647 the Dutch Government decreed that all Tulip Notes had to be honoured with bulbs and so the market crashed. Tulipmania was over.

Ogier Ghislain de Busbecq was the Austrian Emperor's Ambassador to Suleiman the Magnificent in the 16th century. He sent seeds and bulbs of the Tulip back to Vienna — a plant new to the European scene. The name he gave was an error — he based it on the word for turban rather than using its true Turkish name (lalé). Busbecq also introduced the Crown Imperial

Although other countries had not been caught up in this madness the value of Tulips remained high. They were much admired in Britain and remained expensive until the 19th century. As described below they then came to be classed as Mechanic's Flowers fit only for "shopkeepers and workers".

Holland has long been regarded as the world's leading bulb nation, but the original source of our main types was the Ottoman Empire and not Holland. Before Tulipmania began there were hundreds of flower shops selling bulbs in Constantinople. The Hyacinth came to Western Europe from Turkey a few years before the Tulip, and Clusius took some with him when he moved from Vienna to Leiden in 1593. The Ranunculus, Crown Imperial and Anemone were also introductions from the Ottoman Empire, but the 18th century French writer Tournefort was exaggerating when he wrote that "Except for Pinks and Carnations we have no fine flowers but what originally came from the Levant." The Narcissus is a native of Western Europe and has been grown in cottage gardens since the Middle Ages, and the Snowdrop came to Britain with the Romans.

In the 17th and 18th centuries several bulbs were classed as Florist Flowers — Tulip, Anemone, Ranunculus and Hyacinth. These were colourful plants which could be grown for hybridising, exhibiting etc. Things changed with the Industrial Revolution. Farm labourers left the flowers and crops of the countryside to work in the mills and mines, but they did not forget their own roots.

Gardening on the grand scale was of course impossible and so were the exotic plants being introduced into the country in the 19th century. So they turned to the old favourites — the Florist Flowers. The Tulip became a working class plant when the price of bulbs fell in Victorian times. These were the flowers for the labourer, miner and the mill-hand, and a guide printed in 1824 warned the estate gardener against plants which had "degenerated" in such a way.

Fortunately this stupid class distinction among plants was swept away with the arrival of the 20th century. Bulbs were for everyone and none were social outcasts. There were cheap ones as well as expensive ones — the new 'King Alfred' Daffodil in 1900 cost the equivalent of a month's salary for a single bulb. Plant hunters had brought all sorts of exciting new genera and species from many parts of the globe — the showy Gladioli from S. Africa, Lilium regale from China and the Tuberous Begonias from S. America and S. Africa. At the same time the plant hybridists were producing new varieties and they continue to do so.

The demand for bulbs continues to increase each year and to satisfy this demand the commercial growers steadily enlarge the acreage devoted to bulb production. It is no surprise that Holland is the world's largest producer of bulbs, but it is perhaps surprising that Britain comes second. Next comes the U.S followed by Japan. Each year the catalogues include exciting new ones for us to try. The Bulb Story continues...

The south west of England has long been an important area for the commercial production of Narcissi for the bulb and cut flower trades. This 1910 illustration shows early blooms being gathered in the Scilly Isles

BUYING & HANDLING

There are some bulbs which are generally bought as leafy plants — at the garden centre you will find examples such as Achimenes, Clivia, Crocosmia and Cyclamen. Most of the ones in this book, however, are bought as dormant tubers, rhizomes, true bulbs etc and choosing the right material is vital. The correct choice involves two quite separate aspects. Firstly, the species or variety must be right for the conditions and secondly the bulbs themselves must be capable of giving you the display you want. In general you get what you pay for — there are times when you may be offered rubbish by a garden centre or you may obtain good quality material as a bargain offer. Despite the exceptions the general rule really does apply — you get what you pay for.

The first step is to make sure that the bulbs are the right size. For large blooms in the first season make sure that true bulbs and tubers are listed as 'top size' in the catalogue or on the garden centre label. With corms look for maximum height and not just circumference. Rhizomes are rather more difficult to judge — firm medium-sized specimens will often do better than over-large corky ones.

With the popular bulbs 'big is best' is a good rule, but such material is also the most expensive. Buy this grade for containers, beds and borders, but do consider the more economical second-size bulbs if you have a large area of grassland or woodland in which you wish to naturalise the plants. Another exception is the choice of Hyacinths for the garden. Top-size bulbs are right for indoors but second-size or 'bedding' Hyacinths are less likely to topple when grown outdoors.

A second rule is to buy bulbs as early in the planting season as possible. At this time the largest selection will be available and at the garden centre they will not have been damaged by constant handling. This rule is even more important in shops, supermarkets etc where warm conditions can lead to deterioration if the bulbs are stored for a long time.

Finally, plant as soon as possible. Open the package and spread out the bulbs in a tray. With bulbs which have a protective outer tunic place the tray in a cool place — with soft-skinned bulbous plants and plants with fleshy roots cover with moist peat before placing in a cool room.

What to look for

Always examine loose bulbs before you buy — reject any rogue ones which may have been accidentally introduced from another box. Look for the bad signs — a poor quality bulb will never produce a good quality plant. This examination is especially important with 'bargain' offers. Low-priced stock is quite acceptable if it is good-quality undersized material for growing on to produce flowers in the second season, but it is not acceptable if it is end-of-season material which is soft, diseased or has started into active growth.

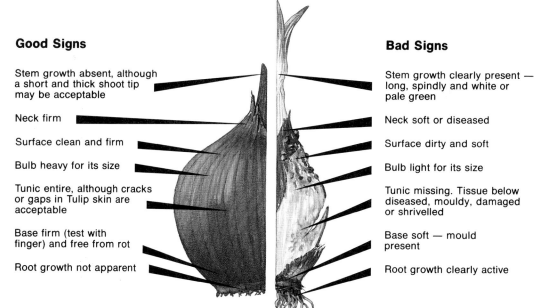

Good Signs

Stem growth absent, although a short and thick shoot tip may be acceptable

Neck firm

Surface clean and firm

Bulb heavy for its size

Tunic entire, although cracks or gaps in Tulip skin are acceptable

Base firm (test with finger) and free from rot

Root growth not apparent

Bad Signs

Stem growth clearly present — long, spindly and white or pale green

Neck soft or diseased

Surface dirty and soft

Bulb light for its size

Tunic missing. Tissue below diseased, mouldy, damaged or shrivelled

Base soft — mould present

Root growth clearly active

Where to buy

GARDEN CENTRE
An excellent place to buy the popular bulbs, either loose or in packs. Your purchase is available for immediate planting and bulbs sold loose can be inspected. Advice is generally available and justifiable complaints will be taken seriously. Many beautiful photographs will be on view but do not buy bulbs you don't know on impulse — check first that they are right for you.

HIGH ST. SHOP
You will find bulbs on offer in garden shops, department stores, supermarkets, greengrocers, florists, market stalls etc at the start of the planting season. That is the time to buy — some bulbs will deteriorate in 10–14 days if the environment is warm. Convenience is the great advantage — you can pick up bulbs with your regular shopping, but choice is often limited.

GENERAL MAIL ORDER
The autumn and spring catalogues of the major plant mail order suppliers contain a bulb section with a colourful range of popular favourites and new introductions. The advantage here is that you have time to plan your requirements and then add them to the order for other plants. Bargain offers from unknown suppliers should be treated with caution.

SPECIALIST MAIL ORDER
A number of nurseries offer catalogues which are devoted exclusively to bulbs. This is the place to look for unusual varieties and the rare genera — the large companies produce catalogues with full colour illustrations but the smaller ones often offer descriptions without illustrations. Finally there are the highly-specialised growers who offer catalogues or lists of a single genus.

What to buy

LOOSE BULBS
There are 2 advantages — the bulbs are usually cheaper than those sold in printed prepacks and they can be inspected before purchase. Handling by other people may have caused damage, however, so look carefully and try to buy your requirements when the bulbs first appear. 'Soft' bulbs such as Lilies should be covered in the box with peat or sawdust.

PACKED BULBS
These bulbs have been spared handling by customers. In addition bags of Daffodils, Tulips etc are often cheaper than buying the bulbs loose. The problem is that you can't see what you are buying, but smaller bulbs are sold in plastic prepacks. Make sure that these bulbs are sound and see that ventilation holes are present.

COLLECTIONS
A collection is an outer container in which there are a number of labelled packs of different bulbs. The collection brings together bulbs of a similar type — '5 Species Tulips', 'Trumpet Lily Collection' etc. It is less expensive to buy these bulbs in this way than ordering them individually, but it is the supplier's choice.

MIXTURES
These are not quite the same thing as Collections. The container (bag, box etc) holds bulbs of several varieties but they are not separated into individually labelled bags. In the catalogues you will find descriptions such as 'Mixed Autumn Crocus', 'Double Freesia Mixture' etc — a mixture of bright but unpredictable colours.

Safe handling

In recent years the products of many industries — toys, patent medicines etc have started to print warnings on their labels where a possible hazard exists, and horticulture is no exception. Warnings now appear on plant labels where necessary.

The risks involved in handling or eating bulbs concern only a few genera, but some are popular ones. The problem can be that the surface of the bulb acts as an irritant, so gloves should be worn when handling. This effect may be restricted to only those people who are allergic to the chemical which causes the problem, so not everyone is at risk.

The other possibility is that the bulb or other parts of the plant may be harmful if eaten. It is therefore wise to tell children that they must never eat any ornamental bulb.

TOXIC IF EATEN, EVEN IN SMALL QUANTITIES
Colchicum
Convallaria
Gloriosa

TOXIC IF EATEN
Arisaema
Arisarum
Arum
Dracunculus

HARMFUL IF EATEN
Amaryllis
Galanthus
Iris
Narcissus
Ornithogalum
Scilla

SKIN IRRITANT
Alstroemeria
Arum
Hyacinthus
Iris
Narcissus
Ornithogalum
Scilla
Tulipa

Colchicum

Convallaria

PRONOUNCING DICTIONARY

Several different bulbs can have the same common or English name, and so it is generally preferable to use the more precise Latin name when ordering or talking about them. The first word is the genus — equivalent to a surname, and this is followed by the species which can be likened to a Christian or given name. The species may have several varieties — a variety which has originated in cultivation rather than in the wild is properly called a cultivar. The cultivar name is usually not in Latin — examples are Fritillaria meleagris 'Aphrodite' and Chionodoxa luciliae 'Pink Giant'.

One problem is that learned botanists sometimes decide to change the genus name, as has happened with Spring Starflower which now has 5 alternative Latin names! Such changes are generally not popular with gardeners and the old Latin name may be retained — the English Bluebell is still frequently referred to as Scilla non-scripta rather than using the more modern name Hyacinthoides non-scripta. Another difficulty with Latin names is that there are no rules for correct pronunciation. The generally agreed genus pronunciations for the bulbs in this book are given below — each name is divided into phonetic syllables, and the stressed syllable is printed in bold type.

ACHIMENES	a-kim-**ee**-nees
ACIDANTHERA	a-kid-**anth**-er-a
AGAPANTHUS	ag-a-**panth**-us
ALBUCA	al-**boo**-ka
ALLIUM	**a**-lee-um
ALSTROEMERIA	al-stroom-**ee**-ree-a
AMARYLLIS	am-a-**rill**-is
ANEMONE	a-**nem**-oh-nee
ANOMATHECA	a-noh-ma-**thee**-ka
ANTHERICUM	an-**ther**-i-kum
ARISAEMA	a-ree-**see**-ma
ARISARUM	a-**rees**-a-rum
ARUM	**a**-rum
ASARUM	a-**sah**-rum
ASPHODELUS	as-**fod**-ell-us
BABIANA	bab-ee-**a**-na
BEGONIA	beh-**goh**-nee-a
BELAMCANDA	bel-am-**kan**-da
BLETILLA	bleh-**till**-a
BRIMEURA	bree-**mew**-ra
BRODIAEA	bro-dee-**ee**-a
BULBOCODIUM	bul-boh-**coh**-dee-um
CAMASSIA	ka-**ma**-see-a
CANNA	**ka**-na
CARDIOCRINUM	kar-dee-oh-**kree**-num
CHIONODOXA	ky-on-oh-**dox**-sa
CHLIDANTHUS	klid-**anth**-us
CLIVIA	**kli**-vee-a
COLCHICUM	**kol**-chee-kum
CONVALLARIA	kon-va-**lah**-ree-a
CORYDALIS	koh-**ree**-dah-lis
CRINUM	**kry**-num
CROCOSMIA	kroh-**koz**-mee-a
CROCUS	**kroh**-kus
CYCLAMEN	**sigh**-kla-men
DAHLIA	**day**-lya or **dah**-lee-a
DIERAMA	dee-a-**rah**-ma
DRACUNCULUS	dra-**kun**-kew-lus
ERANTHIS	eh-**ran**-this
EREMURUS	eh-re-**mew**-rus
ERYTHRONIUM	eh-re-**throw**-nee-um
EUCHARIS	**ew**-ka-ris
EUCOMIS	**ew**-koh-mis
FREESIA	**freez**-ee-a
FRITILLARIA	frit-i-**lah**-ree-a
GALANTHUS	ga-**lan**-thus

GALTONIA	gaul-**toh**-nee-a
GLADIOLUS	glad-ee-**oh**-lus
GLORIOSA	gloh-ree-**oh**-sa
HABRANTHUS	ha-**bran**-thus
HAEMANTHUS	hee-**man**-thus
HEDYCHIUM	hay-**dik**-ee-um
HERMODACTYLUS	her-moh-**dak**-till-us
HIPPEASTRUM	hip-ee-**as**-trum
HOMERIA	hoh-**mere**-ee-a
HYACINTHELLA	high-a-sinth-**ell**-a
HYACINTHUS	high-a-**sinth**-us
HYMENOCALLIS	high-men-oh-**kal**-is
IPHEION	if-**ay**-on
IRIS	**eye**-ris
IXIA	**ix**-see-a
IXIOLIRION	ix-see-oh-**leer**-ee-on
LACHENALIA	lak-eh-**nay**-lee-a
LEUCOJUM	loo-**koh**-jum
LILIUM	**lil**-ee-um
MERENDERA	meh-ren-**deh**-ra
MORAEA	moh-**ree**-a
MUSCARI	mus-**kah**-ree
NARCISSUS	nar-**sis**-us
NECTAROSCORDUM	nek-tah-roh-**skor**-dum
NERINE	nay-**ree**-nay
NOMOCHARIS	no-moh-**ka**-ris
NOTHOLIRION	no-tho-**leer**-ee-on
ORNITHOGALUM	or-ni-**thog**-a-lum
OXALIS	ox-**ah**-lis
PANCRATIUM	pan-**krate**-ee-um
PARADISEA	pa-ra-**dees**-ee-ya
PLEIONE	**play**-oh-nay
POLIANTHES	po-lee-**anth**-eez
PUSCHKINIA	push-**kin**-ee-a
RANUNCULUS	ra-**nung**-kew-lus
RHODOHYPOXIS	roh-doh-hi-**pox**-is
ROMULEA	rom-**ew**-lee-a
ROSCOEA	roz-**koh**-ee-a
SANDERSONIA	san-der-**son**-ee-a
SCADOXUS	scah-**dox**-us
SCHIZOSTYLIS	sky-zoh-**sty**-lis

SCILLA	**sil**-a
SISYRINCHIUM	siz-ee-**ring**-kee-um
SPARAXIS	spa-**rak**-sis
SPREKELIA	spre-**kee**-lee-ya
STERNBERGIA	stern-**bur**-gee-a
TECOPHILAEA	te-koh-fi-**lee**-a
TIGRIDIA	ti-**grid**-ee-a
TRILLIUM	**tril**-ee-um
TRITONIA	try-**toh**-nee-a
TROPAEOLUM	troh-**pee**-oh-lum
TULBAGHIA	tul-**ba**-ghee-ya
TULIPA	**tew**-li-pa
UVULARIA	uv-yew-**lah**-ree-a
VALLOTA	va-**lo**-ta
VELTHEIMIA	vel-**ty**-mee-a
WATSONIA	wot-**son**-ee-a
ZANTEDESCHIA	zan-tee-**dis**-kee-ya
ZEPHYRANTHES	zef-ee-**ranth**-eez

CHAPTER 2

BULBS A-Z

It is worth repeating the definition of bulbous plants which appeared in the Introduction. These plants are species or varieties which form fleshy storage organs and they include true bulbs, corms, tubers, rhizomes and tuberous roots. All of them are referred to under the general term *bulb*.

Not all bulbs, however, qualify for inclusion in this book. First of all we are only dealing with the ornamental types, so the bulbous food plants such as Potato and Onion are not included. Next, the bulb must be available for purchase in its dormant state for it to be included. Some plants such as Caladium, Gloxinia, Hemerocallis and the popular Rhizomatous Irises are bulbs according to the definition given above, but they are bought as plants in leaf.

These exclusions still leave us with a vast range of plants from which to make your choice. Some are available from almost every supplier when the planting season arrives, but many others are either unusual or rare and you will have to search for them. With most of the examples in this book the standard planting material is a dormant bulb, but even with these types the situation has changed slightly in recent years. Garden Tulips, Narcissi and Hyacinths used to be bought almost exclusively as dry bulbs in the autumn, but these days some people prefer to buy pots of growing plants with flower buds for planting up tubs, window boxes etc in spring. Some planting material has long been popular in both the bulb and growing plant form — examples include Tuberous Begonias, Snowdrops, Dahlias and Ranunculus. At the other end of the scale from the plants which are always bought as bulbs are the species which are nearly always bought as growing plants in leaf or flower — most are house or conservatory plants such as Lachenalia, Clivia, Florist Cyclamen, Gloriosa and Nerine.

All the plants mentioned so far bear their bulbous parts below ground, but included in this section are a couple of Orchids which can be grown outdoors. Here the bulbous part is a swollen pseudobulb which is borne above the surface of the compost.

Garden and indoor bulbs from Achimenes to Zephyranthes appear on the following pages. Try a few which are new to you, and also try some of the new varieties of old favourites which appear each year in the shops and catalogues.

KEY TO THE A-Z GUIDE

The recommended home for the plant. *Garden plant* means that it can be grown outdoors, but some types are planted in spring and lifted in autumn.

Indoor plant means that it can be grown in the house, greenhouse or conservatory. It may be a hardy bulb such as Tulip etc which is used for indoor decoration or a half-hardy type not suitable for outdoors

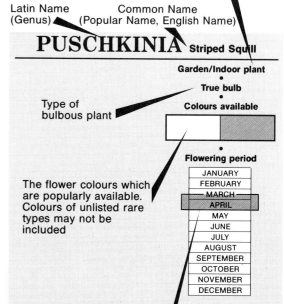

Latin Name (Genus)

Common Name (Popular Name, English Name)

PUSCHKINIA Striped Squill

Garden/Indoor plant

True bulb

Type of bulbous plant

Colours available

The flower colours which are popularly available. Colours of unlisted rare types may not be included

Flowering period

| JANUARY |
| FEBRUARY |
| MARCH |
| APRIL |
| MAY |
| JUNE |
| JULY |
| AUGUST |
| SEPTEMBER |
| OCTOBER |
| NOVEMBER |
| DECEMBER |

Puschkinia is an excellent plant for a rockery. It is completely hardy and trouble-free — the attractive starry flowers appear early in the year and the bulbs increase quite quickly to form large clumps. It is therefore surprising that it is not more popular — it remains a poor relation of the Bluebells. You can them apart by the small fused tube at the base Puschkinia flower which is absent from bloom. The strap-like foliage is derived flower measures about

The main flowering period in the Midlands. In some regions this period may start earlier or finish later. The flowering period of unusual species may not be included — in the case of Garden/Indoor Plant types only the main-use flowering period may be given

VARIETIES: The only spe P. **scilloides (P. lib** Puschkinia is in the r for edging and small flowers which are open blue with a central d rk planted in groups for ma add compost or pe t white variety **'Alba'** is es Puschkinia can be same way as Crocu

SITE & SOIL: Any well light hade.

PLANT DETAILS: Plant He

Description of the basic properties of the genus and its value as a garden and/or indoor plant

Species, varieties and hybrids which are grown in this country. In some cases only a small selection can be shown — this selection features the most widely available types plus a few noteworthy examples which may be listed by only a few suppliers

The planting depth is the height of soil or compost between the surface and the top of the bulb

ACHIMENES Hot Water Plant

Indoor plant
•
Rhizome ('tuber')
•
Colours available

•
Flowering period

| JANUARY |
| FEBRUARY |
| MARCH |
| APRIL |
| MAY |
| JUNE |
| JULY |
| AUGUST |
| SEPTEMBER |
| OCTOBER |
| NOVEMBER |
| DECEMBER |

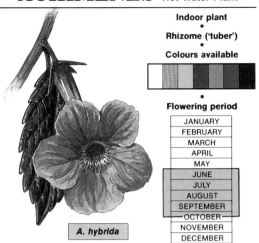

A. hybrida

An easy-to-grow plant — buy the tuber-like rhizomes of named varieties from a mail order bulb company or unnamed plants in flower from a garden centre. The modern varieties produce masses of short-lived trumpet-shaped flowers above the shiny velvety leaves. The stems are weak and so Achimenes is an excellent subject for a hanging basket. Keep the plants reasonably warm (minimum 55°F) and make sure that the compost never dries out. Stop watering once flowering has finished and cut off the withered stems. Plant up in fresh compost in early spring.

VARIETIES: Nearly all the Achimenes offered for sale are hybrids. In the larger bulb catalogues you will find a number of varieties of **A. hybrida**. Examples include **'Snow Queen'** (white), **'Ambroise Verschaffelt'** (white, veined purple), **'Peach Blossom'** and **'Cameo Triumph'** (pink), **'Purple King'** and **'Paul Arnold'** (purple), **'Flamingo'** and **'Master Ingram'** (red), and **'Cattleya'** (blue). You will have to search for the rare yellows such as **'Clouded Yellow'**. Species such as **A. erecta**, **longiflora** and **grandiflora** are larger and much harder to find.

SITE & SOIL: Use a soilless compost — choose a brightly lit spot away from direct sun.

PLANT DETAILS: Planting time: February–March. Planting depth: ¾ in. (2 cm). Spacing: 6 in a 6 in. (15 cm) pot. Height: 6–12 in. (15–30 cm).

PROPAGATION: Separate and pot up rhizomes in early spring. Can be raised from spring-sown seed.

Achimenes hybrida 'Ambroise Verschaffelt'

ACIDANTHERA Acidanthera

Garden/Indoor plant
•
Corm
•
Colour available

•
Flowering period

| JANUARY |
| FEBRUARY |
| MARCH |
| APRIL |
| MAY |
| JUNE |
| JULY |
| AUGUST |
| SEPTEMBER |
| OCTOBER |
| NOVEMBER |
| DECEMBER |

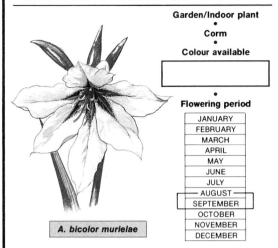

A. bicolor murielae

This Gladiolus-like plant is an excellent choice for sunny borders in the milder parts of the country. It bears 2 ft (60 cm) long sword-shaped leaves and in late summer or autumn up to 10 sweetly-scented blooms appear. The advantage of Acidanthera is that it produces its blooms when most bulbous plants have passed their flowering season, but there is an important drawback. It has to be lifted before the onset of winter — the corms should be stored in a dry and reasonably warm place until the spring. In cold areas Acidanthera may fail to flower — it is better here to grow it as a cool greenhouse plant. Pot up the corms in March.

VARIETIES: There is just one variety. It will be listed as **A. bicolor murielae** or **A. murielae**, although some textbooks call it **Gladiolus callianthus**. Each flower measures 2–3 in. (5–7.5 cm) across — the 6 pure white petals are borne at the end of a long green floral tube. The bloom has a star-like shape and at the centre there is a prominent purple blotch.

SITE & SOIL: Any well-drained soil will do — a warm and sunny site is necessary.

PLANT DETAILS: Planting time: late April. Planting depth: 4 in. (10 cm). Spacing: 8 in. (20 cm). Height: 36 in. (90 cm).

PROPAGATION: Remove cormlets after lifting and store — plant in April. Flowering will take several years.

Acidanthera bicolor murielae

AGAPANTHUS African Lily

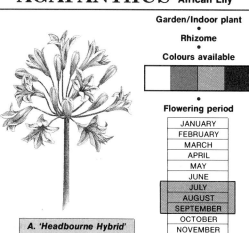

Garden/Indoor plant
•
Rhizome
•
Colours available

Flowering period

JANUARY	
FEBRUARY	
MARCH	
APRIL	
MAY	
JUNE	
JULY	
AUGUST	
SEPTEMBER	
OCTOBER	
NOVEMBER	
DECEMBER	

A. 'Headbourne Hybrid'

In the garden centre you will usually find Agapanthus in the 'border perennial' or 'pot plant' section rather than with the bulbs as it is generally sold as a growing plant. You can, however, buy the fleshy rhizomes from mail order bulb suppliers. From the basal rosette of strap-like leaves the long stems appear on top of which the flowers are clustered. Each trumpet-shaped bloom is about 2 in. (5 cm) long. This showy perennial is a good choice for a tub or border — cover the crown with sand or peat during the winter months. Water copiously in dry weather and do not repot container-grown specimens unless they are pot-bound. In cold exposed areas move tubs indoors in winter or grow as a greenhouse plant.

VARIETIES: The evergreen **A. africanus** with deep blue flowers and **A. orientalis** with white or blue flowers are suitable for indoor cultivation, but both are half hardy. For outdoor planting it is better to choose a hardier species — **A. 'Headbourne Hybrid'** is available in white, pale blue and deep blue. **A. campanulatus** is regarded as the best species for unfavourable situations.

SITE & SOIL: Well-drained soil with adequate organic matter — full sun is essential.

PLANT DETAILS: Planting time: April–May. Planting depth: 4 in. (10 cm). Spacing: 18–24 in. (45–60 cm). Height: 30 in. (75 cm).

PROPAGATION: Divide clumps in April.

Agapanthus africanus

ALBUCA Albuca

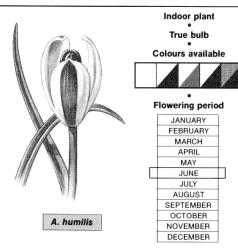

Indoor plant
•
True bulb
•
Colours available

Flowering period

JANUARY	
FEBRUARY	
MARCH	
APRIL	
MAY	
JUNE	
JULY	
AUGUST	
SEPTEMBER	
OCTOBER	
NOVEMBER	
DECEMBER	

A. humilis

Experienced gardeners will recognise many of the entries in this A–Z guide, but very few people will have seen this bulb. The height and appearance of the various species differ widely, but all share a lack of frost resistance which makes them unsuitable as year-round outdoor plants except in the mildest regions of the country. The leaves are narrow and the flowers are borne on short stalks or clustered on tall spires. If you do attempt to grow Albuca in the garden, plant the bulbs in March and lift when the leaves die down in autumn. Store over winter in a dry place.

VARIETIES: You will find Albuca listed in several specialist bulb catalogues. **A. nelsonii** (30 in., fragrant, white flowers striped red) and **A. canadensis** (12 in., yellow flowers striped green) are examples, but the only one you are likely to find is the small **A. humilis**. This alpine house plant bears short flower stems with 1–3 blooms. Each flower has white petals which bear a longitudinal stripe on the outside — green at first and then changing to mauve. Cultivation details are set out below.

SITE & SOIL: Use soil-based or soilless compost — keep in the dark until growth starts.

PLANT DETAILS: Planting time: November. Planting depth: 3 in. (7.5 cm). Spacing 2 in. (5 cm). Height: 4 in. (10 cm).

PROPAGATION: Remove offsets when plants become overcrowded. Pot up in autumn.

Albuca canadensis

ALLIUM **Flowering Onion**

Garden plant
•
True bulb
•
Colours available

•
Flowering period

JANUARY
FEBRUARY
MARCH
APRIL
MAY
JUNE
JULY
AUGUST
SEPTEMBER
OCTOBER
NOVEMBER
DECEMBER

A. albopilosum

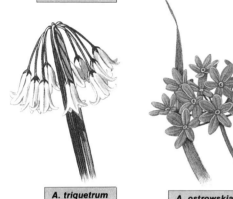

A. triquetrum

A. ostrowskianum

Most of the Alliums are easy to grow but they have never really become popular — perhaps the idea of growing Onions in the bed or border has been a deterrent. There is, however, no problem — the leaves smell only when crushed and some species bear fragrant flowers. It is often the keen flower arranger who chooses to grow Alliums — the blooms are long-lasting in water and they can be dried for winter use. In early or midsummer the clusters of flowers appear on leafless stalks — there are tall species for the back of the border and dwarfs for the rockery. There is no standard shape — the leaves may be wide like Garlic or narrow like Onions. The flowers, too, may be wide- or narrow-petalled. The flower-heads last for about a month.

VARIETIES: There are two basic types of flower-head. Some are spheres made up of many tightly-packed blooms — these are the *Ball-headed* Alliums. The rest bear loose clusters of upright or drooping blooms — these are the *Tufted* Alliums. The giant among the Ball-headed types is **A. giganteum** — 4 ft (120 cm) high with 4 in. (10 cm) wide mauve heads in June. The largest heads are carried by **A. albopilosum** — 2 ft (60 cm) high with 8 in. (20 cm) wide silvery lilac heads in June. Other Ball-headed Alliums include **A. aflatunense** (2–3 ft, pale purple, May), **A. karataviense** (8–10 in., pale lilac purple, May) and **A. sphaerocephalon** (2 ft, red, July). The Tufted Alliums are generally grown at the front of the border or in the rockery. Some of them have drooping flowers like **A. narcissiflorum** (pink), **A. triquetrum** (white) and **A. beesianum** (blue). The popular **A. moly** grows about 9 in. (22.5 cm) high and produces masses of loosely-packed yellow stars in June. **A. ostrowskianum** bears its pink flowers in flat clusters and grows about 6 in. (15 cm) high. There are several other rockery Alliums which are attractive but you should choose with care — several self-seed very freely and are invasive.

SITE & SOIL: Any well-drained soil will do — thrives best in full sun.

PLANT DETAILS: Planting time: September–October. Planting depth: Cover with soil to 3 times the height of the bulb. Spacing: 6–12 in. (15–30 cm). Height: Depends on species — see above.

PROPAGATION: Divide mature clumps in autumn when over-crowding becomes a problem.

Allium giganteum

Allium sphaerocephalon

Allium moly

ALSTROEMERIA Peruvian Lily

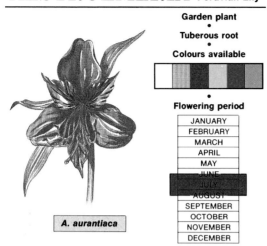

Garden plant
•
Tuberous root
•
Colours available
•
Flowering period

| JANUARY |
| FEBRUARY |
| MARCH |
| APRIL |
| MAY |
| JUNE |
| **JULY** |
| AUGUST |
| SEPTEMBER |
| OCTOBER |
| NOVEMBER |
| DECEMBER |

A. aurantiaca

The 2 in. (5 cm) wide flowers are attractive, variously described as Lily-like, Azalea-like or Orchid-like. They are often streaked or spotted with darker colours and are borne in loose clusters. They are long-lasting in water and you will find them in your local florist, but you will not often see them in gardens. The problem is that few flowers are produced in the first year.

VARIETIES: Choose a variety which is known to be hardy. **A. aurantiaca** (**A. aurea**) is the tall species which bears yellow or orange flowers which are streaked with red. Named varieties include **'Orange King'** (orange) and **'Dover Orange'** (vermilion). **A. 'Ligtu Hybrids'** are shorter and offer a wider range of colours and markings. The secret of success is to plant the fleshy tubers as soon as you receive them and to take care when you spread out the brittle side roots — deep planting is essential. Planting specimens growing in a pot or container is more reliable than starting with tubers. Dead-head faded blooms. Apply a thick mulch in late autumn.

SITE & SOIL: Well-drained, light soil is necessary — thrives in sun or light shade.

PLANT DETAILS: Planting time: March–April. Planting depth: 6 in. (15 cm). Spacing: 12 in. (30 cm). Height: 24–36 in. (60–90 cm).

PROPAGATION: Divide clumps, but only when overcrowding makes it essential.

Alstroemeria 'Frederika'

AMARYLLIS Belladonna Lily

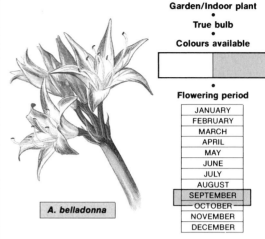

Garden/Indoor plant
•
True bulb
•
Colours available
•
Flowering period

| JANUARY |
| FEBRUARY |
| MARCH |
| APRIL |
| MAY |
| JUNE |
| JULY |
| AUGUST |
| **SEPTEMBER** |
| OCTOBER |
| NOVEMBER |
| DECEMBER |

A. belladonna

The popular 'Amaryllis' bulbs offered for sale in autumn are really varieties of Hippeastrum. There are similarities between the two — both are large bulbs which produce clusters of Lily-like flowers on thick stalks. There are, however, a number of basic differences. The Amaryllis flowers are smaller and appear after the foliage has died down. Another difference is that Hippeastrum is strictly an indoor plant whereas Amaryllis can be grown outdoors in a bed next to a sunny south-facing wall. For indoor display set the bulb in a 6 in. (15 cm) pot in March with its tip just above the compost.

VARIETIES: The only species grown is **A. belladonna** — the usual colour is bright pink. The strap-like leaves appear in spring and then die down in early summer. After a month or two the flower stalks emerge and the buds open to produce clusters of 6–12 fragrant funnel-shaped blooms which are 3 in. (7.5 cm) across. Stake stems to avoid wind damage and cut down once flowering is over. Cover the crown with peat during the winter months.

SITE & SOIL: A bulb for warm areas — full sun is essential. Any well-drained soil will do.

PLANT DETAILS: Planting time: June–July. Planting depth: 6 in. (15 cm). Spacing: 12 in. (30 cm). Height: 24–30 in. (60–75 cm).

PROPAGATION: Buy new bulbs — Amaryllis hates disturbance.

Amaryllis belladonna 'Hathor'

ANEMONE Windflower

Garden plant
•
Rhizome or tuber
•
Colours available

•
Flowering period

| JANUARY |
| FEBRUARY |
| MARCH |
| APRIL |
| MAY |
| JUNE |
| JULY |
| AUGUST |
| SEPTEMBER |
| OCTOBER |
| NOVEMBER |
| DECEMBER |

A. coronaria 'de Caen' strain

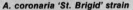

A. coronaria 'St. Brigid' strain

A. nemorosa

The flowers of Anemone species vary widely in shape and colour — from blue Daisies and white star-shaped blooms to the well-known brightly-coloured bowl-like flowers in the florist shop. The use of the different types is as varied as the flower shapes. Some are ideal for naturalising to form large drifts under trees or they can be used to provide early spring colour in the rockery. The popular Florist types are used to provide bold patches of colour in beds, borders and cut flower displays indoors. Anemones can be raised from seed but it is easier to begin with a rootstock, which may be either a tuber or rhizome. You will find a selection of different types in autumn and spring at your garden centre or in the catalogues — all will grow happily in light shade except for A. blanda.

VARIETIES: There are 2 basic types. The *Daisy-flowered* types have narrow petals surrounding a golden disc, the 1½ in. (4 cm) blooms appearing in spring. The first to flower is **A. blanda** (February–April) — the blooms of **A. apennina** (March–April) appear a little later. Both these Daisy-flowered Anemones grow about 6 in. (15 cm) tall and the usual colour is blue although white and pink varieties are available. The white Wood Anemone (**A. nemorosa**) bears starry rather than Daisy-like blooms in April. Plant the tubers about 2 in. (5 cm) deep in September — space them 4 in. (10 cm) apart. More popular but less permanent are the *Florist* or *Poppy-flowered* Anemones (**A. coronaria**). The 2 in. (5 cm) bowl-shaped blooms in bright colours on 6–9 in. (15–22.5 cm) stems are favourite subjects for flower arranging. The **'de Caen'** strain produces single flowers — varieties include **'Mister Fokker'** (blue) and **'Hollandia'** (red). For semi-double or double blooms choose the **'St. Brigid'** strain such as **'The Governor'** (red) and **'The Admiral'** (mauve). Plant in September–October for March–April flowers or in March–April for June–September blooms. Soak the tubers overnight before planting them claws upwards 2 in. (5 cm) deep and 4 in. (10 cm) apart.

SITE & SOIL: Well-drained, humus-rich soil is required — thrives in sun or light shade. The Florist Anemones need a warm and sheltered spot.

PLANT DETAILS: See above.

PROPAGATION: Divide mature clumps in late summer — replant at once.

Anemone blanda

Anemone nemorosa

Anemone coronaria 'de Caen' strain

ANOMATHECA Anomatheca

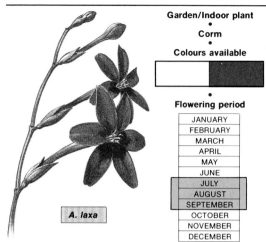

Garden/Indoor plant
•
Corm
•
Colours available

Flowering period

| JANUARY |
| FEBRUARY |
| MARCH |
| APRIL |
| MAY |
| JUNE |
| JULY |
| AUGUST |
| SEPTEMBER |
| OCTOBER |
| NOVEMBER |
| DECEMBER |

A. laxa

An unusual bulb which looks rather like a Freesia when in flower. The leaves at the base are narrow and strap-like, and the flower stems bear a line of trumpet-shaped blooms which all face the same way. After flowering oval pods appear which later open to expose the red seeds. The popular species is relatively hardy, but in cold areas it is best to lift the corms in autumn and store for planting in spring. Alternatively you can grow it indoors as a pot plant.

VARIETIES: The only species you are likely to find is **A. laxa**, sometimes sold as **Lapeirousia laxa** or **cruenta**. The flat-faced flowers measure about 1 in. (2.5 cm) across — the 6 petals on each bloom are bright red with darker blotches on some of the petals. The variety **'Alba'** has white flowers which are flecked with maroon, and for the collector of rarities there is the hard-to-find **A. viridis** which is grown indoors for its green finger-like flowers in February or March.

SITE & SOIL: Well-drained, light soil in a sheltered sunny spot is necessary.

PLANT DETAILS: Planting time: April. Planting depth: 2 in. (5 cm). Spacing: 4 in. (10 cm). Height: 6–12 in. (15–30 cm).

PROPAGATION: Divide overcrowded clumps in autumn and replant. Cormlets can be removed and planted.

Anomatheca laxa

ANTHERICUM St. Bernard's Lily

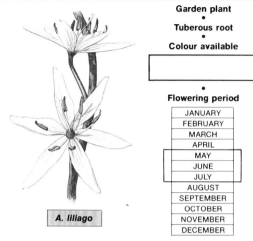

Garden plant
•
Tuberous root
•
Colour available

Flowering period

| JANUARY |
| FEBRUARY |
| MARCH |
| APRIL |
| MAY |
| JUNE |
| JULY |
| AUGUST |
| SEPTEMBER |
| OCTOBER |
| NOVEMBER |
| DECEMBER |

A. liliago

This grassy alpine belongs to the Lily family and has been grown in gardens for hundreds of years, but it has never become popular. It is a slow starter and so the heads of star-shaped blooms do not appear until the second year after planting, but once established Anthericum forms large clumps. It is a bulb for the border, large rockery or for naturalising in grass or open woodland — the tall spires of small flowers appear above the narrow grey-green leaves in early summer and last for about 6–8 weeks. Despite being an alpine this is not a plant for cold and wet areas.

VARIETIES: The species you are most likely to find is **A. liliago** which bears 1½–2 ft (45–60 cm) tall flower stems. The narrow-petalled blooms give a cloud-like effect — each flower measures about 1 in. (2.5 cm) across and bears prominent yellow anthers. **A. ramosus** is a larger plant with branching flower stems which reach 3 ft (90 cm). Both these species are easy to grow and can be cut for indoor decoration.

SITE & SOIL: Well-drained, humus-rich soil in sun or light shade is required.

PLANT DETAILS: Planting time: March or September. Planting depth: 4 in. (10 cm). Spacing: 12 in. (30 cm). Height: 18–36 in. (45–90 cm).

PROPAGATION: Resents root disturbance — divide overcrowded clumps in spring and replant.

Anthericum liliago

ARISAEMA Arisaema

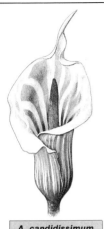

Garden plant
•
Tuber
•
Colours available

Flowering period

| JANUARY |
| FEBRUARY |
| MARCH |
| APRIL |
| **MAY** |
| **JUNE** |
| JULY |
| AUGUST |
| SEPTEMBER |
| OCTOBER |
| NOVEMBER |
| DECEMBER |

A. candidissimum

Arisaema is an excellent choice if you want something unusual to grow in moist soil in the border or woodland garden. It is like an Arum when in bloom — the 'flower' has a large tube (the spathe) which surrounds the pencil-like spadix. The top of the tubular spathe may be turned over as a hood or extended as a tail, and the inner surface is often striped. In late summer the tiny true flowers on this spadix turn into brightly-coloured berries.

VARIETIES: The best one to grow is the easiest one to find — **A. candidissimum**. The flower is about 4 in. (10 cm) high on a 6 in. (15 cm) stalk — the broad 12 in. (30 cm) long leaves appear after flowering has taken place. The pointed flower tube bears pink and white stripes — **A. ringens** is less hardy and has green and white striped flower tubes which are distinctly hooded. The netted and purple **A. griffithii** is even more dramatic. The green-tubed **A. triphyllum** (Jack-in-the-Pulpit) is less colourful but much hardier. Several other species are offered by suppliers of unusual bulbs.

SITE & SOIL: Well-drained, humus-rich soil in sun or partial shade.

PLANT DETAILS: Planting time: September. Planting depth: 6 in. (15 cm). Spacing: 6 in. (15 cm). Height: 12 in. (30 cm).

PROPAGATION: Divide clumps or remove offset tubers and plant in autumn.

Arisaema griffithii

ARISARUM Mouse Plant

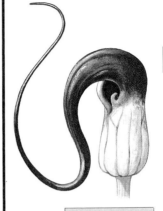

Garden plant
•
Tuber
•
Colour available

Flowering period

| JANUARY |
| FEBRUARY |
| **MARCH** |
| APRIL |
| MAY |
| JUNE |
| JULY |
| AUGUST |
| SEPTEMBER |
| OCTOBER |
| NOVEMBER |
| DECEMBER |

A. proboscideum

This is a 'fun' plant, especially for children — a curiosity rather than a thing of beauty. It is a low-growing ground cover closely related to Arum — in spring it forms a dense mat of arrow-shaped leaves and among this foliage the oddly-shaped flowers appear. It is these blooms which give the plant its common name — the long tail at the top of the flower looks like the rear end of a mouse disappearing down a hole!

VARIETIES: There is an uncommon green species (**A. vulgare**) but the only one you are likely to find is the mouse-like **A. proboscideum**. Like all the aroids there is a spadix and spathe — see Arum for details. The spadix with its tiny flowers is concealed within the 1 in. (2.5 cm) long tubular spathe. Its base is white, but the upper part (the back of the 'mouse') is purplish-brown and the tip (the tail of the mouse) is drawn out into a 6 in. (15 cm) long dark purple thread.

SITE & SOIL: Well-drained, humus-rich soil in partial shade is required.

PLANT DETAILS: Planting time: September–October. Planting depth: 6 in. (15 cm). Spacing: 4 in. (10 cm). Height: 4 in. (10 cm).

PROPAGATION: Divide clumps or remove offset tubers and plant in autumn.

Arisarum proboscideum

ARUM Cuckoo Pint

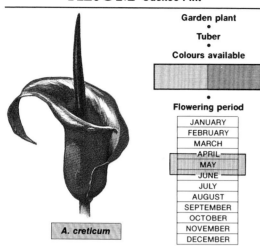

Garden plant
•
Tuber
•
Colours available

Flowering period

JANUARY
FEBRUARY
MARCH
APRIL
MAY
JUNE
JULY
AUGUST
SEPTEMBER
OCTOBER
NOVEMBER
DECEMBER

A. creticum

The 'flower' is strange and interesting. The true flowers are tiny and are clustered on a pencil-like spadix. This is enclosed in a tube-like or sail-like spathe. The leaves are arrow-shaped and berries appear on the spadix in autumn. Depending on the species Arums are grown in the border, rockery or in light woodland for their flowers, attractive leaves or their colourful berries. A word of warning — this plant is poisonous and the berries can look attractive to children.

VARIETIES: Our native species **A. maculatum** has maroon-blotched leaves — for garden use other species are preferred. For floral display the best choice is **A. creticum** — the bottle-shaped yellow spathe is bent back to reveal the prominent pale orange spadix. For a foliage/berry display choose **A. italicum 'Pictum'** or **'Marmoratum'**. The large, wavy-edged leaves have silvery veins — the foliage appears in autumn and lasts until spring. In a sunny spot the pale yellow or greenish-white flowers are followed by bright red berries in autumn.

SITE & SOIL: Well-drained, humus-rich soil in sun or light shade.

PLANT DETAILS: Planting time: August–September. Planting depth: 6 in. (15 cm). Spacing: 4 in. (10 cm). Height: 12 in. (30 cm).

PROPAGATION: Divide clumps or remove offset tubers and plant in autumn.

Arum italicum 'Pictum'

ASARUM Wild Ginger

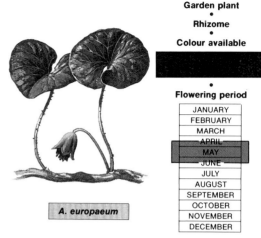

Garden plant
•
Rhizome
•
Colour available

Flowering period

JANUARY
FEBRUARY
MARCH
APRIL
MAY
JUNE
JULY
AUGUST
SEPTEMBER
OCTOBER
NOVEMBER
DECEMBER

A. europaeum

Nearly all bulbs are grown for their floral display, but Asarum is different. It is grown for its evergreen leaves which form a ground-covering carpet. The underground stems spread rapidly in moist soil under trees, producing kidney-shaped leaves on thin stalks. The small bell-shaped flowers which appear in the spring are borne under the leaves and do not add to the display. Not for everyone, of course, but a good choice if you are looking for a glossy and prostrate ground cover.

VARIETIES: A. europaeum is the most popular species. The shiny leathery leaves measure about 3 in. (7.5 cm) across and the tiny pendent flowers are brown or purple. The leaves of **A. caudatum** are dark green and rather larger — the largest foliage is borne by **A. canadense**. The most interesting species is the low-growing and late-flowering **A. hartwegii**. The dark green leaves have narrow silvery veins and the near-black blooms have tail-like lobes. Asarum is sometimes listed as **Hexastylis**.

SITE & SOIL: Thrives in moist, humus-rich soil in partial shade.

PLANT DETAILS: Planting time: September–October. Planting depth: 6 in. (15 cm). Spacing: 12 in. (30 cm). Height: 3–6 in. (7.5–15 cm).

PROPAGATION: Lift and divide clumps in autumn or sow seed in spring.

Asarum canadense

ASPHODELUS Asphodel

Garden plant
•
Tuberous root
•
Colours available

Flowering period

JANUARY
FEBRUARY
MARCH
APRIL
MAY
JUNE
JULY
AUGUST
SEPTEMBER
OCTOBER
NOVEMBER
DECEMBER

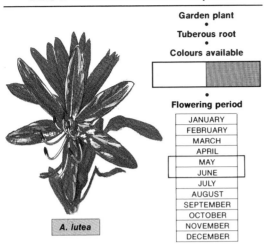

A. lutea

The Asphodels are tall plants with long upright spikes of star-shaped flowers. They will grow quite happily in infertile dry soil and the seed-heads are often decorative. At the base of the plant is a tuft of grass-like leaves. It is not an easy plant to find — you will have to look in the specialist bulb catalogues for the White Asphodel. The tuber- or rhizome-like roots are despatched in spring or autumn for immediate planting.

VARIETIES: White Asphodel (**A. albus**) has white flowers in which each petal has a central green vein. It grows about 3 ft (90 cm) high and the mass of 1½ in. (4 cm) wide blooms is an attractive sight in spring. **A. ramosus** is taller and blooms a little later. The most popular species is the Yellow Asphodel or Jacob's Rod — **A. lutea**. The proper botanical name is **Asphodeline lutea** — a 4 ft (120 cm) high plant with dense spires of bright yellow flowers above the grey-green leaves at the base.

SITE & SOIL: Any well-drained soil will do — thrives in full sun.

PLANT DETAILS: Planting time: March or October. Planting depth: 3 in. (7.5 cm). Spacing: 12 in. (30 cm). Height: 36–48 in. (90–120 cm).

PROPAGATION: Divide overcrowded clumps in spring or autumn.

Asphodelus albus

BABIANA Baboon Root

Garden/Indoor plant
•
Corm
•
Colours available

Flowering period

JANUARY
FEBRUARY
MARCH
APRIL
MAY
JUNE
JULY
AUGUST
SEPTEMBER
OCTOBER
NOVEMBER
DECEMBER

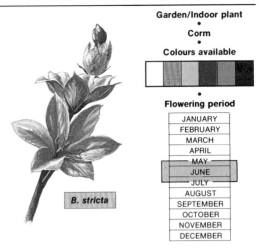

B. stricta

In its native home in S. Africa baboons collect the corms for food — hence the common name. Babiana is related to the Gladiolus but it is a much smaller plant — the strap-like leaves are ribbed and hairy, and the flower stalks bear clusters of 1 in. (2.5 cm) wide blooms. It can be grown outdoors in sheltered areas if you cover the ground with a deep mulch in winter. In colder areas it is better to lift and store the corms in winter or to grow it indoors. For pot culture plant the corms 2 in. (5 cm) deep in compost — when the leaves wither store the corms in dry peat until planting time.

VARIETIES: **B. plicata** is an attractive species — the petals on the 2 in. (5 cm) long tubular flowers are violet with a white or cream blotch. Another colourful species is the red-throated mauve **B. rubro-cyanea**, but it is more usual to grow one of the hybrid varieties of **B. stricta**. Each stalk bears 10 or more 1 in. (2.5 cm) long funnel-shaped blooms which look rather like Freesias, but the spikes are upright and not arching.

SITE & SOIL: Well-drained, humus-rich soil in a sheltered sunny spot is essential.

PLANT DETAILS: Planting time: April. Planting depth: 6 in. (15 cm). Spacing: 4 in. (10 cm). Height: 6–12 in. (15–30 cm).

PROPAGATION: Remove cormlets during the dormant season and plant in April.

Babiana plicata

BEGONIA Tuberous Begonia

Garden/Indoor plant

•

Tuber

•

Colours available

•

Flowering period

JANUARY
FEBRUARY
MARCH
APRIL
MAY
JUNE
JULY
AUGUST
SEPTEMBER
OCTOBER
NOVEMBER
DECEMBER

B. tuberhybrida

B. multiflora

B. pendula

The Begonias dealt with here are the tuberous types which can be bought as flattened 'bulbs' in late winter or spring. All make excellent conservatory plants, but they are best known as bedding plants for beds, borders, hanging baskets, tubs and rockeries. They will flourish in sun or light shade provided that the soil is enriched with organic matter before planting and provided they are watered regularly during dry weather. Press tubers into boxes of damp peat in March or April — place hollow side uppermost. Keep at 60°–70°F and transplant separately into pots of soilless compost when leafy shoots appear. Plant out in June. Feed during the growing season and stake large-flowered forms. With B. tuberhybrida the small female flowers under each showy male one should be pinched off. Lift tubers in mid October — remove stems after the foliage has died down and store tubers in dry peat in a frost-free place.

VARIETIES: The large-flowered **B. tuberhybrida** is the best-known group, its Rose-like or Camellia-like blooms measuring 2–6 in. (5–15 cm) across. There is a wide range of shapes and colours — flowers may be single or double, plain-edged or ruffled and self- or bi-coloured. You will find leafy plants in pots at your garden centre in spring — do not plant out until the danger of frost has gone. Named varieties include **'Diana Wynyard'** (white), **'Fairy Light'** (white, edged red), **'Sugar Candy'** (pink), **'Roy Hartley'** (pink), and **'Guardsman'** (red). **B. multiflora** is smaller than B. tuberhybrida and bears masses of double flowers until the first frost occurs. The hybrid tuberhybrida/multiflora **'Non-Stop'** strain is becoming popular and offers a variety of colours. These Begonias can be raised from January-sown seed but this is not easy and it is better to buy plugs of small seedlings for potting up. In some catalogues you will find **B. bertinii** — an orange single-flowered dwarf species. Finally there are the **B. pendula** varieties (Basket Begonias) bearing slender, drooping stems and flowers which are 1–2 in. (2.5–5 cm) across. Look for the semi-double **'Chanson'** or the double **'Picotee Cascade'**.

SITE & SOIL: Needs soil which is rich in organic matter with little or no lime present. Thrives best in light shade.

PLANT DETAILS: B. tuberhybrida: Height: 9–18 in. (22.5–45 cm). Spacing: 12 in. (30 cm).
B. multiflora: Height: 9 in. (22.5 cm). Spacing: 9 in. (22.5 cm).
B. pendula: Length: 12–24 in. (30–60 cm). Spacing 9 in. (22.5 cm).

PROPAGATION: Tubers can be divided when the shoots are small, but it is better to buy new tubers.

Begonia tuberhybrida 'Masquerade'

Begonia 'Non-Stop Yellow'

Begonia pendula 'Pink Cascade'

BELAMCANDA Leopard Lily

Garden/Indoor plant
•
Rhizome
•
Colour available

•
Flowering period

JANUARY
FEBRUARY
MARCH
APRIL
MAY
JUNE
JULY
AUGUST
SEPTEMBER
OCTOBER
NOVEMBER
DECEMBER

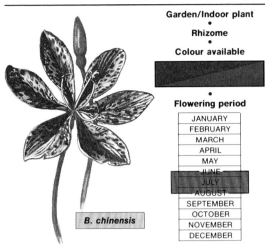

B. chinensis

This member of the Iris family should be more widely grown — despite its reputation for tenderness it will grow quite happily in the garden if covered with a thick mulch in winter. The flowers are spotted which gives Belamcanda its common name. In autumn the pods split open to reveal clusters of shiny black seeds — hence the alternative common name of Blackberry Lily. If the site or soil is unsuitable grow Belamcanda as a conservatory plant. Set 5 rhizomes in a 6 in. (15 cm) pot filled with soilless compost to which extra sand has been added. Keep in the dark until growth appears, water moderately when in flower — dry off and store the rhizomes when flowering is over.

VARIETIES: B. (Pardanthus) chinensis is the only species which is commonly available. The leaves are grouped in a fan like an Iris, but the flowers are quite different. In summer the branched flower stalks bear flat-faced 2 in. wide blooms — the orange petals are spotted or streaked with red. These colourful flowers only last for a day, but new ones continue to appear for several weeks.

SITE & SOIL: Well-drained, humus-rich soil in sun or light shade is necessary.

PLANT DETAILS: Planting time: March–April. Planting depth: 1 in. (2.5 cm). Spacing: 6 in. (15 cm). Height: 30 in. (75 cm).

PROPAGATION: Divide overcrowded clumps in spring.

Belamcanda chinensis

BLETILLA Chinese Ground Orchid

Garden/Indoor plant
•
Pseudobulb
•
Colours available

•
Flowering period

JANUARY
FEBRUARY
MARCH
APRIL
MAY
JUNE
JULY
AUGUST
SEPTEMBER
OCTOBER
NOVEMBER
DECEMBER

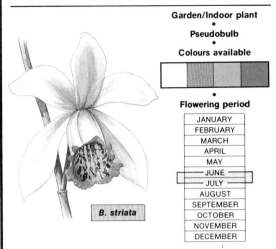

B. striata

Bletilla is a garden Orchid, which means that it can be grown outdoors in well-drained soil in a mild area provided a mulch is placed over the ground in winter. Plant in spring as soon as the pseudobulbs (tuber-like stems) are received — set them 6 in. (15 cm) apart and cover with a 1 in. (2.5 cm) layer of soil. For most areas, however, it is better to grow Bletilla as a pot plant — see below for site, soil and planting details.

VARIETIES: The most popular species is **B. striata** (**B. hyacinthina**) and the usual colour is pink or pale mauve. In early summer the branched flower stalks appear, each one bearing 5-10 showy blooms. These 1–2 in. (2.5–5 cm) wide blooms have a ruffled lip which is darker than the petals. When the foliage withers in autumn keep the compost nearly dry and place the pot in a cool but frost-free place over winter. A white variety (**'Alba'**) is available — there is also a rare yellow species listed as **B. ochracea.**

SITE & SOIL: Use an Orchid compost or loam/leafmould/sand mix. Keep cool and well lit.

PLANT DETAILS: Planting time: March–April. Planting depth: 2 in. (5 cm). Spacing: 1 per 6 in. (15 cm) pot. Height: 12 in. (30 cm).

PROPAGATION: Lift and divide clumps in March every other year.

Bletilla striata

BRIMEURA Spanish Hyacinth

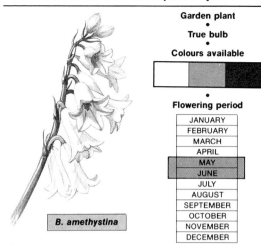

Garden plant
•
True bulb
•
Colours available

•
Flowering period

| JANUARY |
| FEBRUARY |
| MARCH |
| APRIL |
| MAY |
| JUNE |
| JULY |
| AUGUST |
| SEPTEMBER |
| OCTOBER |
| NOVEMBER |
| DECEMBER |

B. amethystina

This small group of plants has been classified with both the Bluebells and the Hyacinths in the past, but is now regarded as a separate genus. The leaves at the base are long and narrow, and from the centre of this tuft of leaves the upright flower stalk appears in late spring or early summer. It bears 10–15 delicate bells, each one looking like a small Bluebell. Brimeura is a good choice for a partially shaded spot in the rockery.

VARIETIES: Unlike the ever-popular Dutch Hyacinth you may have to search for a supplier of the Spanish one. Specialist catalogues offer a single species — **B. amethystina**. The tubular blooms are about ½ in. (1 cm) long and are loosely arranged on the floral spike. The usual colour is pale blue but there are bright blue forms and a white variety (**'Albus'**) is available — this white Spanish Hyacinth is showier, more vigorous and less expensive than the blue one.

SITE & SOIL: Any well-drained soil will do — thrives in sun or partial shade.

PLANT DETAILS: Planting time: September–October. Planting depth: 4 in. (10 cm). Spacing: 4 in. (10 cm). Height: 6–8 in. (15–20 cm).

PROPAGATION: Divide overcrowded clumps in autumn — remove and plant offsets.

Brimeura amethystina

BRODIAEA Brodiaea

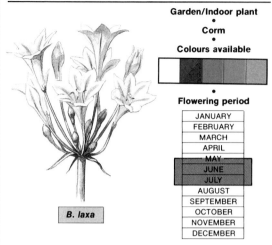

Garden/Indoor plant
•
Corm
•
Colours available

•
Flowering period

| JANUARY |
| FEBRUARY |
| MARCH |
| APRIL |
| MAY |
| JUNE |
| JULY |
| AUGUST |
| SEPTEMBER |
| OCTOBER |
| NOVEMBER |
| DECEMBER |

B. laxa

Brodiaea has a delicate air — this uncommon bulbous plant bears narrow, strap-like leaves and slender flowering stems. These stems carry a cluster of star-shaped or tubular blooms at the top — a plant for people who prefer delicate blooms to big showy ones. Mauve and lavender are the usual colours, ranging from near-blue to near-pink. An excellent cut flower, but don't attempt to grow Brodiaea outdoors if the soil is heavy and the site is exposed. Cultivate it as a pot plant instead.

VARIETIES: Names are rather a muddle — the species may be listed under **Triteleia** or **Dichelostemma**. The most popular Brodiaea is **B. laxa** which bears loose heads of tubular white, blue or lilac flowers and looks like a miniature Agapanthus. **B. tubergenii** is the same size and shape, but the flowers are pale blue inside and dark blue outside. **B. grandiflora** is rather different — the flowers are 1½ in. (4 cm) stars. **B. ida-maia** is quite different — each pendent flower is a bright red tube with green petals.

SITE & SOIL: Well-drained soil, a sheltered spot and full sun are necessary.

PLANT DETAILS: Planting time: September. Planting depth: 3 in. (7.5 cm). Spacing: 4 in. (10 cm). Height: 18–24 in. (45–60 cm).

PROPAGATION: Dislikes disturbance — buy new corms.

Brodiaea laxa

BULBOCODIUM Spring Saffron

Garden/Indoor plant
•
Corm
•
Colour available

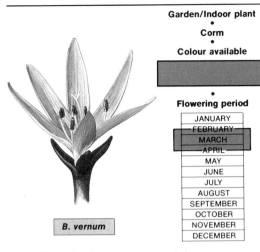

•
Flowering period

JANUARY
FEBRUARY
MARCH
APRIL
MAY
JUNE
JULY
AUGUST
SEPTEMBER
OCTOBER
NOVEMBER
DECEMBER

B. vernum

An early spring bloomer for containers or a sunny rockery. The young flowers of this Colchicum relative look like Crocuses at first glance — the low-growing flowers are goblet-shaped. On closer inspection the differences are seen — the leaves are absent or very small when the blooms appear and the strap-like petals open wide as they mature. The floral display lasts for about 3 weeks, beginning in February in mild districts. It is a good idea to lift and divide the clumps in early autumn every 2–3 years.

VARIETIES: B. vernum is the only species offered for sale. Up to 3 funnel-shaped flowers push through the soil on very short stalks. The petals are lavender-pink with a white base, and the mature blooms are distinctly star-like as the petals open. Bulbocodium can be grown as a pot plant for blooms in January or February. Plant 5 or 6 corms in a bowl filled with compost. Keep in a cool room until the buds appear and then move to the flowering site.

SITE & SOIL: Any well-drained soil will do — thrives best in full sun.

PLANT DETAILS: Planting time: September–October. Planting depth: 3 in. (7.5 cm). Spacing: 4 in. (10 cm). Height: 4 in. (10 cm).

PROPAGATION: Remove cormlets at lifting time and replant.

Bulbocodium vernum

CAMASSIA Quamash

Garden plant
•
True bulb
•
Colours available

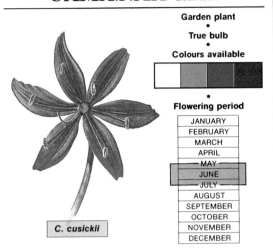

•
Flowering period

JANUARY
FEBRUARY
MARCH
APRIL
MAY
JUNE
JULY
AUGUST
SEPTEMBER
OCTOBER
NOVEMBER
DECEMBER

C. cusickii

Here is a plant which thrives in wet and heavy soil, although prolonged waterlogging throughout the winter months can lead to rot. It is a stately summer flower with stiff floral spikes which are clothed with masses of starry blooms. It is best to plant the bulbs where they can be left undisturbed in grassland or under trees — they are no bother at all but copious watering will be required in prolonged dry weather. Camassia is a plant of the New World and the native Americans used the bulbs for food (quamash) — hence the common name.

VARIETIES: C. leichtlinii is one of the most striking species — the upper part of the 3 ft (90 cm) flowering stem is bedecked with 1½ in. (4 cm) wide blue flowers. It blooms in late May — the variety **'Alba'** bears creamy-white flowers and **'Semiplena'** has semi-double flowers in the same colour. The largest blooms are borne by the lavender-blue variety **'Electra'**. The species **C. quamash** (**C. esculenta**) is shorter, with flowers ranging from white to purple in June. **C. cusickii** is the first to bloom and produces up to 100 blue flowers on each tall spike.

SITE & SOIL: Any moisture-retentive soil will do — thrives in sun or partial shade.

PLANT DETAILS: Planting time: September–October. Planting depth: 4 in. (10 cm). Spacing: 6 in. (15 cm). Height: 24–36 in. (60–90 cm).

PROPAGATION: Lift and divide overcrowded clumps in autumn — replant at once.

Camassia quamash

CANNA Indian Shot

Garden/Indoor plant
•
Rhizome
•
Colours available

•
Flowering period

| JANUARY |
| FEBRUARY |
| MARCH |
| APRIL |
| MAY |
| JUNE |
| JULY |
| AUGUST |
| SEPTEMBER |
| OCTOBER |
| NOVEMBER |
| DECEMBER |

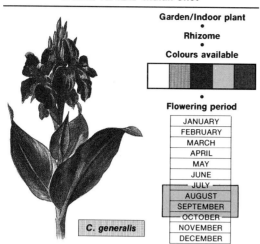

C. generalis

Big, bold and colourful, and so it is a shame that Canna is rarely seen in gardens. It is a half-hardy plant, blooming from midsummer until the onset of frosts, and can be used as a centrepiece in bedding schemes and large containers. The blooms are up to 5 in. (12.5 cm) across and the large leaves are decorative. The rhizomes are started in peat in March and then planted out in early June. The plants are lifted in autumn and the rhizomes are dried before being stored in sand or peat. It can be grown as a pot plant — in March set in compost 1 in. (2.5 cm) below the surface and repot every year.

VARIETIES: Many named varieties of **C. generalis (C. hybrida)** are available. They are divided into 2 groups. The *Coloured-leaved* varieties are highly decorative — examples include **'Dazzler'** (4 ft, red flowers, bronze foliage), **'Assault'** (4 ft, red flowers, purple foliage) and **'Verdi'** (3 ft, orange-blotched yellow and purple flowers, purple foliage). The *Green-leaved* varieties include **'Orchid'** (3 ft, pink flowers), **'President'** (3 ft, red flowers) and **'Lucifer'** (2 ft, red flowers).

SITE & SOIL: Humus-rich soil and full sun are essential.

PLANT DETAILS: Planting time: June. Planting depth: 2 in. (5 cm). Spacing: 12 in. (30 cm). Height: 24–48 in. (60–120 cm).

PROPAGATION: Cut up rhizomes once they have started into growth.

Canna generalis 'J. B. van der Schoot'

CARDIOCRINUM Cardiocrinum

Garden plant
•
True bulb
•
Colour available

•
Flowering period

| JANUARY |
| FEBRUARY |
| MARCH |
| APRIL |
| MAY |
| JUNE |
| JULY |
| AUGUST |
| SEPTEMBER |
| OCTOBER |
| NOVEMBER |
| DECEMBER |

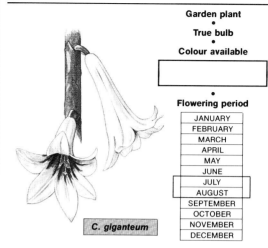

C. giganteum

There is no mistaking Cardiocrinum or the Giant Himalayan Lily when it is in full bloom. Lily-like trumpets about 6 in. (15 cm) long are borne in clusters on a stem above your head. Obviously this giant needs space and it also needs humus-rich soil and some shade — do not grow it in chalky soil nor on a dry, sunny site. It also needs patience — the leafy rosette may take a year or two before sending up the stout flowering stem.

VARIETIES: The giant is **C. giganteum (Lilium giganteum)** which grows up to 9 ft (270 cm) tall. A crown of about 20 large bells clusters above the shiny leaves which spiral the towering stem. Each of these white flowers has reddish markings on the inside and is strongly fragrant. **C. cordatum** grows about 6 ft (180 cm) high — the flowers are fewer in number but no smaller in size. As with its larger sister the main bulb dies after flowering but offsets are produced.

SITE & SOIL: Well-drained, moisture-retentive soil and light shade are essential.

PLANT DETAILS: Planting time: October. Planting depth: ½ in. (1 cm). Spacing: 36 in. (90 cm). Height: 72–108 in. (180–270 cm).

PROPAGATION: Buy new bulbs. Offsets can be planted but will take several years to flower.

Cardiocrinum giganteum

CHIONODOXA Glory of the Snow

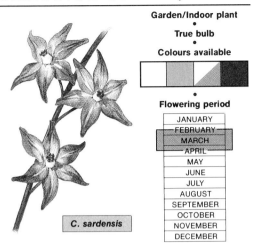

Garden/Indoor plant
•
True bulb
•
Colours available
•
Flowering period

| JANUARY |
| FEBRUARY |
| MARCH |
| APRIL |
| MAY |
| JUNE |
| JULY |
| AUGUST |
| SEPTEMBER |
| OCTOBER |
| NOVEMBER |
| DECEMBER |

C. sardensis

This low-growing early spring bulb is a popular choice for naturalising in the rockery or grassland, but was not grown as a garden plant before the middle of the 19th century. The 6-petalled starry flowers are borne in loose and dainty sprays on upright flower stalks which rise above the strap-like leaves. The foliage withers and dies once flowering is over — the blooms last for 3–4 weeks and can be cut for indoor decoration. Indoors plant the bulbs in September for February flowers.

VARIETIES: The most popular Chionodoxa is **C. luciliae** — about 10 blooms are borne on each flower stalk. Each flower is a pale blue star with a prominent white centre. There are several varieties, including the all-white **'Alba'** and the rosy pink **'Pink Giant'**. **C. sardensis** grows to about the same height (6 in. or 15 cm) and has the same sized flowers (1 in. or 2.5 cm across) but the blooms are all-blue with a tiny white eye. The largest species is the gentian blue **C. gigantea** — 10 in. (25 cm) high with 1½ in. (4 cm) wide flowers.

SITE & SOIL: Any well-drained soil will do — thrives in sun or light shade.

PLANT DETAILS: Planting time: September. Planting depth: 3 in. (7.5 cm). Spacing: 3 in. (7.5 cm). Height: 6–10 in. (15–25 cm).

PROPAGATION: Divide clumps in May — replant at once.

Chionodoxa luciliae

CHLIDANTHUS Delicate Lily

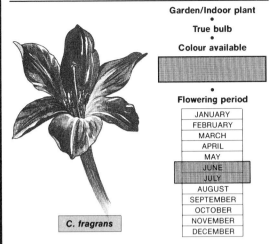

Garden/Indoor plant
•
True bulb
•
Colour available
•
Flowering period

| JANUARY |
| FEBRUARY |
| MARCH |
| APRIL |
| MAY |
| JUNE |
| JULY |
| AUGUST |
| SEPTEMBER |
| OCTOBER |
| NOVEMBER |
| DECEMBER |

C. fragrans

Pick this S. American bulb if you want something different for midsummer colour. The 3 in. (7.5 cm) wide flowers are funnel-shaped and are sweetly fragrant. Unfortunately it is not hardy, so you will have to plant the bulbs in spring and lift in late October. Store them in a cool dry place for planting next April. For indoor cultivation plant 3 bulbs in a 6 in. (15 cm) pot in autumn — cover with ½ in. (1 cm) of compost. Once the flowers appear keep in a cool place.

VARIETIES: There is just one species — **C. fragrans**. In summer the slender flower stalks appear, each one topped with 1–6 bright yellow Lily-like blooms. The narrow grey-green leaves appear shortly after the flowers. A lovely plant, but it sometimes fails to flower in the open garden. Some people prefer to plant them in a compost-filled pot and then in the flowering season bury the container in a bed or border in the garden. The pot is lifted in autumn and the bulbs dried and stored over winter.

SITE & SOIL: Well-drained soil and a sunny site are essential.

PLANT DETAILS: Planting time: April. Planting depth: 1 in. (2.5 cm). Spacing: 6 in. (15 cm). Height: 10 in. (25 cm).

PROPAGATION: Remove bulblets after lifting and store — plant in April.

Chlidanthus fragrans

CLIVIA Kaffir Lily

Indoor plant
•
Bulb-like root
•
Colours available

Flowering period

| JANUARY |
| FEBRUARY |
| MARCH |
| APRIL |
| MAY |
| JUNE |
| JULY |
| AUGUST |
| SEPTEMBER |
| OCTOBER |
| NOVEMBER |
| DECEMBER |

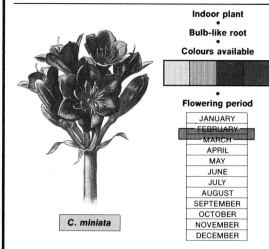

C. miniata

Clivia is a conservatory or house plant, although the pot can be stood outdoors during the summer months. The thick flower stalk bears a cluster of 10–20 flowers at its tip. Each bloom is a fragrant upturned bell, providing a bright display in late winter or early spring. The plant is generally bought as a leafy specimen rather than as a dormant bulb, but you can buy bulbs from some specialist suppliers. To obtain flowers year after year you must provide the plant with winter rest — keep it in an unheated room and provide just enough water to prevent wilting. Do not repot unless the plant is pushing out of the container.

VARIETIES: The Clivias in the catalogues or on the house plant bench are hybrids of **C. miniata**. The usual flower colour is salmon with a yellow throat, but all sorts of blends of cream, yellow, orange and red are available. The evergreen leaves are strap-like and about 18 in. (45 cm) long — they are arranged in a distinctive fan-like pattern.

SITE & SOIL: Bright light — avoid direct sun in summer. Water liberally from spring to autumn.

PLANT DETAILS: Planting time: April–May. Planting depth: ½ in. (1 cm). Spacing: Grow singly in a pot. Height: 12–18 in. (30–45 cm).

PROPAGATION: Repot, when necessary, after flowering. Divide plants at repotting time.

Clivia miniata

COLCHICUM Autumn Crocus

Garden plant
•
Corm
•
Colours available

Flowering period

| JANUARY |
| FEBRUARY |
| MARCH |
| APRIL |
| MAY |
| JUNE |
| JULY |
| AUGUST |
| SEPTEMBER |
| OCTOBER |
| NOVEMBER |
| DECEMBER |

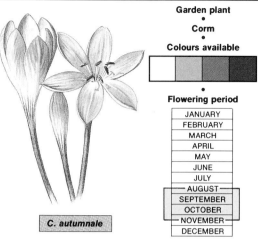

C. autumnale

Despite its common name and the shape of its flowers, Colchicum is not related to the true Crocus. No leaves are present when the wineglass-shaped flowers appear and the long tubes at the base of the petals extend down into the earth. Another difference is that there are 6 showy stamens compared with the 3 stamens in a Crocus flower. It is not a plant for everyone — all parts are poisonous and the large leaves which appear in spring are untidy. In addition the blooms may topple in heavy rain, so plant in grassland to support them or set the corms close together.

VARIETIES: **C. autumnale** bears 2 in. (5 cm) wide pink blooms — **'Album'** is a white variety and **'Roseum Plenum'** a double-flowering one. **C. speciosum** (Meadow Saffron) is larger and has stronger flower tubes to withstand autumn gales. The mauve flowers open out into 8 in. (20 cm) wide stars — **'Album'** is a white form. Named Colchicum hybrids include **'Waterlily'** (pink, double), **'The Giant'** (violet, large single) and **'Princess Astrid'** (pink, single, early-flowering).

SITE & SOIL: Well-drained, humus-rich soil is necessary — thrives in sun or light shade.

PLANT DETAILS: Planting time: July–August. Planting depth: 3 in. (7.5 cm). Spacing: 4–6 in. (10–15 cm). Height: 6–9 in. (15–22.5 cm).

PROPAGATION: Divide clumps in midsummer — replant at once.

Colchicum 'Waterlily'

CONVALLARIA Lily of the Valley

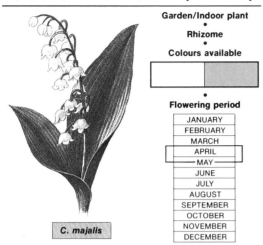

Garden/Indoor plant
•
Rhizome
•
Colours available

•
Flowering period

| JANUARY |
| FEBRUARY |
| MARCH |
| APRIL |
| —— MAY —— |
| JUNE |
| JULY |
| AUGUST |
| SEPTEMBER |
| OCTOBER |
| NOVEMBER |
| DECEMBER |

C. majalis

The dainty fragrant bells on arching flower stems appear at the same time as the large lance-shaped leaves. These leaves are borne in pairs and grow about 6 in. (15 cm) high, partly enclosing the flower stems. The plant spreads by means of underground branching rhizomes — these produce small shoots ('pips') which are used for planting. Convallaria is an excellent choice for spring-flowering ground cover in a shady area. For Christmas flowers indoors you will have to buy specially-prepared pips and plant them in compost in mid November.

VARIETIES: The garden species is **C. majalis**. The stem bears 10–15 pure white bells which are about ¼ in. (0.5 cm) long — these stems can be pulled (not cut) for flower arranging. There are several interesting varieties. Grow **'Fontin's Giant'** for large flowers, **'Prolificans'** for double ones or **'Rosea'** for pink instead of white blooms. For leaf colour there are **'Variegata'** (green, striped gold) and **'Hardwick Hall'** (green, edged gold).

SITE & SOIL: Moisture-retentive soil is essential — thrives best in partial shade.

PLANT DETAILS: Planting time: November–March. Planting depth: 1 in. (2.5 cm). Spacing: 4 in. (10 cm). Height: 8–12 in. (20–30 cm).

PROPAGATION: Divide overcrowded clumps in October — replant at once.

Convallaria majalis 'Variegata'

CORYDALIS Spring Fumitory

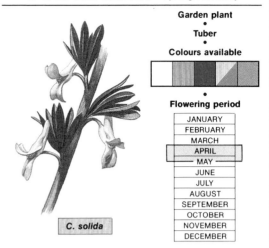

Garden plant
•
Tuber
•
Colours available

•
Flowering period

| JANUARY |
| FEBRUARY |
| MARCH |
| APRIL |
| —— MAY —— |
| JUNE |
| JULY |
| AUGUST |
| SEPTEMBER |
| OCTOBER |
| NOVEMBER |
| DECEMBER |

C. solida

The foliage of Corydalis is ferny and delicate, and each tubular bloom is spurred at the rear and lipped at the front. There are many species, but only a few produce tubers — these can be used for planting in the rock garden or under trees and tall shrubs. They do not like rich soil nor full sun — leave them to naturalise to provide a semi-wild area of pastel colour in spring. The effect is quite subtle and muted — choose something else if you want a bulb to provide a bold and bright effect in the garden.

VARIETIES: **C. solida** (**Fumaria bulbosa**) is the most popular tuberous species. The 6 in. (15 cm) flower spikes are borne in large numbers, each trumpet-like flower being either pink-purple or cream-coloured with a lilac mouth. Look for the variety **'George Baker'** (4–6 in.) — the wide-mouthed blooms are deep rosy-red. **C. cava** is somewhat taller, growing to about 8 in. (20 cm), and with a mixture of white and red flowers. **C. ambigua** bears attractive foliage and clear blue blooms. You will have to search for **C. bracteata** (yellow).

SITE & SOIL: Thrives in moist soil in partial shade.

PLANT DETAILS: Planting time: October–November. Planting depth: 3 in. (7.5 cm). Spacing: 4 in. (10 cm). Height: 4–8 in. (10–20 cm).

PROPAGATION: Divide overcrowded clumps before the leaves have withered — remove and plant offsets.

Corydalis ambigua

CRINUM Swamp Lily

Garden/Indoor plant
•
True bulb
•
Colours available

Flowering period

JANUARY
FEBRUARY
MARCH
APRIL
MAY
JUNE
JULY
AUGUST
SEPTEMBER
OCTOBER
NOVEMBER
DECEMBER

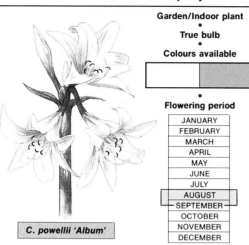

C. powellii 'Album'

Everything about Crinum is large — 6 in. bulbs, 3 ft tall flower stalks and 6 in. wide sweet-smelling Lily-like flowers. It is a pity that it does not have a hardier constitution as it is undoubtedly one of the finest of all late summer bulbs. It needs the protection of a sheltered sunny site during the growing season and a mulch of peat or straw in winter. The strap-like leaves are long and untidy, and perhaps the best way to grow Crinum is in a large container which is moved into a greenhouse before the onset of winter.

VARIETIES: The most reliable outdoor species is **C. powellii**.The flower stem bears a terminal cluster of about 10 blooms which open in succession. Each one of these trumpet-like flowers is about 4 in. (10 cm) long. Pink is the usual colour but a white variety (**'Album'**) is available. Water freely and feed regularly during the growing season. For conservatory cultivation pot up the bulb in March so that the tip is just above the surface. Water liberally during the growing season but water very sparingly in winter. Repot every 3–4 years.

SITE & SOIL: Well-drained, moisture-retentive soil in a south-facing position is essential.

PLANT DETAILS: Planting time: April–May. Planting depth: 6 in. (15 cm). Spacing: 18 in. (45 cm). Height: 36 in. (90 cm).

PROPAGATION: Buy new bulbs — Crinum hates root disturbance.

Crinum powellii

CROCOSMIA Montbretia

Garden plant
•
Corm
•
Colours available

Flowering period

JANUARY
FEBRUARY
MARCH
APRIL
MAY
JUNE
JULY
AUGUST
SEPTEMBER
OCTOBER
NOVEMBER
DECEMBER

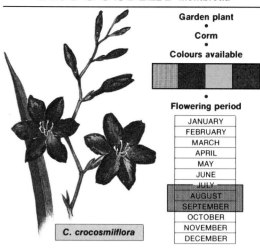

C. crocosmiiflora

Crocosmia is an old favourite which provides tall heads of bright colour when so many garden plants have finished flowering. The arching flower stalks with their tubular or starry blooms are a great favourite with flower arrangers as they are long-lasting in water. Their usual home is the herbaceous border, and it is a good idea to cover the plants with a mulch of peat or straw once the sword-like leaves have withered in late autumn.

VARIETIES: Montbretia is the name which is given to **C. crocosmiiflora** and all its many varieties, although this common name is often applied to all the Crocosmias. The upright flower stalks bear trumpet-shaped 1½ in. (4 cm) blooms in zig-zag fashion. Look for **'Lucifer'** (red, hardy), **'Jenny Bloom'** (yellow, hardy), **'Emberglow'** (orange-red, hardy), **'Solfatare'** (yellow, semi-tender) and **'Emily Mackenzie'** (red-centred orange, semi-tender). A good choice is the fully hardy **C. masonorum** which has arching stems and bright orange-red flowers.

SITE & SOIL: Well-drained, humus-rich soil in a sheltered sunny spot is necessary.

PLANT DETAILS: Planting time: March–April. Planting depth: 3 in. (7.5 cm). Spacing: 6 in. (15 cm). Height: 24–36 in. (60–90 cm).

PROPAGATION: Divide clumps after flowering every 3 years.

Crocosmia 'Lucifer'

CROCUS Crocus

AUTUMN-FLOWERING SPECIES

Flowering period:
September–December

Some produce leaves after flowering

Wide range of colours

C. speciosus

SPRING-FLOWERING CHRYSANTHUS VARIETIES & HYBRIDS

Flowering period:
February–March

All produce leaves before flowers open

Often yellow, but whites, blues and mauves with yellow do occur

C. 'Cream Beauty'

SPRING-FLOWERING SPECIES

Flowering period:
January–April

All produce leaves before flowers open

Wide range of colours

C. tommasinianus

Garden/Indoor plant
•
Corm
•
Colours available

Flowering period

| JANUARY |
| FEBRUARY |
| MARCH |
| APRIL |
| MAY |
| JUNE |
| JULY |
| AUGUST |
| SEPTEMBER |
| OCTOBER |
| NOVEMBER |
| DECEMBER |

SPRING-FLOWERING DUTCH HYBRIDS

Flowering period:
March–April

All produce leaves before flowers open

Often blue, purple or white, but yellows do occur

C. 'Pickwick'

Everyone can recognise a Crocus, and for most gardeners the choice is a simple one. A purple or yellow large-flowering Dutch hybrid, or a mixture of both, designed to bloom after the Snowdrops and before the Tulips. The full Crocus story, however, is much more extensive. There are Crocus species which flower in January and the Chrysanthus hybrids produce blooms which are smaller but earlier than the popular Dutch ones. In addition the Autumn-flowering species provide flowers from September to December. They all fit into the 4 groups illustrated on this page — colours, sizes and time of flowering vary quite markedly, but all are upright and goblet-shaped with 6 petals. The flower becomes starry or cup-shaped when fully open and the grass-like leaves sometimes have a white midrib. They are not fussy about soil type and you can grow them in the rockery, under trees, in beds and borders, in containers and for naturalising in grassland. With the latter use it is necessary not to cut the grass until the leaves have died. In addition to all the outdoor uses they are widely grown as indoor plants for early spring decoration. Choose one of the Chrysanthus or Dutch hybrids. Fill a bowl, clay pot, pan or Crocus pot with compost and plant the corms 1 in. (2.5 cm) deep and 1 in. apart. Place the containers outdoors and leave them there until the flower buds have begun to show colour. Now move them indoors — in a shady cool spot for a few days and then to the site chosen for flowering.

VARIETIES: The *Autumn-flowering* Species are easy to grow in a sunny, well-drained spot. **C. speciosus** is the most popular and is often the earliest to flower in September. The blooms are tall with veined petals in violet, blue and white. The Saffron Crocus (**C. sativus**) is smaller and easy to recognise — the 3 stigmas are long and bright red. Other varieties include **C. ochroleucus** (cream), **C. nudiflorus** (purple) and the November-flowering **C. laevigatus** and **C. longiflorus**. The earliest of the *Spring-flowering* Species come into bloom as the latest of the Autumn-flowering ones fade. These January–February bloomers include **C. ancyrensis** (the Golden Bunch Crocus with masses of orange-yellow flowers), **C. angustifolius** (the Cloth-of-Gold Crocus with brown-backed golden flowers) and the early varieties of **C. tommasinianus** (the 'Tommy' Crocus with wide-open blooms in lilac, blue, reddish purple and white). Other Spring-flowering Species include **C. sieberi** (yellow-throated lilac) and its varieties **'Bowles White'** and the gold, white and purple **'Tricolor'**. Others you will find in the catalogues are **C. biflorus** (the Scotch Crocus) and **C. imperati 'De Jager'** (bold purple stripes). One of the Spring-flowering Species has given rise to a large number of Crocus types — the *Chrysanthus* Varieties and Hybrids. The flowers are early, medium-sized and fragrant. At planting time you will find several types at your garden centre — look for **'Blue Pearl'** (blue with a gold base), **'Cream Beauty'** (pale yellow with orange stigmas), **'E. A. Bowles'** (deep yellow, large), **'Ladykiller'** (purple outside and white within), **'Princess Beatrix'** (blue with a yellow base) and **'Snowbunting'** (white with a yellow base). The final group is made up of the *Dutch* Hybrids, listed in some catalogues as the Large-flowering Varieties. They have all been bred from **C. vernus** and are larger and later than the Chrysanthus Varieties and Hybrids. A number of favourites belong here. **'Joan of Arc'** is one of the best whites and **'Mammoth Yellow'** is the largest of the golden Crocuses. **'Pickwick'** is white with purple stripes, **'Remembrance'** is shiny purple and **'Vanguard'** is silvery lilac.

SITE & SOIL: Any well-drained soil in sun or light shade.

PLANT DETAILS: Planting time: September–November (July for Autumn-flowering Species). Planting depth: 3 in. (7.5 cm). Spacing: 4 in. (10 cm). Height: 3–5 in. (7.5–12.5 cm).

PROPAGATION: Divide overcrowded clumps in autumn.

CROCUS continued

Crocus speciosus

Crocus sativus

Crocus ochroleucus

Crocus angustifolius

Crocus sieberi 'Tricolor'

Crocus 'Ladykiller'

Crocus 'Joan of Arc'

Crocus 'Mammoth Yellow'

Crocus 'Remembrance'

CYCLAMEN Cyclamen

Garden/Indoor plant
•
Tuber ('corm')
•

Colours available

•

Flowering period

JANUARY	
FEBRUARY	
MARCH	
APRIL	
MAY	
JUNE	
JULY	
AUGUST	
SEPTEMBER	
OCTOBER	
NOVEMBER	
DECEMBER	

C. persicum

For most of us the Cyclamen is a pot plant — large, long-stemmed flowers with swept-back petals rising above heart-shaped silver-patterned leaves. These are the Florist Cyclamens and are bought in flower rather than as dormant tubers. You should buy the plant in autumn and not midwinter, and choose one with plenty of buds. Provide a cool spot away from direct sunlight. Reduce watering when flowers fade — place the pot on its side and keep dry until midsummer. Then repot using fresh compost, burying the tuber so that the top is just above the surface. Keep the compost barely moist until the shoots appear. If this flower form appeals to you there are small Hardy Cyclamens with 1 in. (2.5 cm) flowers for growing outdoors. They are a good choice for carpeting under trees or shrubs and for a shady part of the rockery. There are winter, spring, summer and autumn varieties — see below for details.

VARIETIES: The *Florist* Cyclamens are hybrids of **C. persicum**. These plants have wide petals which may be frilled and are available in many colours. The foliage is usually edged, marbled or lined in white. This leaf patterning may be bold enough to rival the flowers in display value. Once there were only 12 in. (30 cm) high standard-sized varieties but now there are dwarfs with scented blooms on stalks only a few inches high. The *Hardy* Cyclamens are usually bought as tubers (often listed as corms) and planted with the smooth side down in late summer. The most popular species is **C. hederifolium** (**C. neapolitanum**) which has marbled leaves and bears white, pink or red flowers in September–November. Almost as easy to grow is **C. coum**. The white, pink or red flowers are blotched with purple and appear in December–March — the round leaves are usually all-green. **C. purpurascens** (**C. europaeum**) bears fragrant red flowers in July–September above the silver-zoned leaves and the marbled-leaved **C. repandum** has red, pink or white flowers in April.

SITE & SOIL: Well-drained, humus-rich soil in partial shade is necessary.

PLANT DETAILS: Planting time: July–September. Planting depth: 1 in. (2.5 cm). Spacing: 6 in. (15 cm). Height: 4–6 in. (10–15 cm).

PROPAGATION: Cyclamens hate disturbance — do not divide. Seed can be sown under glass in summer.

C. coum

C. hederifolium

Cyclamen persicum

Cyclamen hederifolium 'Moira Reid'

Cyclamen coum 'Roseum'

DAHLIA Dahlia

Garden plant
•
Tuberous root
•
Colours available

Flowering period

| JANUARY |
| FEBRUARY |
| MARCH |
| APRIL |
| MAY |
| JUNE |
| JULY |
| AUGUST |
| SEPTEMBER |
| OCTOBER |
| NOVEMBER |
| DECEMBER |

D. 'Athalie'

D. 'Little John'

Dahlias are a basic feature of the late summer garden. The giant Border varieties with blooms 10 in. (25 cm) across are the stars of the show, but you can also buy Bedding and Lilliput Dahlias with small flowers and a compact growth habit. The favourite types of Border Dahlia are the Decorative, Semi-Cactus and Cactus groups, and their usual home is the herbaceous border or in a bed of their own. The Bedding and Lilliput varieties on the other hand are grown in rockeries, containers and bedded-out areas. All Dahlias provide excellent material for flower arranging. You can start by planting out rooted cuttings or sprouted tubers in late May or early June, but it is more usual to plant dormant tubers and set them out about a month earlier. Border Dahlias will require staking — insert a stout cane or wooden stake to a depth of 12 in. (30 cm) before planting. You can increase the bushiness of the plant by pinching out the tips of the main stems about 3 weeks after planting. Water thoroughly during dry spells — once the buds have appeared it will be necessary to water every few days if rain does not fall. Do not hoe — keep weeds down by applying a 2 in. (5 cm) mulch of peat or compost around the plant. For larger (but fewer) flowers it is necessary to remove the sidebuds in the cluster, leaving just the terminal flower bud. The regular removal of faded blooms will prolong the flowering life of the specimen. When the first frosts have blackened the foliage cut off the stems about 6 in. (15 cm) above the ground. Gently fork out the tubers and discard surplus soil and broken roots. Stand the tubers upside down for a week to drain off excess moisture and then place them on a layer of peat in a box and cover the roots but not the crowns with more peat. Store in a cool but frost-free place until planting time arrives.

SITE & SOIL: Any well-drained garden soil will do — choose a spot which receives at least a few hours sunshine on a bright day.

PLANT DETAILS: Planting time: Late April-early May. Planting depth: Border varieties 3 in. (7.5 cm). Bedding & Lilliput varieties 2 in. (5 cm).
Spacing: Tall Border varieties 36 in. (90 cm).
Medium Border varieties 24 in. (60 cm).
Bedding & Lilliput varieties 12 in. (30 cm).
Height: See page 35.

PROPAGATION: Carefully divide tubers every 2 years — make sure that each division has a piece of stem with swollen tubers attached.

FLOWER SIZE

Some catalogues use words to describe the bloom diameters of well-grown Decorative and Cactus varieties. The key below will guide you in making your choice.

Giant	More than 10 in. (25 cm)
Large	8–10 in. (20–25 cm)
Medium	6–8 in. (15–20 cm)
Small	4–6 in. (10–15 cm)
Miniature	Less than 4 in. (10 cm)

Dahlia blooms are made up of miniature flowers known as florets. The types of florets present are a key to identification.

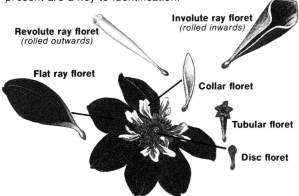

Revolute ray floret
(rolled outwards)

Involute ray floret
(rolled inwards)

Flat ray floret

Collar floret

Tubular floret

Disc floret

DAHLIA continued

BORDER & BEDDING DAHLIAS

PLANT HEIGHT

Some catalogues use words to describe the average height of a variety grown under good conditions. Do remember that the stated height is only an average — the actual height achieved by a plant will depend upon location, weather and cultural conditions.

Tall Border variety
  More than 4 ft (120 cm)

Medium Border variety
  3–4 ft (90–120 cm)

Small Border variety
  2–3 ft (60–90 cm)

Bedding variety
  1–2 ft (30–60 cm)

Lilliput variety
  Less than 1 ft (30 cm)

SINGLE-FLOWERED

One ring of ray florets. Central group of disc florets. Height 1½–2 ft (45–60 cm). Blooms up to 4 in. (10 cm).
Examples: **'Murillo'** (light red edged blood red), **'Yellow Hammer'** (yellow), **'Sneezy'** (white)

ANEMONE-FLOWERED

One or more rings of ray florets. Central group of tubular florets. Height 2–3 ft (60–90 cm). Blooms up to 4 in. (10 cm).
Examples: **'Comet'** (dark red), **'Lucy'** (purple and yellow), **'Vera Higgins'** (bronze)

COLLERETTE

One outer ring of flat ray florets plus an inner ring of collar florets and a central group of disc florets. Height 2½–4 ft (75–120 cm). Blooms up to 4 in. (10 cm).
Examples: **'La Gioconda'** (scarlet and gold), **'Claire de Lune'** (yellow)

WATER-LILY

Fully double, flattened shape. Ray florets are flat or with slightly curved margins. Height up to 4 ft (120 cm). Blooms up to 6 in. (15 cm).
Examples: **'Scarlet Beauty'** (red), **'Gerrie Hoek'** (pale and dark pink), **'Vicky Crutchfield'** (pink)

DECORATIVE

Fully double. Flat ray florets are broad and blunt-ended. Height up to 5 ft (150 cm). Blooms up to 10 in. (25 cm) or more.
Examples: **'Jocondo'** (Giant red), **'House of Orange'** (Medium orange), **'David Howard'** (Miniature orange)

BALL

Fully double, ball-shaped — often flattened. Involute ray florets are blunt- or round-ended. Height up to 4 ft (120 cm). Blooms up to 6 in. (15 cm).
Examples: **'Wootton Cupid'** (pink), **'Cherida'** (bronze-lilac), **'Stolze von Berlin'** (pink)

POMPON

Fully double, globe-shaped. Involute ray florets are blunt- or round-ended. Height 2½–4 ft (75–120 cm). Blooms less than 2 in. (5 cm).
Examples: **'Willo's Violet'** (pale purple), **'Moor Place'** (purple), **'Noreen'** (pink)

CACTUS

Fully double. Revolute ray florets are narrow and pointed. Height up to 5 ft (150 cm). Blooms up to 10 in. (25 cm) or more.
Examples: **'Irish Visit'** (Large red), **'Doris Day'** (Small red), **'Athalie'** (Small pink)

SEMI-CACTUS

Fully double. Pointed ray florets are revolute for half their length or less. Height up to 5 ft (150 cm). Blooms up to 10 in. (25 cm) or more.
Examples: **'Golden Crown'** (Large golden yellow), **'Symbol'** (Medium orange), **'Park Princess'** (Miniature pink)

MISCELLANEOUS

Flower form not belonging to any of the other 9 groups.
Examples: **'Bishop of Llandaff'** (red), **'Andries Wonder'** (salmon), **'Giraffe'** (yellow and bronze-red), **D. coccinea** (red), **D. merkii** (rose-lilac), **'Jescot Julie'** (orange-purple)

LILLIPUT DAHLIAS

Single — one ring of ray florets. Central group of disc florets. Height less than 1 ft (30 cm). Blooms up to 1½ in. (4 cm).
Examples: **'Bambino'** (creamy white), **'Little John'** (yellow), **'Red Riding Hood'** (vermilion)

DAHLIA continued

Dahlia 'Yellow Hammer'

Dahlia 'Comet'

Dahlia 'Gerrie Hoek'

Dahlia 'House of Orange'

Dahlia 'Cherida'

Dahlia 'Willo's Violet'

Dahlia 'Doris Day'

Dahlia 'Symbol'

Dahlia 'Bishop of Llandaff'

DIERAMA Wand Flower

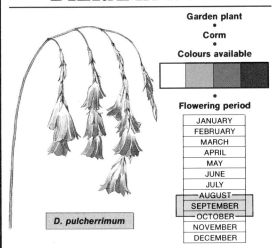

Garden plant
•
Corm
•
Colours available

•
Flowering period

JANUARY
FEBRUARY
MARCH
APRIL
MAY
JUNE
JULY
AUGUST
SEPTEMBER
OCTOBER
NOVEMBER
DECEMBER

D. pulcherrimum

A stunning plant when grown in the right situation, but not often seen. It needs space — the most popular one (D. pulcherrimum) grows about 5 ft (150 cm) high. It also needs shelter and a sunny spot, but Dierama is not as tender as is often supposed. The tall grassy leaves are semi-evergreen and in late summer the wiry arching stems appear, each one bowed down by the numerous tubular or bell-shaped flowers it bears. These tassels of 1 in. (2.5 cm) long blooms wave in the breeze — hence the common name.

VARIETIES: D. pulcherrimum is a tall species which bears deep pink or purplish red blooms. There are several varieties listed in the specialist catalogues, including the large-flowered **'Major'** and with colours ranging from **'Album'** (white), **'Moonlight'** (pale lilac) and **'Blackbird'** (violet) to the wine-red **'Heron'** and purple **'Nigra'**. **D. pendulum** is similar in growth habit but smaller, reaching 3–4 ft (90–120 cm). The baby is **D. pumilum** (**D. dracomontanum**) which grows about 2½ ft (75 cm) high with pink or lilac blooms.

SITE & SOIL: Well-drained soil and full sun are necessary.

PLANT DETAILS: Planting time: October–November. Planting depth: 3 in. (7.5 cm). Spacing: 12 in. (30 cm). Height: 30–60 in. (75–150 cm).

PROPAGATION: Hates root disturbance — transplant seedlings rather than lifting clumps for division.

Dierama pendulum

DRACUNCULUS Dragon Arum

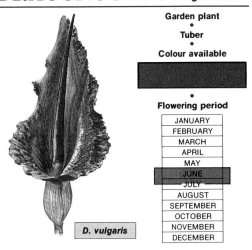

Garden plant
•
Tuber
•
Colour available

•
Flowering period

JANUARY
FEBRUARY
MARCH
APRIL
MAY
JUNE
JULY
AUGUST
SEPTEMBER
OCTOBER
NOVEMBER
DECEMBER

D. vulgaris

A plant which is bizarre rather than beautiful. It is a member of the aroid family and has a complex flower made up of a spathe and spadix like an Arum — see page 20. Everything about it is large — the leaves which spread out like a fan and the flowers which appear in summer. It is an easy plant to grow in a sunny spot and is certainly eye-catching when in bloom, but it is a rarity and you will have to search for a supplier. The problem is the putrid smell which is attractive to moths but not to people.

VARIETIES: The only species you are likely to find in the catalogues is **D. vulgaris (Arum dracunculus)**. The leaves grow up to 8 in. (20 cm) long and are divided into finger-like segments. The leaf stalks and fleshy stems are blotched with brown, giving a snakeskin effect. On top of each stem the complex flower appears in early summer. The wavy-edged spathe reaches about 18 in. (45 cm) — pale green on the outside and maroon-purple within. The dark purple spadix reaches to the top of the spathe.

SITE & SOIL: Any well-drained soil will do — thrives best in full sun.

PLANT DETAILS: Planting time: August–September. Planting depth: 3 in. (7.5 cm). Spacing: 18 in. (45 cm). Height: 36 in. (90 cm).

PROPAGATION: Divide clumps or remove offset tubers and plant in autumn.

Dracunculus vulgaris

ERANTHIS Winter Aconite

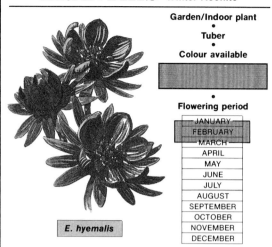

Garden/Indoor plant
•
Tuber
•
Colour available

Flowering period

JANUARY
FEBRUARY
MARCH
APRIL
MAY
JUNE
JULY
AUGUST
SEPTEMBER
OCTOBER
NOVEMBER
DECEMBER

E. hyemalis

Plant Winter Aconites with the Snowdrops in autumn under shrubs or deciduous trees — in February or even earlier you will be rewarded with a glossy yellow carpet of flowers when so much of the garden is bare. These blooms are borne on 3 in. (7.5 cm) stalks and bear a frilly green collar. This collar is really a bract — the true leaves do not appear until the plant is in flower. Eranthis can be grown as a house plant — plant the tubers in compost in September for January blooms.

VARIETIES: The usual Eranthis is **E. hyemalis** — 1 in. lemon yellow flowers and deeply divided green leaves. This is the one to choose for very early flowers, but it can become a nuisance in confined areas as it produces an abundance of self-sown plants. The hybrid **E. tubergenii** is less invasive, more robust and the flowers are larger. **E. cilicica** is another large-flowering Winter Aconite — the leaves have a bronzy tinge. Remember to plant Eranthis as soon as the tubers arrive.

SITE & SOIL: Any well-drained soil will do — thrives in sun or partial shade.

PLANT DETAILS: Planting time: September. Planting depth: 2 in. (5 cm). Spacing: 4 in. (10 cm). Height: 3–5 in. (7.5–12.5 cm).

PROPAGATION: Lift and divide clumps in early summer every few years — replant immediately.

Eranthis cilicica

EREMURUS Foxtail Lily

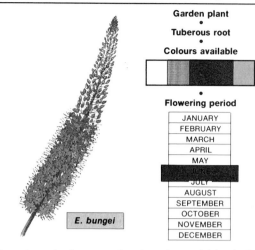

Garden plant
•
Tuberous root
•
Colours available

Flowering period

JANUARY
FEBRUARY
MARCH
APRIL
MAY
JUNE
JULY
AUGUST
SEPTEMBER
OCTOBER
NOVEMBER
DECEMBER

E. bungei

Here is a herbaceous border plant which rivals Delphinium in stateliness — colourful and massive upright spikes rising shoulder high or even higher. Their make-up, however, is quite unlike the Delphinium — Eremurus flower-heads are made up of countless starry flowers. Unfortunately it is a fussy plant and you will have to choose the site carefully — it needs really good drainage and both sun and protection from cold winds are essential. Copious watering in dry weather is required. When planting, rest the roots of the crown on a bed of sand.

VARIETIES: The giant Eremurus is **E. robustus** which grows 8 ft (240 cm) high and bears pale pink flowers in early June. It is too tall for many gardens. A more popular species is **E. bungei (E. stenophyllus)** — 5 ft (150 cm) high with yellow or orange blooms. The easiest ones to grow are the **'Shelford'** and **'Ruiter'** hybrids which are available in a wide range of colours. Another easy one is the fully hardy **E. himalaicus** (4 ft, white). Prolonged hard frost in winter can be fatal to the more delicate types — cover the crowns with bracken or peat in late autumn.

SITE & SOIL: Well-drained, light soil with sun in the afternoon and evening are necessary.

PLANT DETAILS: Planting time: September–October. Planting depth: 3 in. (7.5 cm). Spacing: 24–36 in. (60–90 cm). Height: 48–96 in. (120–240 cm).

PROPAGATION: Divide clumps in autumn or early spring.

Eremurus robustus

ERYTHRONIUM Erythronium

Garden/Indoor plant
•
Corm
•
Colours available

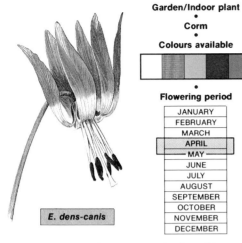

Flowering period

JANUARY
FEBRUARY
MARCH
APRIL
MAY
JUNE
JULY
AUGUST
SEPTEMBER
OCTOBER
NOVEMBER
DECEMBER

E. dens-canis

The key feature of Erythronium is the wide-open starry flower which droops at the top of a wiry stem. The petals are usually bent backwards and the foliage is often blotched or streaked with brown. These plants are most at home in a woodland setting around shrubs or trees. They are not difficult to grow, but there are two rules. Never let the corms dry out between lifting or purchase and planting, and do not disturb established clumps unless it is really necessary.

VARIETIES: E. dens-canis (Dog's-tooth Violet) is the usual type — the name comes from the shape of the corm and not the leaves. The rose-coloured flowers are 2 in. (5 cm) across and the leaves are marked with brown blotches — varieties with flowers in white, pink and violet are available. It grows about 6 in. (15 cm) high — for taller plants with yellow flowers grow **E. 'Pagoda'**. A smaller yellow is the Trout Lily (**E. americanum**). The aristocrat is **E. 'White Beauty'** — red-eyed pure white flowers on 12 in. (30 cm) stems.

SITE & SOIL: Well-drained but moisture-retentive soil is required — thrives best in partial shade.

PLANT DETAILS: Planting time: August–October. Planting depth: 3 in. (7.5 cm). Spacing: 4 in. (10 cm). Height: 6–12 in. (15–30 cm).

PROPAGATION: Resents root disturbance — divide over-crowded clumps in late summer and replant immediately.

Erythronium 'Pagoda'

EUCHARIS Amazon Lily

Indoor plant
•
True bulb
•
Colour available

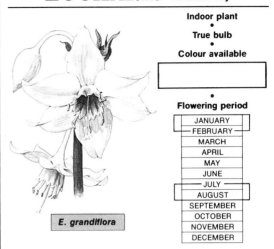

Flowering period

JANUARY
FEBRUARY
MARCH
APRIL
MAY
JUNE
JULY
AUGUST
SEPTEMBER
OCTOBER
NOVEMBER
DECEMBER

E. grandiflora

This showy bulb from S. America has been grown in conservatories and greenhouses since Victorian times, but it is not for you unless you can provide a minimum temperature of 65°F (18°C) during the growing season. The usual blooming period is late summer and again in winter if a period of rest is provided. The routine is to water copiously and feed regularly during active growth and then withhold fertilizer and only give enough water to prevent wilting once the flowers have faded. Resume regular watering and feeding when new leaves have started to grow.

VARIETIES: E. grandiflora (**E. amazonica**) has 3 in. (7.5 cm) wide fragrant blooms which look like a white Narcissus with a spiky trumpet. About 3–6 are borne on each 2 ft (60 cm) stalk. Eucharis is an evergreen which generally blooms between the end of summer and midwinter, but it can flower at other times of the year. The secret of success is to provide the right amount of water to keep the plant alive but not active during the resting period. Repot in spring every 3–4 years.

SITE & SOIL: Use a soilless compost — choose a brightly-lit spot away from direct sun.

PLANT DETAILS: Planting time: April–May. Planting depth: Tip should be just above the surface. Spacing: 1 in a 5 in. (12.5 cm) pot. Height: 24 in. (60 cm).

PROPAGATION: Remove and plant up bulblets when repotting.

Eucharis grandiflora

EUCOMIS Pineapple Lily

Garden/Indoor plant
•
True bulb
•
Colours available

Flowering period

JANUARY
FEBRUARY
MARCH
APRIL
MAY
JUNE
JULY
AUGUST
SEPTEMBER
OCTOBER
NOVEMBER
DECEMBER

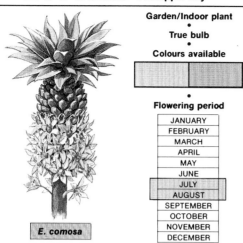

E. comosa

It is easy to see the origin of the common name when this plant is in flower — there is a leafy crown above the floral spike. Do not try to plant it outdoors unless you live in a sheltered mild area — it is much better to treat it as a container plant which is stood outdoors during the growing season and brought into the greenhouse before the onset of frosts. The leaves die down in winter — keep the compost dry until growth starts again in spring.

VARIETIES: E. comosa (E. punctata) needs lots of space — the 1½ ft (45 cm) long leaves form a large rosette and the 1 ft (30 cm) tall flower-head bears masses of fragrant creamy-white flowers. This plant grows about 2 ft (60 cm) high — for something shorter choose **E. bicolor** which grows about 1½ ft (45 cm) high. Its 1 in. (2.5 cm) wide flowers are pale green with a lilac edge. Water container-grown plants copiously during summer and repot every year in spring.

SITE & SOIL: Use a soil-based compost — place in a brightly-lit spot in a greenhouse or on a window sill. Outdoors a sunny spot is required.

PLANT DETAILS: Planting time: March–April. Planting depth: Tip should be level with the surface. Spacing: 1 in a 6 in. (15 cm) pot. Height: 18–24 in. (45–60 cm).

PROPAGATION: Remove and pot up bulblets when repotting.

Eucomis bicolor

FREESIA Freesia

Garden/Indoor plant
•
Corm
•
Colours available

Flowering period

JANUARY
FEBRUARY
MARCH
APRIL
MAY
JUNE
JULY
AUGUST
SEPTEMBER
OCTOBER
NOVEMBER
DECEMBER

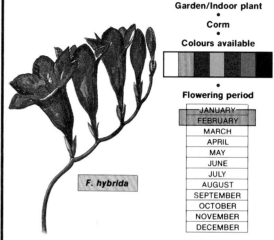

F. hybrida

Outdoor Freesias can be grown in a sheltered sunny spot — buy specially prepared corms and plant 2 in. (5 cm) deep in April for flowers in August–October. Much more popular, however, are the Florist Freesias grown in the greenhouse for winter blooms, and their varieties and cultivation are described below. After planting stand the pots outdoors until early autumn. Bring indoors and the flowers will begin to appear in January. Keep the greenhouse cool. When flowers and leaves have died down, store the corms in dry peat and repot in summer.

VARIETIES: The 2 in. long tubular flowers of **F. hybrida** grow on one side of the wiry stems. Fragrance is an important feature and the floral sprays are popular with flower arrangers. Mixtures of various colours are often chosen but you can buy named varieties. Examples include **'Ballerina'** (white), **'Aurora'** (cream), **'Wintergold'** (yellow), **'Oberon'** (bronze), **'Red Lion'** (vermilion), **'Marie Louise'** (white-throated pink) and **'Royal Blue'** (white-throated blue). Double-flowering varieties are available.

SITE & SOIL: Use a soilless or soil-based compost — place close to the glass and provide support.

PLANT DETAILS: Planting time: July–August. Planting depth: 2 in. (5 cm). Spacing: 6 in a 5 in. (12.5 cm) pot. Height: 12–18 in. (30–45 cm).

PROPAGATION: Separate cormlets after lifting and store for planting up in summer.

Freesia hybrida 'Marie Louise'

FRITILLARIA Fritillary

Garden plant

•

True bulb

•

Colours available

•

Flowering period

JANUARY
FEBRUARY
MARCH
APRIL
— MAY —
JUNE
JULY
AUGUST
SEPTEMBER
OCTOBER
NOVEMBER
DECEMBER

F. meleagris

F. imperialis

F. persica

All the Fritillarias have bell-like blooms which generally hang downwards from the top of upright stems which bear narrow leaves. There the family likenesses end. Some are easy to grow, such as the dainty Snake's Head Fritillary, and others like F. grayana need the shelter of an alpine house. There is also a large difference in heights — F. pluriflora is compact enough for a small rockery whereas F. persica bears its flowers on a 3–4 ft (90–120 cm) stalk. The 2 most popular ones are Snake's Head Fritillary and Crown Imperial, and all they need is a site which is free-draining and receives some sunshine. This does not mean that they are trouble-free — you must take care at planting time. The bulbs are made up of fleshy scales — do not let them dry out and handle carefully. Put some coarse sand in the planting hole and place the bulbs sideways. Cover with sand and replace the soil.

VARIETIES: **F. meleagris** (Snake's Head Fritillary) is a plant for the rockery, front of the border or for naturalising in grass. Each 1 ft (30 cm) stem bears 1 or 2 pendent 1½ in. (4 cm) bells. The usual petal pattern is a checkerboard, although there are all-white varieties (**'Alba'**, **'Aphrodite'**) available. **F. imperialis** (Crown Imperial) is a much more imposing plant than its lowly but popular relative. At the top of each stout 2–3 ft (60–90 cm) stem is a cluster of pendent blooms — 2 in. (5 cm) cups in yellow (**'Maxima Lutea'**), orange (**'Aurora'**) or red (**'Rubra'**). The flower-head is unusual — the odour is peculiar and there is a crown of short green leaves. This is a plant for the herbaceous or mixed border, as is the equally imposing **F. persica** with tall green stems from which hang purple bell-shaped flowers. In contrast there is the 6 in. (15 cm) high **F. michailowskyi** which bears purple bells edged with yellow. Another colourful species is **F. acmopetala** —1½ ft (45 cm) with purple- and yellow-striped flowers.

SITE & SOIL: Any well-drained soil will do — thrives best in light shade.

PLANT DETAILS: Planting time: September–November. Planting depth: Short varieties — 5 in. (12.5 cm). Tall varieties — 8 in. (20 cm). Spacing: Short varieties — 6 in. (15 cm). Tall varieties — 18 in. (45 cm). Height: 6–48 in. (15–120 cm).

PROPAGATION: Divide clumps in summer every 4 years.

Fritillaria meleagris 'Alba'

Fritillaria imperialis 'Maxima Lutea'

Fritillaria michailowskyi

GALANTHUS Snowdrop

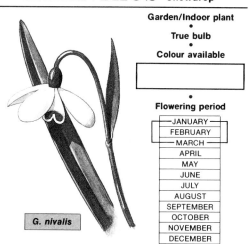

G. nivalis

Garden/Indoor plant
•
True bulb
•
Colour available

•
Flowering period

| JANUARY |
| FEBRUARY |
| MARCH |
| APRIL |
| MAY |
| JUNE |
| JULY |
| AUGUST |
| SEPTEMBER |
| OCTOBER |
| NOVEMBER |
| DECEMBER |

There are several bulbs in this A–Z section which flower in February or even earlier, but nearly every gardener relies on the Snowdrop to herald that spring is on the way. The pendent white bells can be distinguished from the Snowflake (Leucojum) by the 3 inner green-tipped petals and the 3 outer all-white ones. Dried-out bulbs transplant badly so always plant Snowdrops as soon as you buy them. For indoor blooms plant the bulbs ½ in. (1 cm) deep in compost-filled pots in September — treat as Crocus (page 31).

VARIETIES: The Common Snowdrop is **G. nivalis** — 1 in. (2.5 cm) long flowers on 6 in. (15 cm) stalks. There are several interesting varieties, such as the double-flowering **'Ophelia'**, **'Flore Pleno'** and **'Pusey Green Tip'**, the tall **'Viridapicis'** and the yellow-marked **'Lutescens'**. As a change from the Common Snowdrop and its varieties you can grow the large **G. elwesii** with 10 in. (25 cm) stems and globular flowers. Best of all, perhaps, are the two hybrids — **G. 'Atkinsii'** (early, tall) and **G. 'S. Arnott'** (large-flowered, scented).

SITE & SOIL: Moist soil and light shade are required.

PLANT DETAILS: Planting time: September–October. Planting depth: 4 in. (10 cm). Spacing: 4 in. (10 cm). Height: 4–10 in. (10–25 cm).

PROPAGATION: Lift and divide clumps while the leaves are still green — replant immediately.

Galanthus 'Atkinsii'

GALTONIA Summer Hyacinth

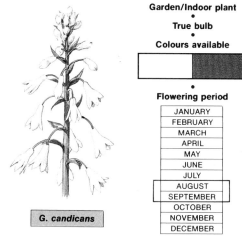

G. candicans

Garden/Indoor plant
•
True bulb
•
Colours available

•
Flowering period

| JANUARY |
| FEBRUARY |
| MARCH |
| APRIL |
| MAY |
| JUNE |
| JULY |
| AUGUST |
| SEPTEMBER |
| OCTOBER |
| NOVEMBER |
| DECEMBER |

Galtonia is an imposing plant for the herbaceous or mixed border. In summer the tall flower stalk is clothed with 20 or more pendulous bell-like blooms. The leaves are long and strap-like — the effect is that of a giant and elongated Hyacinth. Cut off the flower stalks once they have withered and cover the crown with a thick mulch of leafmould or peat to protect against winter frosts. Galtonia can be grown as a greenhouse plant — set the bulbs 4 in. (10 cm) deep in large pots in September for May–June flowers.

VARIETIES: The popular species is **G. candicans (Hyacinthus candicans)**. The leaves are about 2 ft (60 cm) long and the flowers are white with green markings. With its 3 ft (90 cm) stalk it is much more impressive than an ordinary Hyacinth, of course, but it is also less fragrant. It is an easy bulb if you plant deeply enough and let the clumps grow undisturbed. **G. viridiflora** is an equally tall species but the leaves are wide and the flowers are pale green. Another pale green Galtonia is the 2 ft (60 cm) **G. princeps**.

SITE & SOIL: Well-drained, humus-rich soil is required — thrives best in full sun.

PLANT DETAILS: Planting time: March–April. Planting depth: 7 in. (17.5 cm). Spacing: 12 in. (30 cm). Height: 24–36 in. (60–90 cm).

PROPAGATION: Dislikes disturbance — buy new bulbs.

Galtonia candicans

GLADIOLUS Sword Lily

SPECIES
Garden/Indoor plant

G. 'The Bride'

MINIATURE HYBRIDS
Garden/Indoor plant

G. 'Greenbird'

LARGE-FLOWERED HYBRIDS
Garden plant

G. 'Flower Song'

PRIMULINUS HYBRIDS
Garden/Indoor plant

G. 'Columbine'

BUTTERFLY HYBRIDS
Garden plant

G. 'Melodie'

Garden/Indoor plant

•

Corm

•

Colours available

•

Flowering period

JANUARY
FEBRUARY
MARCH
APRIL
MAY
JUNE
JULY
AUGUST
SEPTEMBER
OCTOBER
NOVEMBER
DECEMBER

Gladiolus is one of the handful of bulbous plants which everyone can recognise. Its sword-like leaves, upright stems and one-sided spikes of irregular-shaped open trumpets are a common sight in borders outside and vases inside the house during the summer months. All quite similar at first glance, perhaps, but the differences between the various types are surprisingly wide. The height of the flower stalk which rises from the corm may reach little more than 1 ft (30 cm) or as much as 4 ft (120 cm). Flowers range from the width of an eggcup to the size of a saucer and the colours span the rainbow. The petal edge is often plain, but it may be hooded, frilled or ruffled. There are a few species and their varieties which are hardy, but the popular ones are half-hardy hybrids. They are planted in spring for summer flowering and are then lifted during October. Shake off the soil and dry for a few days in a warm room before storing in a cool but frost-free place until the spring. They are easy to grow in good soil and a sunny spot — water thoroughly during dry weather once the flower spikes have appeared. Gladioli make excellent cut flowers but they do have a few drawbacks as bedding plants. Staking of the Large-flowered hybrids is usually necessary and the flowering period is quite short. The trick here is to plant at fortnightly intervals so that a succession of blooms is obtained. Gladioli are not usually thought of as indoor bulbs and the Large-flowered varieties are not suitable. You can, however, grow one of the short Primulinus or Miniature hybrids as a house plant or you can pick one of the G. colvillii varieties.

VARIETIES: There are several ways of classifying Gladioli, depending on whether you are a botanist, an exhibitor or a gardener looking for something to buy. For the gardener the following division will help when looking around the garden centre or in the catalogues. There are 5 basic groups. The first and most popular one contains the *Large-flowered* Hybrids. Here are the largest plants which grow 3–4 ft (90–120 cm) high with triangular flowers 4½–7 in. (11–17.5 cm) across. The flower spikes are 16–20 in. (40–50 cm) high. The range of varieties is vast — a few popular ones are **'White Friendship'** (Giant white), **'Peter Pears'** (Large red-throated salmon), **'Royal Dutch'** (Large white-throated lavender), **'Flower Song'** (Large frilled yellow) and **'Spic and Span'** (Large yellow-blotched pink). The *Primulinus* Hybrids grow 1½–3 ft (45–90 cm) high — the flowers are loosely arranged on the stem and the top petal is hooded (bent forward). Average bloom width is 3 in. (7.5 cm) and examples are **'Robin'** (rose-purple), **'Leonore'** (yellow), **'Columbine'** (pink and white) and **'Essex'** (red). Staking is not necessary and it is not often needed for the third group — the *Butterfly* Hybrids. These grow 2–3 ft (60–90 cm) high with 2–4 in. (5–10 cm) wide flowers. The 2 basic features of most of these hybrids are the close packing of the ruffled flowers on the stem and the striking colours of the throats. These features can be clearly seen in such varieties as **'Melodie'** (red-throated pink) and **'Georgette'** (yellow-throated red). The *Miniature* Hybrids are like small Primulinus varieties — height 1½–2 ft (45–60 cm), flower size 2 in. (5 cm) with petals frequently frilled or ruffled. Examples include **'Bo Peep'** (apricot) and **'Greenbird'** (yellowish-green). The final group are the *Species* which are hardy or moderately hardy and flower in May or June. Examples include the 2 ft (60 cm) **G. byzantinus** (Small red) and the hybrids or varieties of **G. colvillei** such as **'The Bride'** (Small white).

SITE & SOIL: Any well-drained soil will do — thrives best in full sun.

PLANT DETAILS: Planting time: Hybrids — March–May. Species — October. Planting depth: 4–5 in. (10–12.5 cm). Spacing: 4–6 in. (10–15 cm). Height: Depends on variety — see above.

PROPAGATION: Remove and store cormlets at lifting time. Plant in spring — they will take 2–3 years to flower.

GLADIOLUS continued

FLOWER SIZE

Catalogues sometimes express the size of Gladioli flowers in words rather than figures. These terms refer to the width of the bottom flower in the spike when it is fully open and when grown under good conditions.

GIANT
over 5½ in. (14 cm)

LARGE
4½–5½ in. (11–14 cm)

MEDIUM
3½–4½ in. (9–11 cm)

SMALL
2½–3½ in. (6–9 cm)

MINIATURE
less than 2½ in. (6 cm)

Gladiolus 'Peter Pears'

Gladiolus 'Flower Song'

Gladiolus 'Columbine'

Gladiolus 'Melodie'

Gladiolus 'Greenbird'

Gladiolus byzantinus

Gladiolus 'The Bride'

GLORIOSA Glory Lily

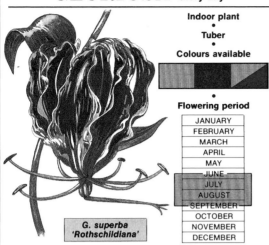

Indoor plant
•
Tuber
•
Colours available
•
Flowering period

JANUARY
FEBRUARY
MARCH
APRIL
MAY
JUNE
JULY
AUGUST
SEPTEMBER
OCTOBER
NOVEMBER
DECEMBER

G. superba 'Rothschildiana'

As its name suggests, the Glory Lily is a glorious sight when in full bloom in summer. It is either bought in flower or raised in the greenhouse from a tuber planted early in the year. Water sparingly at first, then more freely as the stems begin to grow. The slender stems need support — the 6 in. (15 cm) oval leaves bear tendrils at the tips. Water liberally during the growing season — after flowering give less water and then stop altogether to let the tubers dry out. Leave them in the pots at a minimum of 55°F (13°C) and repot in the spring.

VARIETIES: The usual species is **G. superba**. The 4 in. wide flowers have swept-back petals like a Turk's-cap Lily. These wavy-edged petals are orange at first and turn to deep red as they mature. **G. superba 'Rothschildiana'** is similar in growth habit and flower form. Like its parent the stamens and style are prominently displayed, but each petal is red with a yellow base and sides. The all-yellow **G. lutea** is rare.

SITE & SOIL: Use a soil-based or soilless compost — choose a brightly lit spot but shade from hot summer sun.

PLANT DETAILS: Planting time: January–March. Planting depth: 2 in. (5 cm). Spacing: 1 in a 6 in. (15 cm) pot. Height: 5–8 ft (150–240 cm).

PROPAGATION: Divide and then plant sprouting tubers in March — each piece must have a bud or shoot.

Gloriosa superba

HABRANTHUS Habranthus

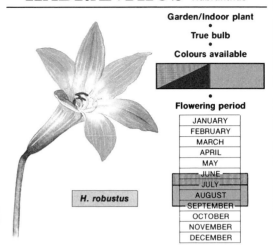

Garden/Indoor plant
•
True bulb
•
Colours available
•
Flowering period

JANUARY
FEBRUARY
MARCH
APRIL
MAY
JUNE
JULY
AUGUST
SEPTEMBER
OCTOBER
NOVEMBER
DECEMBER

H. robustus

This dainty bulb is related to Hippeastrum, but it has none of the grandeur of its showy cousin. Instead it looks like a Crocus borne on top of an upright stalk — a characteristic feature is that the bloom is held at an angle. There are several species but most are tender. You will find a couple of the hardier ones in some specialist catalogues — flower colour, time of flowering and frost resistance will depend on the species you choose.

VARIETIES: **H. tubispathus** (**H. andersonii**) is the species which is reliably hardy. In June the flower stalks appear at intervals while the leaves are still absent. The blooms are borne singly on top of each stalk — yellow inside and coppery orange outside. These golden trumpets are about 1 in. (2.5 cm) long — for larger blooms you will have to grow **H. robustus**. This species produces 2–3 in. (5–7.5 cm) flowers from midsummer to early autumn, but it is not fully hardy and so needs a sunny and sheltered border. Alternatively you can grow it indoors as a greenhouse plant.

SITE & SOIL: Well-drained, humus-rich soil is necessary — thrives in full sun.

PLANT DETAILS: Planting time: October–November. Planting depth: 4 in. (10 cm). Spacing: 6 in. (15 cm). Height: 9–12 in. (22.5–30 cm).

PROPAGATION: Lift and divide clumps in autumn.

Habranthus tubispathus

HAEMANTHUS Blood Lily

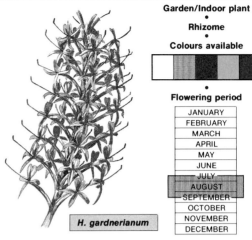

Garden/Indoor plant
•
True bulb
•
Colours available

Flowering period

| JANUARY |
| FEBRUARY |
| MARCH |
| APRIL |
| MAY |
| JUNE |
| JULY |
| AUGUST |
| SEPTEMBER |
| OCTOBER |
| NOVEMBER |
| DECEMBER |

H. coccineus

The genus Haemanthus has been divided — the species which bear petal-like bracts below the true flowers have been retained as Haemanthus and the ones with large round heads of spiky flowers have been transferred to the genus Scadoxus. The Haemanthus species have a brush-like flower-head and are quite tender. You can try growing them outdoors by planting just below the surface in April, but it is better to treat them as greenhouse or house plants. Use a pot which is about twice the width of the bulb — water sparingly until growth starts and then water freely. Water very sparingly in winter and allow the plant to rest until spring. Repot every 4–5 years.

VARIETIES: H. albiflos (Paint Brush) blooms in early summer. It has brush-like heads of tiny white flowers surrounded by white bracts. The flower stalks are leafless but there are 2–5 wide evergreen leaves at the base. With **H. coccineus** the flowers (6 petal-like bracts below a mass of true flowers) open in September. They are pink or red and the foliage which appears after the flowers withers in late autumn.

SITE & SOIL: Use a soilless compost — grow in a brightly lit spot.

PLANT DETAILS: Planting time: March–May. Planting depth: Tip should be just above the surface. Spacing: 1 in a pot — see above. Height: 12 in. (30 cm).

PROPAGATION: Pot up bulblets at repotting time.

Haemanthus albiflos

HEDYCHIUM Ginger Lily

Garden/Indoor plant
•
Rhizome
•
Colours available

Flowering period

| JANUARY |
| FEBRUARY |
| MARCH |
| APRIL |
| MAY |
| JUNE |
| JULY |
| AUGUST |
| SEPTEMBER |
| OCTOBER |
| NOVEMBER |
| DECEMBER |

H. gardnerianum

Grow this eye-catching plant from India as a summer bedding plant like Canna or as a greenhouse plant. The tall stem bears long leaves and at the top there is the spectacular flower-head in summer or autumn — this is up to 1 ft (30 cm) or more in height with rows of 2 in. (5 cm) long fragrant flowers bearing prominent stamens. For outdoor cultivation treat as Canna — for growing as a pot plant water copiously between spring and late autumn and then very sparingly in winter. Cut down flower stems when flowering has finished.

VARIETIES: There are several species which make excellent dot plants in a large container for the summer garden. The easiest one to grow is **H. gardnerianum** — the yellow flowers bear striking red filaments. It needs a minimum temperature of 40°–45°F (4°–7°C), but the white-flowered **H. coronarium** needs a minimum temperature of 50°F (10°C). Other types are more difficult to find — there are the orange **H. flavescens** and the red, pink or orange **H. coccineum**.

SITE & SOIL: Soil-based or soilless compost — choose a brightly lit spot.

PLANT DETAILS: Planting time: March–April. Planting depth: Tip should be just below the surface. Spacing: 24 in. (60 cm). Height: 48–72 in. (120–180 cm).

PROPAGATION: Divide rhizomes in spring.

Hedychium coronarium

HERMODACTYLUS Widow Iris

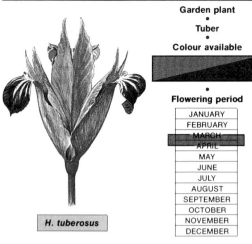

Garden plant
•
Tuber
•
Colour available

•
Flowering period

| JANUARY |
| FEBRUARY |
| MARCH |
| APRIL |
| MAY |
| JUNE |
| JULY |
| AUGUST |
| SEPTEMBER |
| OCTOBER |
| NOVEMBER |
| DECEMBER |

H. tuberosus

This unusual bulb is an Iris-like plant which blooms early in the year. It is small and not particularly colourful but it has its uses. It will grow in chalky soil and makes an excellent cut flower for spring displays. It has a reputation for being rather tender but it will grow quite happily in the rockery if it is provided with a peat or leafmould mulch in winter. In summer the foliage dies down and during this period it requires dry conditions.

VARIETIES: There is just one species — **H. tuberosus** known as the Snake's Head or Widow Iris. The finger-like tubers fork and spread in the soil and the clumps should not be disturbed unless it is really necessary. The grey-green leaves are long and narrow and in early spring the 2 in. (5 cm) wide flowers appear singly on the upright stalks. The upright inner petals are translucent pale green and the outer petals are dark brown or purple with a pale edge. These curiously-coloured fragrant blooms always attract attention, but not everyone likes them.

SITE & SOIL: Any well-drained, non-acid soil will do — full sun is essential.

PLANT DETAILS: Planting time: October–November. Planting depth: 2 in. (5 cm). Spacing: 4 in. (10 cm). Height: 12 in. (30 cm).

PROPAGATION: Divide overcrowded clumps in spring.

Hermodactylus tuberosus

HIPPEASTRUM Amaryllis

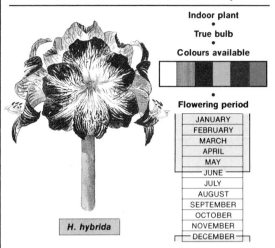

Indoor plant
•
True bulb
•
Colours available

•
Flowering period

| JANUARY |
| FEBRUARY |
| MARCH |
| APRIL |
| MAY |
| JUNE |
| JULY |
| AUGUST |
| SEPTEMBER |
| OCTOBER |
| NOVEMBER |
| DECEMBER |

H. hybrida

The large bulb is planted in compost (do not let the roots dry out) and watered sparingly until the shoot has emerged. Water freely once active growth has started and feed at weekly intervals. Hippeastrums bloom about 8 weeks after planting — for Christmas flowers plant prepared bulbs in late October. The thick stem bears 2-6 trumpets which are up to 6 in. (15 cm) wide. Remove the flower stalk when blooms wither — stop watering and feeding when the leaves have yellowed. Bring back into growth by starting to water after a period of rest. Repot every 3 years.

VARIETIES: All the popular Hippeastrums are large-flowering varieties of **H. hybrida**. They are often sold on the basis of their colour, which may be any shade from white to pale purple. Streaked, veined and edged varieties are common but yellow Hippeastrums are rare. Varieties include **'Apple Blossom'** (white/pink), **'Red Lion'** (red), **'Picotee'** (red-edged white), **'Bouquet'** (salmon), **'Belinda'** (dark red) and **'Yellow Pioneer'** (yellow).

SITE & SOIL: Use a soilless compost — a brightly lit spot is essential.

PLANT DETAILS: Planting time: Mid October–April. Planting depth: Half the bulb above the surface. Spacing: 1 per 7 in. (17.5 cm) pot. Height: 18–30 in. (45–75 cm).

PROPAGATION: Remove and plant up offsets in spring.

Hippeastrum hybrida 'Apple Blossom'

HOMERIA Homeria

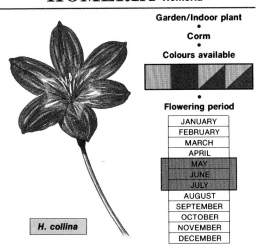

Garden/Indoor plant
•
Corm
•
Colours available
•
Flowering period

| JANUARY |
| FEBRUARY |
| MARCH |
| APRIL |
| MAY |
| JUNE |
| JULY |
| AUGUST |
| SEPTEMBER |
| OCTOBER |
| NOVEMBER |
| DECEMBER |

H. collina

These unusual spring- and summer-flowering plants belong to the Iris family. Starry or cup-shaped blooms are borne on top of wiry stems — the leaves are long and narrow. This is a tender plant but you can try it outdoors if you have well-drained soil in a sunny spot. Plant the corms 3 in. deep in January and lift again in October. For nearly all gardeners, however, this is an indoor bulb. After planting place the pot under peat in a cold frame and bring into the greenhouse when the shoots have appeared. Water very sparingly after flowering — repot in autumn.

VARIETIES: None of the Homerias is popular — you will have to look through the catalogues. There are just 2 which you are likely to find. **H. collina (H. breyniana)** has 2–3 in. (5–7.5 cm) wide flowers in spring — these open-faced cups are dark orange with a yellow centre. **H. ochroleuca** blooms later and is taller — the flowers are yellow. In one or two catalogues you will find **H. flaccida** (red and yellow).

SITE & SOIL: Use a soil-based or soilless compost — choose a brightly lit spot away from direct sun.

PLANT DETAILS: Planting time: September–October. Planting depth: 1 in. (2.5 cm). Spacing: 5 in a 5 in. (12.5 cm) pot. Height: 12–18 in. (30–45 cm).

PROPAGATION: Remove and plant offsets when repotting in autumn.

Homeria ochroleuca

HYACINTHELLA Hyacinthella

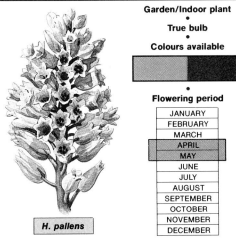

Garden/Indoor plant
•
True bulb
•
Colours available
•
Flowering period

| JANUARY |
| FEBRUARY |
| MARCH |
| APRIL |
| MAY |
| JUNE |
| JULY |
| AUGUST |
| SEPTEMBER |
| OCTOBER |
| NOVEMBER |
| DECEMBER |

H. pallens

This is not a particularly showy plant and there are not many suppliers, so it is one for the collector of rarities. Hyacinthella is small with short floral spikes. Depending on the variety this spike bears a few or a mass of bell-shaped flowers. Each bloom is somewhere between a Hyacinth and a Grape Hyacinth in shape — the lobes at the end of the bell-like flower are much shorter than those on a Hyacinth but much more pronounced than the virtually absent lobes on a Grape Hyacinth.

VARIETIES: This is a plant for the rockery or the greenhouse. Outdoors it needs a dry and sunny spot as it requires a dormant period during the summer months. There are several species hidden away in the specialist catalogues — the one to be found on offer by several suppliers is **H. acutiloba**. This has a couple of strap-like leaves at the base and a cluster of mid blue flowers in May. **H. pallens** has a mass of small azure blue flowers, in contrast to **H. leucophaea** which has just a few near-white blooms at the top of the flower stem.

SITE & SOIL: Well-drained light soil is necessary — thrives in sun or light shade.

PLANT DETAILS: Planting time: September–October. Planting depth: 2 in. (5 cm). Spacing: 3 in. (7.5 cm). Height: 4 in. (10 cm).

PROPAGATION: Divide clumps in autumn every 3 years.

Hyacinthella leucophaea

HYACINTHUS Hyacinth

DUTCH HYACINTHS

H. orientalis
'Pink Pearl'

Garden/Indoor plant

•

True bulb

•

Colours available

•

Flowering period

| JANUARY |
| FEBRUARY |
| MARCH |
| APRIL |
| MAY |
| JUNE |
| JULY |
| AUGUST |
| SEPTEMBER |
| OCTOBER |
| NOVEMBER |
| DECEMBER |

ROMAN HYACINTHS

H. orientalis
albulus

MULTIFLORA HYACINTHS

H. orientalis
'Multiflora'

CYNTHELLA HYACINTHS

H. orientalis
'Lord Balfour'

As a spring-flowering indoor pot plant the Hyacinth has few rivals. Leafless flower stalks bear scores of star-faced bells and there is a fragrance that can fill the room. Outdoors they are bedding plants with a lot of merit — neat growth, a long flowering period, a wide range of colours and a sweet smell. Despite these merits they have never been able to match Tulips, Daffodils or Crocuses in popularity. The probable reasons are that they cost more than the other spring favourites and there is little variety among the popular types apart from colour. In most soils you can leave the bulbs of Dutch Hyacinths outdoors over winter, but the display in the second year will not be as good. It is generally better to let the foliage die down, lift the bulbs and then store them in dry peat until planting time comes round again. When planting follow the depth, spacing etc details set out below, and also remember 2 special points. Don't pick the largest bulbs which are used for indoors — buy instead the medium-sized ones ('Bedding Hyacinths') which produce flower stalks that are less susceptible to weather damage. Secondly, add well-rotted compost or peat to the soil before putting in the bulbs. Before planting Hyacinths in bowls or pots for indoor display read the section on the forcing technique for garden bulbs. This involves keeping the pots in the dark until the green shoots begin to appear. The container is then moved to a shady and cool spot indoors. After a few days move it close to the window — leave it in this location until the flower buds appear. Now is the time to move the pot or bowl to where the bulbs are to flower. October and November are the planting months. You can buy specially prepared bulbs for Christmas flowering — these should be planted during the first 3 weeks of September. Watering should be withheld after indoor Hyacinths have flowered to let the foliage wither and then the bulbs should be removed. Clean them and store for planting in the garden in early autumn.

VARIETIES: By far the most popular Hyacinths are the *Dutch* Hybrids of **H. orientalis**. In April or early May the tightly-packed flower-heads appear, ranging in colour from pure white to deep purple. The stem is 10–12 in. (25–30 cm) high of which about half is clothed with 1 in. (2.5 cm) long waxy flowers. Grow these Dutch Hybrids in large groups in beds or containers rather than as single specimens. Varieties include **'Amethyst'** (early, lilac), **'Amsterdam'** (early, red), **'Anne Marie'** (early, light pink), **'Blue Magic'** (mid-season, purple-blue), **'Carnegie'** (late, white), **'City of Haarlem'** (late, yellow), **'Delft Blue'** (mid-season, pale blue), **'Jan Bos'** (early, red), **'Lady Derby'** (mid-season, pink), **'Lord Balfour'** (mid-season, wine red), **'L'Innocence'** (mid-season, white), **'Ostara'** (mid-season, dark blue), **'Pink Pearl'** (early, pink) and **'Violet Pearl'** (early, silver-edged lilac-rose). An unusual indoor group are the *Roman* Hyacinths which are varieties of **H. orientalis albulus** (**Bellevalia romana**). The flowers of white, pink or blue are smaller and less tightly packed on short 6 in. (15 cm) stalks. A third group, the *Multiflora* Varieties, also have the flowers loosely arranged and each bulb produces several flower stems. They can be grown indoors or out and white, pink and blue flowers are available. Both Roman and Multiflora Hyacinths bloom earlier than the Dutch ones. The final group are the *Cynthella* or *Miniature* Hyacinths. These are small 5–6 in. (12.5–15 cm) versions of well-known Dutch Hyacinths such as 'Delft Blue', 'Jan Bos', 'Lady Derby', 'City of Haarlem' and 'Lord Balfour'.

SITE & SOIL: Any reasonable garden soil adequately supplied with humus will do — thrives in sun or light shade.

PLANT DETAILS: Planting time: September–October. Planting depth: 6 in. (15 cm). Spacing: 8 in. (20 cm). Height: 5–12 in. (12.5–30 cm).

PROPAGATION: Remove offsets at lifting time — plant in autumn.

HYACINTHUS continued

Hyacinthus 'Anne Marie'

Hyacinthus 'Jan Bos'

Hyacinthus 'Delft Blue'

Hyacinthus 'Carnegie'

Hyacinthus 'City of Haarlem'

Hyacinthus 'Lord Balfour'

Hyacinthus orientalis albulus 'Pale Blue'

Hyacinthus orientalis albulus 'Pink'

Hyacinthus orientalis albulus 'Blue'

HYMENOCALLIS Spider Lily

Garden/Indoor plant
•
True bulb
•
Colours available

Flowering period

JANUARY
FEBRUARY
MARCH
APRIL
MAY
JUNE
JULY
AUGUST
SEPTEMBER
OCTOBER
NOVEMBER
DECEMBER

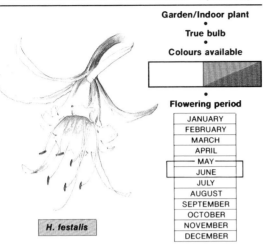

H. festalis

Despite its common name Hymenocallis is more like a Daffodil than a Lily. Each large flower has a long cup (corona) with projecting stamens and at the base a ring of narrow petals. These fragrant blooms are borne on top of leafless stalks. It is usually grown as a greenhouse plant (see below) but you can grow it in a sunny spot outdoors. Plant the bulbs 5 in. (12.5 cm) deep in late May and water during dry spells. Flowering takes place in August — in late autumn lift the bulbs for storage over winter or cover the ground with a deep mulch of peat or leafmould.

VARIETIES: H. festalis (**Ismene festalis**) is the most popular species. About 6 fragrant white blooms are borne on top of the 1½–2 ft (45–60 cm) stem — each flower measures 4–6 in. (10–15 cm) across. A minimum temperature of 55°F (13°C) is necessary — water sparingly until the green shoot appears. Stop watering when the leaves wither in autumn — leave dormant over winter and repot in spring every 2–3 years. H. **'Sulphur Queen'** has green-veined yellow flowers.

SITE & SOIL: Use a soilless compost — choose a brightly lit spot away from hot summer sun.

PLANT DETAILS: Planting time: March. Planting depth: Tip should be just above the surface. Spacing: 1 in a 5 in. (12.5 cm) pot. Height: 18–24 in. (45–60 cm).

PROPAGATION: Remove and plant offsets at repotting time.

Hymenocallis 'Sulphur Queen'

IPHEION Spring Starflower

Garden plant
•
True bulb
•
Colours available

Flowering period

JANUARY
FEBRUARY
MARCH
APRIL
MAY
JUNE
JULY
AUGUST
SEPTEMBER
OCTOBER
NOVEMBER
DECEMBER

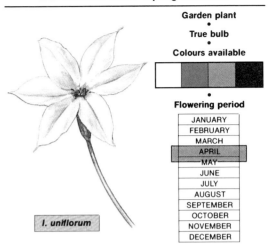

I. uniflorum

A pretty bulb for the rockery, woodland or front of the border. It is a trouble-free plant which has 6 in. (15 cm) strap-like arching leaves and in spring several stalks which are each topped by a starry flower. These blooms have a pleasant smell, but the leaves emit the pungent odour of garlic when crushed. It is a slow starter and the number of blooms may be disappointing in the first year, but after a few years a large clump is formed which flowers profusely.

VARIETIES: The basic species is **I. uniflorum**. Few plants have been given more alternative names — **Brodiaea uniflora**, **Milla uniflora**, **Triteleia uniflora** and **Tristigma uniflorum**! The flowers, unlike the names, are delightfully simple — 1 in. (2.5 cm) wide 6-pointed stars with pale blue petals which have a violet line on the reverse. The white variety **'Album'** has larger flowers and the popular **'Wisley Blue'** has flowers which are violet-blue. The darkest Ipheion is **'Froyle Mill'** and the most eye-catching is the electric blue but rather tender **I. 'Rolf Fiedler'**.

SITE & SOIL: Any well-drained soil in sun or light shade. Dislikes an exposed, windy site.

PLANT DETAILS: Planting time: September–October. Planting depth: 2 in. (5 cm). Spacing: 3 in. (7.5 cm). Height: 4–6 in. (10–15 cm).

PROPAGATION: Lift and divide clumps in autumn every 3–4 years. Replant at once.

Ipheion 'Rolf Fiedler'

IRIS Iris

RETICULATA GROUP
Leaves narrow,
round, pointed
3–6 in. (7.5–15 cm)
Flowers February–March

I. reticulata

Garden/Indoor plant
•
True bulb
•
Colours available

•
Flowering period

JANUARY
FEBRUARY
MARCH
APRIL
MAY
JUNE
JULY
AUGUST
SEPTEMBER
OCTOBER
NOVEMBER
DECEMBER

JUNO GROUP
Leaves flat — lower part
clasps the stem
1–2 ft (30–60 cm)
Flowers April–May

XIPHIUM GROUP
Leaves sword-like, flat
or angular
1½–2 ft (45–60 cm)
Flowers June–July

I. 'Lemon Queen'

I. bucharica

Irises are a vast genus of plants ranging from bold-flowering specimens with 4 ft (120 cm) stems to tiny alpines peeping above the earth. Nearly all, however, have the same flower pattern — 3 inner petals ('standards') generally standing erect and 3 outer petals ('falls') generally hanging downwards. There are 2 basic types. The Rhizome Irises spread by means of thickened underground stems — the really large and showy Irises belong here, the Flag Iris, Bearded Iris, Water Iris etc. They are planted as leafy specimens on the surface of the ground and are therefore not dealt with in this book — see The Flower Expert. The second type are the Bulb Irises and these are described below. They are smaller plants than the Rhizome ones and are often grown in rockeries or at the front of the border. Flowers appear in winter, spring or summer depending on the species grown and most will thrive in chalky soil. Do not disturb the clumps — lifting and division should not take place for 4–5 years after planting.

VARIETIES: There are 3 groups of Bulb Irises. The *Reticulata* group are the well-known dwarfs which grow 3–6 in. (7.5–15 cm) high and bloom in February or March. The popular yellow fragrant one is **I. danfordiae** — the brown-spotted petals appear before the leaves. Even more popular is **I. reticulata** — purplish-blue scented flowers with yellow markings. It grows about 6 in. (15 cm) high and the flowers are 2–3 in. (5–7.5 cm) across — in the catalogues or garden centre you may find varieties and hybrids such as **'Cantab'** (pale blue, orange markings), **'Pauline'** (deep mauve, white markings), **'Katharine Hodgkin'** (pale blue, yellow markings), **'Joyce'** (sky blue, reddish markings) and **'J. S. Dijt'** (reddish purple, orange markings). For larger flowers grow **I. histrioides 'Major'** — gentian blue blooms with white spots. The bulbs in this Reticulata group are covered with a fibrous net — plant them 3 in. (7.5 cm) deep and 4 in. (10 cm) apart in September–October. All can be grown as indoor pot plants for January–February blooms. The *Xiphium* group are quite different. They are summer-flowering and the stems are 1½–2 ft (45–60 cm) tall. All of them are sun-loving plants and not as hardy as the Reticulata group. The first ones to bloom are the Dutch Irises, which are great favourites with flower arrangers. The white, yellow, blue or purple blooms appear in June — named varieties include **'Ideal'** (blue, falls blotched yellow), **'Symphony'** (pale yellow, falls deep yellow), **'Wedgwood'** (pale blue), **'White Excelsior'** (white, falls blotched yellow), **'Royal Yellow'** (yellow, falls deep yellow) and **'Lemon Queen'** (yellow). Next to bloom are the English Irises (June–July) which are combinations of white, mauve, blue and purple — an example is **I. latifolia** with 4 in. (10 cm) wide blooms which are violet with yellow stripes. The final section of the Xiphium group are the Spanish Irises which flower in July. They need moist soil and should be lifted each year after the foliage has withered and then stored for autumn planting. The Dutch, English and Spanish Irises which make up the Xiphium group should be planted 4–6 in. (10–15 cm) deep and 6 in. (15 cm) apart in September–October. The 2 main groups of Bulb Irises described above (the Reticulatas and the Xiphiums) are well-known, but the spring-flowering *Juno* group are unusual and uncommon. The standards are horizontal and not upright, and they need humus-rich soil in full sun. Examples include **I. bucharica** with ivory and yellow flowers in April on 1 ft (30 cm) stems, **I. magnifica** which bears lavender and white flowers in May on 2 ft (60 cm) stems and **I. graeberiana** with blue and white flowers in April on 6–12 in. (15–30 cm) stems. I. graeberiana is easier to grow than the other Juno Irises. Plant bulbs of the Juno group 2 in. (5 cm) deep and 6–9 in. (15–22.5 cm) apart in September–October. Do not break the fleshy roots at the base.

SITE & SOIL: For most types well-drained, light soil is essential — thrives best in full sun.

PLANT DETAILS: See above.

PROPAGATION: Divide clumps when lifting is necessary.

IRIS continued

Iris danfordiae

Iris reticulata 'Cantab'

Iris reticulata 'Joyce'

Iris reticulata 'Katharine Hodgkin'

Iris reticulata 'J. S. Dijt'

Iris histrioides 'Major'

Iris 'White Excelsior'

Iris 'Wedgwood'

Iris magnifica

IXIA Corn Lily

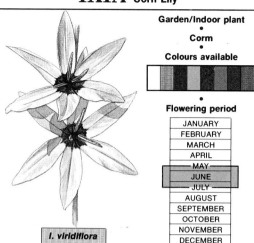

Garden/Indoor plant

●

Corm

●

Colours available

●

Flowering period

| JANUARY |
| FEBRUARY |
| MARCH |
| APRIL |
| MAY |
| JUNE |
| JULY |
| AUGUST |
| SEPTEMBER |
| OCTOBER |
| NOVEMBER |
| DECEMBER |

I. viridiflora

About a dozen 6-petalled stars are borne on wiry stems in late spring or summer above a fan of sword-shaped leaves. You can leave it outdoors if your soil is light and the climate is mild, but it is safer to plant the corms 3 in. (7.5 cm) deep in March and then lift them in late summer when the foliage has died down. Store in a dry place until planting time. In most areas it is best to grow Ixia as an indoor plant as described below. Keep the compost fairly dry until growth starts, then water freely. Remove and store corms when the foliage has withered.

VARIETIES: The colours of Ixia blooms are usually bright and the centres are generally dark red or brown. When open the flowers are 1–2 in. (2.5–5 cm) across, but they close on dull days. Several species are listed in specialist catalogues — you may find **I. paniculata**, the yellow-flowered **I. maculata** or the green **I. viridiflora**. It is more usual to buy one of the hybrids rather than a species as they are easier to grow — examples include **I. 'Hogarth'** (yellow), **'Mabel'** (rose red), **'Nelson'** (white) and **'Englishton'** (pink).

SITE & SOIL: Use a soilless compost — choose a brightly lit spot in a cold or cool greenhouse.

PLANT DETAILS: Planting time: October. Planting depth: 2 in. (5 cm). Spacing: 5 in a 5 in. (12.5 cm) pot. Height: 12–18 in. (30–45 cm).

PROPAGATION: Remove cormlets after lifting and store — plant in autumn.

Ixia 'Mabel'

IXIOLIRION Ixia Lily

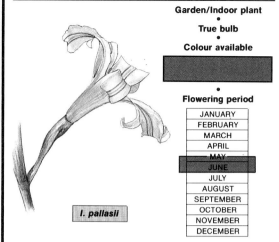

Garden/Indoor plant

●

True bulb

●

Colour available

●

Flowering period

| JANUARY |
| FEBRUARY |
| MARCH |
| APRIL |
| MAY |
| JUNE |
| JULY |
| AUGUST |
| SEPTEMBER |
| OCTOBER |
| NOVEMBER |
| DECEMBER |

I. pallasii

A plant with a couple of surprises. It is not related to Ixia despite its Latin and common names, and it is quite tender despite being a native of Siberia. It can be grown as a greenhouse plant in the same way as Ixia, but you can cultivate it in a warm and sheltered spot outdoors if the soil is sandy and a mulch of peat or leafmould is applied during the winter months. In less favourable situations the bulbs should be lifted in autumn and stored in dry peat for planting in March. An unusual bulb, but worth considering if you are a keen flower arranger.

VARIETIES: The funnel-shaped flowers are borne loosely on thin stems — each bloom has 6 petals which open widely to form a 2 in. (5 cm) star. The narrow grey-green leaves appear before the flowers. There are just 2 species from which to make your choice. **I. pallasii** (**I. montanum, I. tataricum**) produces flower stems which are about 1½ ft (45 cm) high — the lavender- or violet-blue flowers bear reflexed petals which have longitudinal dark stripes. The other species (**I. ledebourii**) is very similar but is shorter and blooms earlier.

SITE & SOIL: Well-drained, light soil in a sheltered sunny spot is necessary.

PLANT DETAILS: Planting time: September–October. Planting depth: 3 in. (7.5 cm). Spacing: 6 in. (15 cm). Height: 12–18 in. (30–45 cm).

PROPAGATION: Remove and replant bulblets at lifting time.

Ixiolirion pallasii

LACHENALIA Cape Cowslip

Indoor plant
•
True bulb
•
Colours available
•
Flowering period

JANUARY
FEBRUARY
MARCH
APRIL
MAY
JUNE
JULY
AUGUST
SEPTEMBER
OCTOBER
NOVEMBER
DECEMBER

L. aloides

Lachenalia is an attractive house plant, providing a mass of waxy tubular flowers for about a month in winter. Despite its colourful and novel appearance it has never become popular because of its inability to live in a heated room. After planting keep it in a cool bright place, water once and then leave until shoots appear. Water and feed regularly during the flowering season — after flowering continue watering for several weeks and then reduce and stop. Keep the compost dry and repot in autumn.

VARIETIES: The most popular species is **L. aloides** (**L. tricolor**). The 1 in. blooms are red at the bud stage and then yellow tinged with green and red as they mature. The flower stalks and fleshy leaves are blotched with brown or purple. The variety **'Aurea'** has all-orange flowers — choose **'Lutea'** for all-yellow blooms. The easiest Lachenalia to grow is **L. pendula** (**L. bulbifera**). It is taller than L. aloides and the blooms are red with green and purple tips. It is early-flowering, sometimes producing its bright flower-heads as early as Christmas.

SITE & SOIL: Use a soilless compost — choose a brightly lit spot with some direct sun.

PLANT DETAILS: Planting time: August–September. Planting depth: Tip should be just below the surface. Spacing: 5 in a 5 in. (12.5 cm) pot. Height: 8–12 in. (20–30 cm).

PROPAGATION: Remove and plant bulblets at repotting time.

Lachenalia aloides 'Aurea'

LEUCOJUM Snowflake

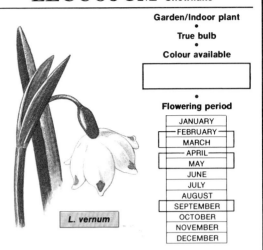

Garden/Indoor plant
•
True bulb
•
Colour available
•
Flowering period

JANUARY
FEBRUARY
MARCH
APRIL
MAY
JUNE
JULY
AUGUST
SEPTEMBER
OCTOBER
NOVEMBER
DECEMBER

L. vernum

The white bell-shaped flowers of the Spring Snowflake are sometimes confused with Snowdrops. Both appear in early spring and both bear nodding blooms made up of 6 petals. But Leucojum is taller and all the petals are the same size — at the tip of each petal there is a green or yellow spot. There are spring-, summer- and autumn-flowering species. Use the spring-flowering types for rockeries, the front of the border or for growing indoors like Snowdrops — the tall summer ones belong in the herbaceous or mixed border.

VARIETIES: The Spring Snowflake is **L. vernum** — a tolerant plant which thrives in both shade and moist soil. The cup-shaped flowers are ¾ in. (2 cm) across and are borne in February or March on 8 in. (20 cm) stalks above strap-like leaves. The variety **'Carpathicum'** has yellow- rather than green-spotted petals. The Summer Snowflake (**L. aestivum**) has 2 ft (60 cm) stems — **'Gravetye Giant'** is the best variety. The Autumn Snowflake (**L. autumnale**) grows only 5 in. (12.5 cm) high and unlike the others requires full sun and sandy soil.

SITE & SOIL: Moisture-retentive soil in sun or partial shade.

PLANT DETAILS: Planting time: September–October. Planting depth: 3 in. (7.5 cm). Spacing: 4–8 in. (10–20 cm). Height: 5–24 in. (12.5–60 cm).

PROPAGATION: Divide mature clumps when foliage has died down — replant at once.

Leucojum aestivum

LILIUM Lily

Garden/Indoor plant
•
True bulb
•
Colours available

•
Flowering period

JANUARY
FEBRUARY
MARCH
APRIL
MAY
JUNE
JULY
AUGUST
SEPTEMBER
OCTOBER
NOVEMBER
DECEMBER

TURK'S-CAP SHAPED
The petals are rolled and swept back. The flowers are usually small.

Examples: **L. martagon, L. 'Mrs R O Backhouse', L. hansonii, L. 'Dalhansonii'**

TRUMPET SHAPED
The petals are grouped together for part of the length of the flower to produce a basal tube.

Examples: **L. regale, L. 'Limelight', L. candidum, L. longiflorum**

BOWL SHAPED
The petals flare open to produce a wide bowl. The flowers are usually large.

Examples: **L. auratum, L. 'Pink Glory', L. speciosum, L. 'Crimson Beauty'**

The word 'Lily' conjures up a picture of a stately plant with leafy stems and fragrant flowers which delight the eye. Nearly all produce bulbs made up of loose scales and the flowers are borne singly or in loose groups. Early summer is the usual flowering season and nearly all of them are hardy enough to be grown anywhere in the country. However, it is impossible to generalise about a group of plants as large and diverse as the Lily genus. Flowers range from 1 in. (2.5 cm) to 1 ft (30 cm) in diameter and have a scent which extends from delightful to disagreeable. The colour range spans the whole floral spectrum with the exception of blue. There are dwarfs such as the 1 ft (30 cm) L. pumilum for the container or rock garden and the 8 ft (240 cm) giants such as L. henryi for the back of the border. Most are 3–5 ft (90–150 cm) high and are at home in the herbaceous and mixed border or in a bed on their own. There is a Lily for practically every garden, but many gardeners shy away from these lovely bulbs because of their reputation for being hard to grow. This is true for some of the more difficult species, but during this century a number of tolerant species have been discovered and during the past 40 years the Hybrid Lilies have set new standards in flower size, vigour and disease resistance. The basic requirement is for free-draining soil — waterlogging in winter will quickly lead to rot. Another essential is to plant the bulbs as soon as they arrive — they must not be allowed to dry out. Depth of planting depends on the rooting habit of the variety. Stem-rooting Lilies produce roots just above the bulb as well as at the base, and so need to be planted deeply. A few species are Basal-rooting Lilies and so need shallow planting in autumn. Sprinkle coarse sand in the bottom of the hole before planting. Spread out the roots and sprinkle sand between them. Once the plants are actively growing they must not be allowed to dry out at the roots — water thoroughly and regularly during dry weather and feed occasionally with a liquid fertilizer. Do not hoe — place a peat or compost mulch around the stems instead. Not all Lilies require staking, but it is advisable for any variety likely to grow over 3 ft (90 cm) high. Dead-head faded blooms and cut off the stems at ground level when they have died down at the end of the season. Apply a fresh mulch of peat or leafmould for the winter. Many species and hybrids can be grown in containers outdoors — use a large pot or tub and plant 3 or 4 bulbs. Remember that Stem-rooting Lilies require deep planting. Lilies can also be grown as house plants or conservatory specimens, but here the choice is more limited. Both the white Easter Lily (L. longiflorum) and the Mid-Century Hybrids are easy to grow indoors. Cool conditions are necessary and the plant must be shaded from summer sun.

SITE & SOIL: A well-drained site is essential — enrich the soil with well-rotted organic matter. A few Lilies such as L. auratum require lime but most species will not thrive if chalk is present — the modern hybrids are not bothered either way. Choose a sunny spot but a little shade during the day will not be a problem. Shade the lower part of the plant if possible by growing short plants around the base.

PLANT DETAILS: Planting time: August–March — autumn is the best time. Planting depth: Stem-rooting Lilies 6–8 in. (15–20 cm). Basal-rooting Lilies 2 in. (5 cm).
Spacing: 6–18 in. (15–45 cm) — see page 58 for details.
Height: 12–96 in. (30–240 cm) — see page 58 for details.

PROPAGATION: The easiest method is to divide the mature clumps in autumn and replant immediately. Another method is scaling — pull off plump scales from a bulb and place them in a sealed bag of moist peat until rooted. Plant in compost-filled pots.

LILIUM continued

ASIATIC HYBRIDS

Height 2–5 ft (60–150 cm). Spacing 1½ ft (45 cm). Flowers 4–5 in. (10–12.5 cm) across — Turk's-cap, Trumpet or Bowl shaped. Flowering period June–July.

By far the most numerous group. Many of the varieties have upright or outward-facing blooms — examples are **'Sterling Star'** (white), **'Corsage'** (ivory-shaded pink), **'Orange Triumph'** (violet-spotted gold) and the Mid-Century Hybrids such as **'Enchantment'** (red), **'Harmony'** (orange-yellow), **'Red Lion'** (red), **'Destiny'** (yellow), **'Brandywine'** (orange), **'Cinnabar'** (maroon) and **'Paprika'** (deep red). The Turk's-cap Asiatic Hybrids have pendent flowers — examples include **'Citronella'** (yellow), **'Connecticut Yankee'** (orange-red) and the brown-spotted Fiesta Hybrids.

MARTAGON HYBRIDS

Height 4–6 ft (120–180 cm). Spacing 1 ft (30 cm). Flowers 2–3 in. (5–7.5 cm) across — Turk's-cap shaped. Flowering period June–July.

About 25 pendent blooms are borne at the top of the flower stalk — the petals are usually spotted and varieties are available in a wide range of colours. These hybrids thrive best in partial shade and can tolerate alkaline soil. The usual parents are L. martagon and L. hansonii. Not many types are available — look for **L. 'Dalhansonii'** (orange-spotted maroon, unpleasant smell), the Backhouse Hybrids such as **'Mrs R O Backhouse'** (purple-spotted gold), **'Marhan'** (brown-spotted orange) and **'Jacques S Dijt'** (purple-spotted ivory). The Paisley Hybrids (red-spotted white, yellow, orange etc) also belong here.

CANDIDUM HYBRIDS

Height 4–6 ft (120–180 cm). Spacing 1 ft (30 cm). Flowers 4–5 in. (10–12.5 cm) across — Trumpet shaped with strongly reflexed petals. Flowering period June–July.

It is strange that this is the smallest group of all, and yet is represented by the oldest known Lily hybrid — **L. testaceum** or the Nankeen Lily. The fragrant flowers have a Turk's-cap appearance — about 10 are borne at the top of the flower stalk. These pendulous blooms have bright red anthers and the waxy petals are in various shades of yellow ranging from cream to deep apricot. This Lily is basal-rooting so shallow planting in autumn is necessary — it is lime tolerant. Other Candidum Hybrids include **'Apollo'** (white), **'Artemis'** (apricot), **'Prelude'** (vermilion) and **'Ares'** (orange).

AMERICAN HYBRIDS

Height 4–7 ft (120–210 cm). Spacing 1½ ft (45 cm). Flowers 4–5 in. (10–12.5 cm) across — most are Turk's-cap shaped. Flowering period July.

These spotted hybrids have been bred from American species such as L. pardalinum. The 20 nodding blooms are borne in a pyramid-shaped head — they are excellent for flower arranging. The best-known varieties belong to the Bellingham Hybrids and flourish in lime-free soil and light shade — yellow, orange or red bi-colours with prominent dark red or black spots. **'Shuksan'** is the favourite choice — the golden yellow petals are spotted with brown and may be tipped with pink. Another group are the Bullwood Hybrids such as the red **'Cherrywood'**. The American Hybrids produce rhizomes.

TRUMPET HYBRIDS

Height 4–6 ft (120–180 cm). Spacing 1½ ft (45 cm). Flowers up to 8 in. (20 cm) long — Trumpet or Bowl shaped. Flowering period July–August.

The Trumpet group includes the Aurelian and Olympic Hybrids. Typical examples are **'African Queen'** (orange), **'Pink Perfection'** (pink), **'Black Dragon'** (white inside, purple-brown outside), **'Golden Splendour'** (golden yellow), **'Green Dragon'** (white inside, green outside) and **'Limelight'** (lime-yellow). For Bowl-shaped blooms there are **'Heart's Desire'** (orange-throated ivory) and **'Thunderbolt'** (orange). For nodding Bowl-shaped flowers grow **'Golden Showers'** — for starry Bowl-shaped flowers with flat-faced blooms choose one of the **'Sunburst'** varieties.

ORIENTAL HYBRIDS

Height 2–8 ft (60–240 cm). Spacing 1–1½ ft (30–45 cm). Flowers up to 1 ft (30 cm) across — Bowl shaped. Flowering period August–September.

Here you will find the largest and some of the most beautiful of all the Lily hybrids, but they are harder to grow than many others. The Orientals need well-drained, acid and rich soil in a sunny sheltered position. Bowl-shaped varieties include **'Crimson Beauty'** (red-striped white), **'Empress of China'** (red-spotted white), **'Pink Glory'** (white-edged pink) and **'Bonfire'** (red and white). For starry Bowl-shaped flowers grow one of the Imperial varieties such as **'Imperial Silver'** (red-spotted white) or the popular **'Stargazer'** (white-edged pink). **'Journey's End'** has white-edged recurved pink petals.

SPECIES

L. amabile Height 4 ft (120 cm). Spacing 1½ ft (45 cm). Stem-rooting. 3 in. (7.5 cm) Turk's-cap flowers — red with black spots. Disagreeable odour. June–July.

L. auratum (Golden-rayed Lily) Height 5–8 ft (150–240 cm). Spacing 1 ft (30 cm). Stem-rooting. 8–10 in. (20–25 cm) Bowl-shaped flowers — white with yellow stripes, brown spots. August–September.

L. bulbiferum (Orange Lily) Height 2–4 ft (60–120 cm). Spacing 9 in. (22.5 cm). Stem-rooting. 3 in. (7.5 cm) Trumpet-shaped flowers — orange with purple spots. June–July.

L. canadense (Canada Lily) Height 4–6 ft (120–180 cm). Spacing 1 ft (30 cm). Basal-rooting. 2 in. (5 cm) Trumpet-shaped flowers — yellow with brown spots. September–October.

L. candidum (Madonna Lily) Height 4–5 ft (120–150 cm). Spacing 9 in. (22.5 cm). Basal-rooting. 3 in. (7.5 cm) Trumpet-shaped flowers — pure white. June–July.

L. hansonii (Golden Turk's-cap Lily) Height 4–5 ft (120–150 cm). Spacing 1 ft (30 cm). Stem-rooting. 1½ in. (4 cm) Turk's-cap flowers — yellow with brown spots. June–July.

L. henryi (Henry's Lily) Height 6–8 ft (180–240 cm). Spacing 1½ ft (45 cm). Stem-rooting. 3 in. (7.5 cm) Turk's-cap flowers — yellow with dark red spots. August–September.

L. longiflorum (Easter Lily) Height 2½–3 ft (75–90 cm). Spacing 9 in. (22.5 cm). Stem-rooting. 5–6 in. (12.5–15 cm) Trumpet-shaped flowers — white. July–August. Half hardy.

L. martagon (Turk's-cap Lily) Height 3–5 ft (90–150 cm). Spacing 1 ft (30 cm). Basal-rooting. 1½ in. (4 cm) Turk's-cap flowers — purplish-brown with dark spots. Disagreeable odour. June–July.

L. pardalinum (Leopard Lily) Height 3–6 ft (90–180 cm). Spacing 1 ft (30 cm). Basal-rooting. 2½ in. (6 cm) Turk's-cap flowers — dark orange with purple spots. July.

L. pumilum (Coral Lily) Height 1–1½ ft (30–45 cm). Spacing 6 in. (15 cm). Stem-rooting. 1½ in. (4 cm) Turk's-cap flowers — scarlet. June.

L. regale (Regal Lily) Height 3–6 ft (90–180 cm). Spacing 1½ ft (45 cm). Stem-rooting. 5 in. (12.5 cm) Trumpet-shaped flowers — white with yellow throat. July–August.

L. speciosum Height 3–5 ft (90–150 cm). Spacing 1½ ft (45 cm). Stem-rooting. 3–5 in. (7.5–12.5 cm) Bowl-shaped flowers — white with red markings. Fragrant. August–September. Half hardy — grow under glass.

L. tigrinum (Tiger Lily) Height 3–5 ft (90–150 cm). Spacing 1½ ft (45 cm). Stem-rooting. 3–4 in. (7.5–10 cm) Turk's-cap flowers — orange with purple spots. July–September.

LILIUM continued

Lilium 'Cinnabar'

Lilium 'Mrs R O Backhouse'

Lilium testaceum

Lilium 'Shuksan'

Lilium 'Thunderbolt'

Lilium 'Stargazer'

Lilium auratum

Lilium regale

Lilium tigrinum

MERENDERA Merendera

Garden plant
•
Corm
•
Colours available
•
Flowering period

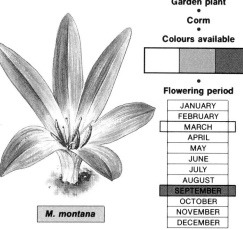

JANUARY	
FEBRUARY	
MARCH	
APRIL	
MAY	
JUNE	
JULY	
AUGUST	
SEPTEMBER	
OCTOBER	
NOVEMBER	
DECEMBER	

M. montana

There are a couple of requirements for this small bulb outdoors — a vacant spot at the front of a sunny rockery and a desire to grow something which the visitor is most unlikely to have seen before. It is very closely related to Colchicum — the main difference is that the 6 petals of Merendera are separate and do not form a tube at the base. You will not see it at the garden centre but you should be able to find M. montana in some specialist catalogues. It is quite hardy, but because of its small size it is more often grown in an alpine house rather than in a rockery.

VARIETIES: M. montana is the species you are most likely to find. The flowers appear singly or in pairs, the 6 rosy pink or lilac petals opening wide before the narrow leaves appear. The blooms are about 1½ in. (4 cm) wide and the yellow anthers are prominently displayed. It blooms in September — for spring blooms grow the pale purple **M. trigyna**. A few bulb growers offer the tiny **M. sobolifera** — this white-flowering dwarf is a plant for the alpine house rather than the open garden where it is just too small to be seen.

SITE & SOIL: Well-drained soil in a sunny location, or grow under glass.

PLANT DETAILS: Planting time: July. Planting depth: 2 in. (5 cm). Spacing: 3 in. (7.5 cm). Height: 2 in. (5 cm).

PROPAGATION: Divide clumps in autumn when leaves have withered.

Merendera montana

MORAEA Butterfly Iris

Garden/Indoor plant
•
Corm or rhizome
•
Colours available
•
Flowering period

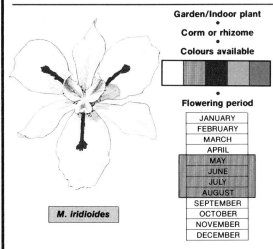

JANUARY	
FEBRUARY	
MARCH	
APRIL	
MAY	
JUNE	
JULY	
AUGUST	
SEPTEMBER	
OCTOBER	
NOVEMBER	
DECEMBER	

M. iridioides

These Iris-like plants are colourful and often attractively patterned, but they are rarely grown. The problem is that these 'African Irises' have none of the hardiness of the true Irises, which means that they have to be lifted in autumn and stored over winter for planting in the spring. The 'bulb' is generally a corm, but there are a few (more correctly listed under Dietes rather than Moraea) which are raised from rhizomes. Moraea can be grown as a house plant.

VARIETIES: The one you are most likely to find is the yellow-flowering **M. spathulata** which grows 2 ft (60 cm) high and produces bright yellow flowers in summer. Another species which has Iris-like flowers is **M. iridioides (Dietes vegeta)** which reaches the same height but has blooms which are white with yellow and blue markings. The Peacock Moraeas are more spectacular — they have 3 large outer petals which bear dark-coloured blotches at the base. Examples include **M. aristata** (white with blue blotch), **M. pavonia** (orange or yellow with blue blotch) and **M. villosa** (various colours with blue blotch).

SITE & SOIL: Well-drained, light soil — a sunny, sheltered site is essential.

PLANT DETAILS: Planting time: April. Planting depth: 2 in. (5 cm). Spacing: 9 in. (22.5 cm). Height: 18–36 in. (45–90 cm).

PROPAGATION: Remove offsets at lifting time — plant in spring.

Moraea spathulata

MUSCARI Grape Hyacinth

M. armeniacum

Garden/Indoor plant

•

True bulb

•

Colours available

•

Flowering period

| JANUARY |
| FEBRUARY |
| MARCH |
| APRIL |
| MAY |
| JUNE |
| JULY |
| AUGUST |
| SEPTEMBER |
| OCTOBER |
| NOVEMBER |
| DECEMBER |

Nobody sings the praises of this old favourite because it has none of the glamour of the many showy bulbs in this chapter, but our gardens would be poorer without it. It is a popular choice for gaps in the rockery, the front of borders and for planting with Tulips, Daffodils, Primulas etc. Muscari can be used for naturalising in woodland or in a grassy area, and are often grown in outdoor containers beneath conifers and taller plants. They can also be grown indoors in the same way as Crocus corms — plant the bulbs closely together in compost-filled pots or bowls in September for January–March flowers. The flowers are easily recognised by most gardeners — tiny, bell- or flask-shaped blooms on top of a leafless and fleshy stem. The strap-like leaves appear before the flowers — these blooms are usually but not always blue. The flowers can be cut for small-scale indoor arrangements.

VARIETIES: The usual choice is **M. armeniacum** or one of its varieties. The basic type grows about 6–9 in. (15–22.5 cm) high and bears blue flowers which have a white rim — these blooms measure ¼ in. (0.5 cm) long and are fragrant. The foliage season is often quite long, starting in autumn and lasting until after the April blooms have withered. **'Blue Spike'** is a popular variety — it is shorter than the species and the double flowers are pale blue. Other varieties include **'Fantasy Creation'** (double greeny-yellow) and **'Saffier'** (white-rimmed deep blue). **M. azureum** bears its dark-striped bright blue flowers in March — **'Album'** is a white-flowering dwarf variety. **M. botryoides 'Album'** is another white Muscari. There are several species which look quite different from the all-blue or all-white varieties. The 12 in. (30 cm) **M. comosum 'Plumosum'** has large and feathery violet-coloured blooms and **M. macrocarpum** bears brown-rimmed yellow flowers — both these novelties bloom in May. **M. ambrosiacum** is another May flowerer — its purple blooms fade to pale green and then to cream as they mature. The Oxford & Cambridge Muscari (**M. tubergenianum**) has pale blue flowers at the top of the stalk and dark blue ones below.

SITE & SOIL: Any well-drained soil will do — thrives best in full sun.

PLANT DETAILS: Planting time: September–October. Planting depth: 3 in. (7.5 cm). Spacing: 4 in. (10 cm). Height 4–12 in. (10–30 cm).

PROPAGATION: Divide clumps in autumn every 3 years — replant at once.

M. botryoides 'Album'

M. macrocarpum

Muscari armeniacum 'Blue Spike'

Muscari comosum 'Plumosum'

Muscari tubergenianum

NARCISSUS Narcissus, Daffodil

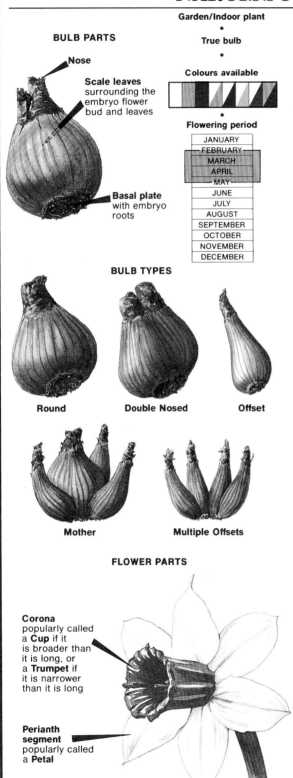

BULB PARTS

Nose

Scale leaves surrounding the embryo flower bud and leaves

Basal plate with embryo roots

Garden/Indoor plant
•
True bulb
•

Colours available

•

Flowering period

| JANUARY |
| FEBRUARY |
| MARCH |
| APRIL |
| MAY |
| JUNE |
| JULY |
| AUGUST |
| SEPTEMBER |
| OCTOBER |
| NOVEMBER |
| DECEMBER |

BULB TYPES

Round　　Double Nosed　　Offset

Mother　　Multiple Offsets

FLOWER PARTS

Corona popularly called a **Cup** if it is broader than it is long, or a **Trumpet** if it is narrower than it is long

Perianth segment popularly called a **Petal**

A walk down any suburban street in March or April will quickly convince you that the Narcissus is our most popular spring flower, but it comes as a surprise to read that various surveys have shown that it is also our overall favourite flower, beating even the Rose. Too well-known to need a detailed description, of course, but not everyone realises the range of shapes, sizes and colours among the thousand or two which are commercially available. The heights vary from 3 in. (7.5 cm) to 2 ft (60 cm) and the colours include oranges, pinks, apricots and reds as well as the familiar white and yellows. You can also find split corona and double varieties as well as the simple perianth/corona arrangement illustrated on the left. With all varieties the leafless flower stalk arises among the strap-like leaves. The flowers range from 1–3 in. (2.5–7.5 cm) across and are generally but not always borne singly on the top of the stalk. They are easy to grow, which is one of the reasons for their great popularity. They will grow in any reasonable soil, although they grow best in fertile moist soil, and apart from the Tazetta varieties are fully hardy. This means that Narcissi can be left in the ground over winter and will spread into large clumps in a few years. They have all sorts of uses in the garden — the dwarfs are excellent in rockeries, pots, bed and border edges etc and the taller ones can be used in beds, borders, under trees, in grassland and so on. As a general rule Narcissi are better grown in informal groups than in regular-spaced neat rows, but it is a matter of personal taste. Dwarf varieties are popular as container plants — N. triandrus, N. bulbocodium and N. 'Minnow' are typical examples. To make a start in the garden, look through the bulb catalogues or the wide selection at your garden centre in early autumn. To make your choice easier this genus has been split into 12 groups, and the Division numbers appear in the rest of this section and in many catalogues. Choose your bulbs carefully (see the section on Buying & Handling) and plant them as soon as possible after buying. Do not use offsets or multiple offsets if you want blooms next spring. If your soil is heavy sprinkle some coarse sand in the hole before planting. The time to feed the soil is before planting or in February — there is little point in feeding at or after flowering. Remove dead flower-heads if practical and let the foliage die down naturally. Don't tie it into a knot and do not cut the grass above the bulbs for at least a month after the flowers have faded. The clumps should not be disturbed unless it is necessary — they can be lifted every 4–5 years in July or August for division and then replanted immediately. Pots of Narcissi act as heralds of spring in countless homes. Nearly all types can be grown indoors, but the most reliable groups are considered to be the Trumpet and Large-cupped Narcissi together with the Cyclamineus and Tazetta varieties. Read the section on Bulbs In The Home before you begin. Then plant the bulbs in August–October for flowers in January–April — set them close together with their noses just above the surface. The Tazetta varieties bear bunches of flowers on each stem at Christmas or early in the New Year. Prepared bulbs of several other types can be bought for planting in September for Christmas blooming.

SITE & SOIL: Any well-drained garden soil will do — thrives in sun or light shade.

PLANT DETAILS: Planting time: August–October. Planting depth: Cover with soil to twice the height of the bulb. Spacing: 4–8 in. (10–20 cm). Height: 3–24 in. (7.5–60 cm).

PROPAGATION: Lift overcrowded clumps in summer — divide, separate offsets and replant without delay.

NARCISSUS continued

Division 1:
TRUMPET DAFFODILS

One flower per stem — trumpet at least as long as the petals. Height 6 in.–1½ ft (15–45 cm).

By popular usage the word 'Daffodil' is the common name for all the varieties in this Division — the common name 'Narcissus' is used for all other types. **'King Alfred'** (golden yellow, early) once dominated this group, but it has died out and the word is used by some suppliers for other all-yellow varieties. Its place has been taken by **'Golden Harvest'** (golden yellow, very early), **'Dutch Master'** (golden yellow, early), **'Rembrandt'** (yellow, early) and **'Unsurpassable'** (yellow, mid-season, good indoors). The best-known all-white is **'Mount Hood'** (mid-season) — others include **'Empress of Ireland'** (large, early), **'April Love'** (large, early) and **'Beersheba'** (early, good indoors). There are numberous bi-colours — examples are **'Magnet'** (white with yellow trumpet, early), **'Spellbinder'** (yellow, trumpet fading to white, early) and **'Bravoure'** (white with yellow trumpet, early). There are some 6 in. (15 cm) dwarfs such as **'Topolino'** (white with yellow trumpet, early) and **'W. P. Milner'** (white, very early).

Narcissus 'Mount Hood'

Narcissus 'Golden Harvest'

Narcissus 'Spellbinder'

Narcissus 'Bravoure'

Narcissus 'Topolino'

Narcissus 'King Alfred'

Narcissus 'Magnet'

NARCISSUS continued

Division 2:
LARGE-CUPPED NARCISSI

One flower per stem — cup more than ⅓ the length of the petals. Height 1–2 ft (30–60 cm).

There are some fine yellows. The large and popular **'Carlton'** (early) is good for planting indoors, and so is **'Yellow Sun'** (very early). Other popular all-yellows include the narrow-cupped **'St. Keverne'** (early) and **'Gigantic Star'** (early). All-whites are less common, but you should be able to find **'Easter Moon'** (mid-season) and **'Desdemona'** (mid-season). For something different look for the all-white **'Sea Urchin'** (late) with its deeply serrated cup. This group has many splendid bi-colours in all sorts of combinations — examples include **'Carbineer'** (yellow with orange-red cup, late), **'Professor Einstein'** (white with orange cup, very early), **'Sempre Avanti'** (cream with orange cup, early), **'Flower Record'** (white with orange-rimmed yellow cup, early) and **'Fortune'** for indoors or out (yellow with orange cup, early). The first white variety with a pink cup was **'Mrs R O Backhouse'** — modern ones include **'Salome'**, **'Rosy Sunrise'** and **'Salmon Trout'**.

Narcissus 'Carlton'

Narcissus 'Desdemona'

Narcissus 'Professor Einstein'

Narcissus 'Sempre Avanti'

Division 3:
SMALL-CUPPED NARCISSI

One flower per stem — cup less than ⅓ the length of the petals. Height 1–1½ ft (30–45 cm).

There are a number of all-white varieties such as **'Angel'** (very late) and **'Frigid'** (late) but most types are bi-colours with a red or orange cup. The petals may be yellow, as with **'Birma'** (mid-season) and **'Edward Buxton'** (early) or white like **'Barrett Browning'** (early) and **'Aflame'** (early).

Narcissus 'Edward Buxton'

Narcissus 'Barrett Browning'

NARCISSUS continued

Division 4:
DOUBLE NARCISSI

One or more flowers per stem — more than one ring of petals. Height 6 in.–1½ ft (15–45 cm).

New double varieties in a wide range of colours and shapes continue to appear each year, but the old **'Telamonius Plenus'** (all-yellow, early) continues to be one of the most reliable. A more popular yellow these days is **'Golden Ducat'** (mid-season). There are several all-whites with one flower on each stem, including **'Ice King'** (mid-season). Most people pick a bi-colour, and there are lots from which to make your choice — look for **'Irene Copeland'** (white and apricot, mid-season), **'Texas'** (yellow and orange, early) and **'White Lion'** (white and yellow, late). Some varieties have several blooms on each stem — popular ones include **'Cheerfulness'** (pale cream, mid-season), **'White Marvel'** (white, late) and **'Sir Winston Churchill'** (white and orange-red, mid-season). For the rockery and the front of the border there are several 6 in. (15 cm) dwarfs like **'Rip Van Winkle'** (yellow, mid-season) and **'Pencrebar'** (yellow, mid-season).

Narcissus 'Telamonius Plenus'

Narcissus 'Texas'

Narcissus 'Golden Ducat'

Narcissus 'White Lion'

Division 5:
TRIANDRUS NARCISSI

Usually several flowers per stem — drooping flowers and slightly reflexed petals. Height 6 in.–1½ ft (15–45 cm).

These varieties have been bred from N. triandrus — good for indoors, garden beds and containers. The all-white mid-season **'Thalia'** is the popular one, but there are others to try. **'Angel's Tears'** (mid-season) is creamy-white, **'Ice Wings'** (mid-season) is pure white and **'Liberty Bells'** (late) is yellow.

Narcissus 'Thalia'

Narcissus 'Liberty Bells'

NARCISSUS continued

Division 6:
CYCLAMINEUS NARCISSI

Nearly always one flower per stem — drooping flowers with long trumpets and strongly reflexed petals. Height 6 in.–1 ft (15–30 cm).

These varieties have been bred from N. cyclamineus. Because of their small size they are frequently used in pots, window boxes, containers etc as well as in grassland, beds and borders. In this group are some of the earliest Narcissi — the frilly trumpets and swept-back petals of **'February Gold'** (all-yellow) and **'Peeping Tom'** (all-yellow) appear in February or early March. Shortly afterwards the March ones appear — the popular **'Jack Snipe'** and **'February Silver'** with their white petals and yellow trumpets, and the all-yellow **'Tête-à Tête'** with several flowers on each stem. **'Jenny'** is white and cream — **'Garden Princess'** is all-yellow. **'Itzim'** is an attractive deep yellow dwarf for the rockery. There is no need to restrict yourself to whites and yellows — there are Cyclamineus Narcissi with pink trumpets and white petals which bloom later in spring. The first one was **'Foundling'** and more recent ones include **'Lilac Charm'** and **'Lavender Lace'**. For orange trumpets and yellow petals choose **'Jetfire'** (early).

Narcissus 'February Gold'

Narcissus 'Jenny'

Narcissus 'Itzim'

Narcissus 'Jack Snipe'

Division 7:
JONQUILLA NARCISSI

Usually more than one flower per stem — cup shorter than the petals. Height 6 in.–1 ft (15–30 cm).

The Jonquils have been bred from N. jonquilla. The leaves are narrow and the fragrant flowers have broad petals. All-yellows include **'Sun Disc'** (late) and **'Trevithian'** (mid-season). Other Jonquils include **'Suzy'** (yellow and orange, mid-season), **'Lintie'** (yellow and orange, late), **'Pipit'** (yellow and white, mid-season) and **'Waterperry'** (white and pink, mid-season).

Narcissus 'Suzy'

Narcissus 'Pipit'

NARCISSUS continued

Division 8:
TAZETTA NARCISSI

Several flowers per stem — small flowers with short cups and rounded petals. Height 6 in.–1½ ft (15–45 cm).

These varieties have been bred from N. tazetta. The true Tazettas have the tenderness of their parent — vigorous growers but they are only suitable outdoors for mild areas. The flowers are fragrant and these bulbs are best known as indoor plants or cut flowers. **'Paper White'** (all-white, very early) is an old favourite for planting indoors for Christmas flowers — another Christmas Tazetta is **'Grand Soleil d'Or'** (yellow petals and orange cup, early). New ones have appeared in recent years, such as the **'Chinese Sacred Lily'** (white petals and golden-yellow cup, early) from the East and **'Matador'** (yellow petals and orange cup, early) from the U.S. Also included in this Division are the Poetaz Narcissi (Tazetta/Poeticus hybrids) which are much hardier and can be grown outdoors. Look for **'Cragford'** (white and orange, early), **'Geranium'** (white and orange, mid-season), **'Silver Chimes'** (white and pale yellow, mid-season) and the dwarf **'Minnow'** (cream and yellow, mid-season).

Narcissus 'Paper White'

Narcissus 'Grand Soleil d'Or'

Narcissus 'Minnow'

Narcissus 'Geranium'

Division 9:
POETICUS NARCISSI

Usually one flower per stem — white petals with a frilled red-edged cup. Height 1–1½ ft (30–45 cm).

The most popular variety is **'Actaea'** (yellow cup, mid-season) although many people prefer the age-old **'Pheasant's Eye'** with its deep orange cup and very late flowers in May. Others include **'Cantabile'** (green cup, late) and the **'Double White Poeticus'** (white cup, late). All the Poeticus Narcissi are sweetly scented.

Narcissus 'Actaea'

Narcissus 'Double White Poeticus'

NARCISSUS continued

Division 10:
WILD NARCISSI

All species, varieties and natural hybrids found in the wild. Height less than 1 ft (30 cm).

The dividing line between this Division and all the others should be clear-cut. Grouped here are the natural forms of Narcissus — all the others are of garden origin. In practice it is not so simple because some of these natural forms have been given common names and appear with their offsprings in the appropriate Division. For example, **N. triandrus albus** appears as **'Angel's Tears'** in Division 5 and **N. poeticus recurvus** appears as **'Pheasant's Eye'** in Division 9. Species and varieties which do belong here are the 4 in. (10 cm) **N. asturiensis** with its tiny yellow Trumpet Daffodils, **N. canaliculatus** (white and yellow) which is a tiny Tazetta Narcissus, **N. cyclamineus** with swept-back petals and the Hoop Petticoat (**N. bulbocodium**) with its wide trumpet and narrow petals. **N. pseudonarcissus** is the Wild Daffodil which grows 6-9 in. (15-22.5 cm) high. The Tenby Daffodil **N. obvallaris** is a small golden Trumpet Daffodil. Most Wild Narcissi are very early and all are excellent in rockeries.

Narcissus asturiensis

Narcissus canaliculatus

Narcissus cyclamineus

Narcissus bulbocodium

Division 11:
SPLIT-CORONA NARCISSI

One flower per stem — corona split for at least ⅓ of its length. Height 1-1½ ft (30-45 cm).

This is the latest and most unusual of the Narcissus Divisions. The split sections of the corona usually spread outwards — hence the common names Butterfly and Orchid Narcissi. Examples include **'Chanterelle'** (white petals and yellow corona), **'Orangery'** (white and orange), **'Papillon Blanc'** (all-white) and **'Lemon Beauty'** (yellow and orange).

Narcissus 'Orangery'

Division 12:
MISCELLANEOUS NARCISSI

Types which belong nowhere else.

Very uncommon. Specialist catalogues list some N. bulbocodium hybrids such as **'Kenellis'** and **'Taffeta'**.

Narcissus 'Kenellis'

NECTAROSCORDUM

Garden plant
•
True bulb
•
Colours available

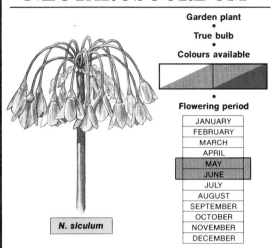

•
Flowering period

JANUARY	
FEBRUARY	
MARCH	
APRIL	
MAY	
JUNE	
JULY	
AUGUST	
SEPTEMBER	
OCTOBER	
NOVEMBER	
DECEMBER	

N. siculum

This tall plant is closely related to Allium (Flowering Onion) — you will detect the connection if you crush the foliage. These leaves have a distinct keel along their length, and in late spring or early summer the long and leafless flower stems appear. From the top of these stems the bell-shaped flowers hang down on thin stalks. A curious effect is seen after the flowers have been fertilised. As the seed pods form the stalks stiffen and turn upwards, so that the seed-heads have a shuttlecock appearance.

VARIETIES: The only species which is generally available is **N. siculum** (**N. dioscoridis**). It is sometimes listed as **Allium siculum**, and like some Alliums bears a loose cluster of drooping flowers. These 1 in. (2.5 cm) blooms are green with purple markings. The variety **'Bulgaricus'** is very similar in appearance and growth habit, but the flowers are white shaded with green. Both are easy to grow in herbaceous or mixed borders and they are useful plants for naturalising in grassland. Their greatest appeal is to the flower arranger as the dried seed-heads provide unusual material for their displays.

SITE & SOIL: Any well-drained soil will do — thrives best in full sun.

PLANT DETAILS: Planting time: September–October. Planting depth: 4 in. (10 cm). Spacing: 12 in. (30 cm). Height: 36–48 in. (90–120 cm).

PROPAGATION: Divide mature clumps in autumn when overcrowding becomes a problem.

Nectaroscordum siculum

NERINE Nerine

Garden/Indoor plant
•
True bulb
•
Colours available

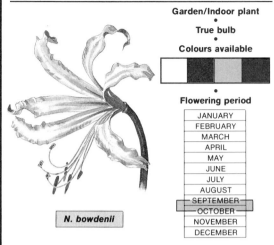

•
Flowering period

JANUARY	
FEBRUARY	
MARCH	
APRIL	
MAY	
JUNE	
JULY	
AUGUST	
SEPTEMBER	
OCTOBER	
NOVEMBER	
DECEMBER	

N. bowdenii

The Nerine flower-head consists of a cluster of stalked blooms on top of a leafless stem — each flower is funnel-shaped with wavy narrow petals which curl backwards. Nearly all are too tender to grow outdoors and should be grown as indoor plants — set the bulbs in compost with their necks well above the surface. This planting should take place in late summer. When shoots emerge in late spring stand the pot outdoors until the flower buds appear — then move indoors. There is one species which is hardy enough to grow outdoors if it is protected with a mulch in winter.

VARIETIES: For indoor blooms there are **N. flexuosa** which grows to 3 ft (90 cm) and bears pink or white flowers, and the Guernsey Lily (**N. sarniensis**) which produces a tight group of white, orange or red blooms on 1–1½ ft (30–45 cm) stems. **N. undulata** bears nodding pink flowers. **N. bowdenii** is the species to grow outdoors — see details below. The colour is deep pink — the variety **'Pink Triumph'** has silvery pink blooms. The foliage grows in spring and dies down in summer.

SITE & SOIL: Well-drained soil, a sheltered spot and full sun are necessary.

PLANT DETAILS: Planting time: April or August. Planting depth: 4 in. (10 cm). Spacing: 6 in. (15 cm). Height: 24 in. (60 cm).

PROPAGATION: Divide overcrowded clumps in spring — replant at once.

Nerine sarniensis

NOMOCHARIS Nomocharis

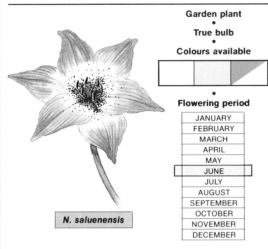

Garden plant
•
True bulb
•
Colours available

Flowering period

JANUARY
FEBRUARY
MARCH
APRIL
MAY
JUNE
JULY
AUGUST
SEPTEMBER
OCTOBER
NOVEMBER
DECEMBER

N. saluenensis

This one is a challenge. First of all you will have to find the Lily-like bulbs, and there are not many suppliers. Next you have to grow them, and they have specific needs. For numerous bulbs in this A–Z section the instruction is to choose a warm and sheltered spot, but for this Himalayan plant you need the wet and cool climate of the north and west. The soil must be peaty and should never be allowed to dry out. The reward for success is an eye-catching show of beautiful starry flowers with petals which are often fringed and spotted. Do not lift and divide established clumps.

VARIETIES: The most popular species is **N. aperta**. In summer 3–6 pale pink flowers appear at the top of the leafy stems — each bloom measures up to 6 in. (15 cm) across and has a dark and spotted centre. **N. mairei** has fringed flowers which are white or pale pink with a dark purple eye — this species is often confused with the similar **N. pardanthina**. The most colourful Nomocharis and the easiest to grow is **N. saluenensis** — the star-shaped blooms are white or pale pink flushed with deep pink at the tips.

SITE & SOIL: Well-drained, humus-rich soil in partial shade.

PLANT DETAILS: Planting time: November. Planting depth: 4 in. (10 cm). Spacing: 12 in. (30 cm). Height: 24–36 in. (60–90 cm).

PROPAGATION: Dislikes disturbance — buy new bulbs.

Nomocharis pardanthina

NOTHOLIRION Notholirion

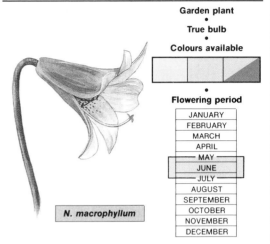

Garden plant
•
True bulb
•
Colours available

Flowering period

JANUARY
FEBRUARY
MARCH
APRIL
MAY
JUNE
JULY
AUGUST
SEPTEMBER
OCTOBER
NOVEMBER
DECEMBER

N. macrophyllum

This rarity shares an unusual feature with the better-known Cardiocrinum — the bulb dies after flowering and it is the offsets which produce next year's growth. The blooms are open-mouthed trumpets but they are much smaller than the Cardiocrinum ones and the plants are much shorter. The long and narrow leaves appear at the base of the plant from autumn until early spring and the flowers appear in late spring or summer on leafy stems. Choose a spot near low-growing evergreens so that the winter leaves can be given some protection.

VARIETIES: The easiest one to find is **N. bulbiferum** (**N. hyacinthinum**). In midsummer about 20 bells appear on each 2–3 ft (60–90 cm) stem — these blooms are lilac with green-flushed petal tips. **N. thomsonianum** reaches about the same height but differs by having 2 in. (5 cm) long pale pink blooms in late spring. The most colourful species is **N. macrophyllum** — the flowers are deep mauve on the outside and purple-spotted pale lavender within. Unfortunately only a few of these 1 in. (2.5 cm) long trumpets appear on each stem.

SITE & SOIL: Well-drained, humus-rich soil in sun or light shade.

PLANT DETAILS: Planting time: October–November. Planting depth: 4 in. (10 cm). Spacing: 12 in. (30 cm). Height: 24–36 in. (60–90 cm).

PROPAGATION: Remove and plant offsets in autumn.

Notholirion thomsonianum

ORNITHOGALUM

Garden/Indoor plant
•
True bulb
•
Colours available

Flowering period

| JANUARY |
| FEBRUARY |
| MARCH |
| APRIL |
| MAY |
| JUNE |
| JULY |
| AUGUST |
| SEPTEMBER |
| OCTOBER |
| NOVEMBER |
| DECEMBER |

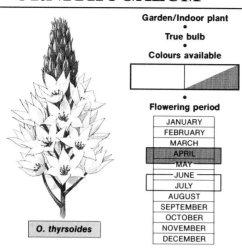

O. thyrsoides

There are 2 distinct groups. The first one contains the species which are not hardy and so are grown as pot plants indoors. Alternatively they are planted outdoors in April for late summer flowers and are then discarded. For indoor culture plant about 6 bulbs in a 6 in. (15 cm) pot in autumn — reduce watering once flowering is over and repot each autumn. The second group consists of the few species which are hardy and can be grown in grassland or in the rockery.

VARIETIES: The best known of the tender species is Chincherinchee (**O. thyrsoides**). It bears 1 ft (30 cm) long strap-like leaves and in early summer the 1½ ft (45 cm) high stems appear. These stems are crowned by a crowded spike of 20–30 white starry flowers. The hardy species bloom in spring — basic details are set out below. **O. nutans** is a good one to buy — about a dozen pendent silvery flowers with green backs are borne on each stem. The popular Star of Bethlehem (**O. umbellatum**) grows to the same height (1 ft or 30 cm) but it has a different growth habit — the starry flowers face upwards and close during the night.

SITE & SOIL: Any well-drained soil will do — thrives in sun or partial shade.

PLANT DETAILS: Planting time: October. Planting depth: 2 in. (5 cm). Spacing: 4–6 in. (10–15 cm). Height: 6–18 in. (15–45 cm).

PROPAGATION: Divide clumps in summer — replant at once.

Ornithogalum umbellatum

OXALIS Wood Sorrel

Garden/Indoor plant
•
Tuber, rhizome or true bulb
•
Colours available

Flowering period

| JANUARY |
| FEBRUARY |
| MARCH |
| APRIL |
| MAY |
| JUNE |
| JULY |
| AUGUST |
| SEPTEMBER |
| OCTOBER |
| NOVEMBER |
| DECEMBER |

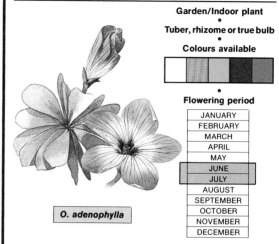

O. adenophylla

You should never plant a clump of Oxalis (Sorrel, Clover and Shamrock are common names) unless you know the species. Some spread rapidly and can ruin part of a rockery, and others are half hardy and need to be grown indoors. For outdoors you should choose a hardy non-invasive Oxalis. They are undemanding plants — simply dig in some peat or compost before planting. For indoor flowers plant the bulbs 1 in. deep in compost in spring or autumn. Keep moist during the growing season but water very sparingly after the leaves wither.

VARIETIES: Oxalis grows as a rounded clump of clover-like leaves and 5-petalled flowers which open wide when the sun shines. Tender species include **O. tetraphylla** (pink flowers, brown-marked leaves) and **O. cernua** (yellow flowers). The most popular garden Oxalis is **O. adenophylla** which grows about 3 in. (7.5 cm) high. The leaves are grey-green and the flowers are silver splashed and veined with pink. It spreads to about 6 in. (15 cm) — **O. enneaphylla** in white, pink or red is even more restrained. **O. laciniata** has mauve flowers and the creeper **O. chrysantha** is yellow.

SITE & SOIL: Any well-drained soil will do — thrives best in full sun.

PLANT DETAILS: Planting time: September–November. Planting depth: 3 in. (7.5 cm). Spacing: 4 in. (10 cm). Height: 2–6 in. (5–15 cm).

PROPAGATION: Divide clumps in summer.

Oxalis laciniata

PANCRATIUM Sea Lily

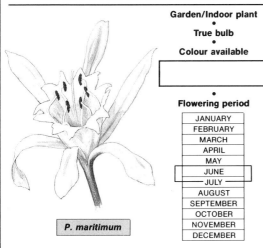

Garden/Indoor plant
•
True bulb
•
Colour available

Flowering period

JANUARY
FEBRUARY
MARCH
APRIL
MAY
JUNE
JULY
AUGUST
SEPTEMBER
OCTOBER
NOVEMBER
DECEMBER

P. maritimum

This plant from the Mediterranean seashore is very similar to the American Spider Lily (Hymenocallis) and its cultural needs are even more demanding. It is sometimes recommended as an outdoor plant for warm and sheltered sites but it is risky and sometimes refuses to flower. It will need a thick mulch in winter and a spell of warm dry weather after flowering. If you want to try it outdoors plant the bulbs 5 in. (12.5 cm) deep in May and water during dry spells. Leave undisturbed for 4–5 years.

VARIETIES: P. maritimum is the only species you are likely to find. The stalk bears a loose head of up to 10 blooms. Each white fragrant flower looks rather like a Narcissus — there is a wide cup with long stamens and a ring of 6 narrow petals. For growing indoors a minimum temperature of 55°F (13°C) is necessary. Water sparingly until the shoot appears and then keep the compost moist as long as the foliage remains green. Pots can be stood outdoors when in flower. Stop watering when the leaves wither — leave dormant over winter and repot in spring every 2–3 years.

SITE & SOIL: Use a soilless compost — choose a brightly lit spot away from hot summer sun.

PLANT DETAILS: Planting time: March. Planting depth: Tip should be just above the surface. Spacing: 1 in a 5 in. (12.5 cm) pot. Height: 12–18 in. (30–45 cm).

PROPAGATION: Remove and plant offsets at repotting time.

Pancratium maritimum

PARADISEA St. Bernard's Lily

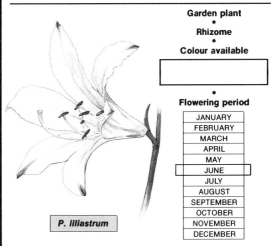

Garden plant
•
Rhizome
•
Colour available

Flowering period

JANUARY
FEBRUARY
MARCH
APRIL
MAY
JUNE
JULY
AUGUST
SEPTEMBER
OCTOBER
NOVEMBER
DECEMBER

P. liliastrum

Unlike the other plant on this page St. Bernard's Lily is completely hardy and should be more widely grown. It is an excellent choice for open woodland, a partially shaded rock garden or for naturalising in grassland. The leaves are grass-like and the stems bear Lily-like flowers. The rhizomes bear fleshy roots and not dormant organs, so they cannot be dried and stored. For this reason Paradisea is often bought as a growing plant, but roots can be obtained and should be planted immediately.

VARIETIES: The species which is usually grown is **P. liliastrum**. The flower spike bears up to 10 tubular flowers along one side — each fragrant bloom is about 2 in. (5 cm) long and you can recognise this plant by the small green blotch at the tip of each petal. Be careful how you handle the brittle roots when planting and in autumn apply a mulch of compost or well-rotted manure over the crown. Do not disturb the clumps unless it is necessary as few flowers appear in the year after transplanting. The variety **'Major'** is a little larger than the species.

SITE & SOIL: Well-drained, humus-rich soil is necessary — thrives in partial shade.

PLANT DETAILS: Planting time: September or March. Planting depth: 3 in. (7.5 cm). Spacing: 12 in. (30 cm). Height: 12–24 in. (30–60 cm).

PROPAGATION: Divide overcrowded clumps in early autumn.

Paradisea liliastrum

PLEIONE Rockery Orchid

Garden/Indoor plant
•
Pseudobulb
•
Colours available

Flowering period

JANUARY
FEBRUARY
MARCH
APRIL
MAY
JUNE
JULY
AUGUST
SEPTEMBER
OCTOBER
NOVEMBER
DECEMBER

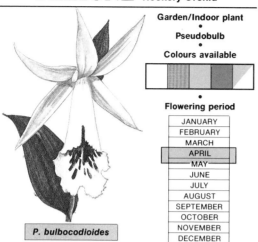

P. bulbocodioides

There is something really satisfying about growing an Orchid in the garden, and this small Orchid from China has become quite widely available in recent years. It is not for everyone — you will need a sheltered site in a mild locality and the protection of a cloche or bell jar from autumn until spring. No special compost is needed — just enrich the soil with peat and leafmould plus some sharp sand. Where outdoor conditions are unsuitable grow Pleione as a house plant — set the pseudobulbs to half their depth in orchid compost in spring. Water with rainwater and feed regularly.

VARIETIES: P. **bulbocodioides** (**P. formosana**) and its varieties are the Pleiones chosen for growing outdoors. The showy 3 in. (7.5 cm) blooms have narrow petals around a fringed yellow, white or pink central tube. The inside of this tube is streaked or mottled. The species is pink with red markings inside the tube. There are several varieties which are quite similar apart from the inside colour — for example **'Oriental Grace'** (yellow markings) and **'Piton'** (violet markings). For other petal colours choose **'Snowcap'** (white) or **'Shantung'** (yellow).

SITE & SOIL: Well-drained, humus-rich soil in a mild area — thrives best in partial shade.

PLANT DETAILS: Planting time: May. Planting depth: Top of pseudobulb should be above the surface. Spacing: 6 in. (15 cm). Height: 3 in. (7.5 cm).

PROPAGATION: Collect and pot up detached pseudobulbs from the base of the plant in late spring.

Pleione bulbocodioides 'Shantung'

POLIANTHES Tuberose

Indoor plant
•
Tuber
•
Colour available

Flowering period

JANUARY
FEBRUARY
MARCH
APRIL
MAY
JUNE
JULY
AUGUST
SEPTEMBER
OCTOBER
NOVEMBER
DECEMBER

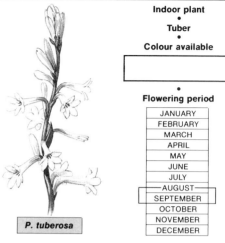

P. tuberosa

The Tuberose was a popular conservatory plant in Victorian times — the pure white waxy blooms filled the air with fragrance. Then, surprisingly, it lost its appeal, perhaps because of its association with funerals. It can be found in a few catalogues and is well worth cultivating if you have a heated greenhouse. Plant the tubers in spring and do not water until the leaves appear. Water freely when the plant is actively growing — 2–6 flower stalks will emerge in autumn. The stems can be cut for flower arranging. When the blooms fade the tubers are discarded as they will not flower in the following season.

VARIETIES: The basic species is **P. tuberosa**. At the base there is a clump of grassy 1 ft (30 cm) long leaves and above them are the 3 ft (90 cm) high flowering stems. The tubular flowers are borne along the upper half of each stem — the petals open out as the blooms mature to form a 1–2 in. (2.5–5 cm) star. You are more likely to find the double-flowering variety **'The Pearl'** rather than the single-flowering species. This variety is shorter than its parent, growing to 1½–2 ft (45–60 cm) but its blooms are just as fragrant.

SITE & SOIL: Use soil-based or soilless compost — choose a brightly lit spot away from direct sun.

PLANT DETAILS: Planting time: March. Planting depth: 1 in. (2.5 cm). Spacing: 1 in a 5 in. (12.5 cm) pot. Height: 18–36 in. (45–90 cm).

PROPAGATION: Buy new tubers.

Polianthes tuberosa 'The Pearl'

PUSCHKINIA Striped Squill

Garden/Indoor plant
•
True bulb
•
Colours available

Flowering period

JANUARY
FEBRUARY
MARCH
APRIL
MAY
JUNE
JULY
AUGUST
SEPTEMBER
OCTOBER
NOVEMBER
DECEMBER

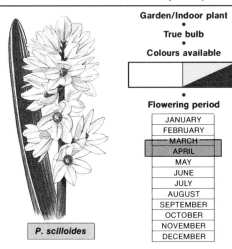

P. scilloides

Puschkinia is an excellent plant for a rockery. It is completely hardy and trouble-free — the attractive starry flowers appear early in the year and the bulbs increase quite quickly to form large clumps. It is therefore surprising that it is not more popular — it remains a poor relation of the Bluebells. You can tell them apart by the small fused tube at the base of the Puschkinia flower which is absent from the Scilla bloom. The strap-like foliage is dark green and each flower measures about ½ in. (1 cm) across.

VARIETIES: The only species grown as a garden plant is **P. scilloides (P. libanotica)**. The usual place for Puschkinia is in the rockery, but it is also a good choice for edging and small containers. Each stem carries 6–12 flowers which are open bells — each petal is pale silvery blue with a central dark blue stripe. The bulbs are best planted in groups for maximum effect, and it is helpful to add compost or peat to the soil before planting. The white variety **'Alba'** is less eye-catching than the species. Puschkinia can be grown as a pot plant indoors in the same way as Crocus or Squill.

SITE & SOIL: Any well-drained soil will do — thrives in sun or light shade.

PLANT DETAILS: Planting time: September–October. Planting depth: 2 in. (5 cm). Spacing: 3 in. (7.5 cm). Height: 4–6 in. (10–15 cm).

PROPAGATION: Divide clumps in summer — replant at once.

Puschkinia scilloides 'Alba'

RANUNCULUS Persian Buttercup

Garden/Indoor plant
•
Tuberous root
•
Colours available

Flowering period

JANUARY
FEBRUARY
MARCH
APRIL
MAY
JUNE
JULY
AUGUST
SEPTEMBER
OCTOBER
NOVEMBER
DECEMBER

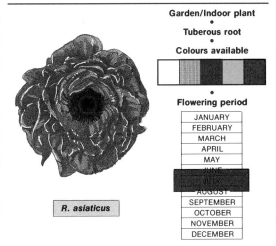

R. asiaticus

This showy Buttercup is an excellent plant for the border — each stem bears several 3–5 in. (7.5–12.5 cm) wide blooms in summer. These flowers are useful for cutting as they are long-lasting in water. The ferny foliage which appears in spring is attractive but it dies down in summer. Soak the tuberous roots in cold water for several hours and then plant them claws downwards in spring. Lift in late summer when the foliage has withered and store the 'tubers' over winter in dry peat in a frost-free place.

VARIETIES: R. asiaticus is the only species you are likely to find. There are several forms including the *Persians* which are rather small and sometimes single and the *French* which are semi-double. The most popular form is the *Paeony-flowered* which are large and often fully double. The *Turban* Buttercups are fully double and ball-like. These groups are represented by scores of hybrids, but Ranunculus is nearly always bought as a multi-coloured mixture of semi-double and double types rather than as a single variety.

SITE & SOIL: Any well-drained soil will do — thrives best in full sun.

PLANT DETAILS: Planting time: March–April. Planting depth: 1 in. (2.5 cm). Spacing: 6 in. (15 cm). Height: 12 in. (30 cm).

PROPAGATION: Divide clumps of tuberous roots after lifting — replant in spring.

Ranunculus asiaticus

RHODOHYPOXIS

Garden plant
•
Tuber
•
Colours available

Flowering period

JANUARY	
FEBRUARY	
MARCH	
APRIL	
MAY	■
JUNE	■
JULY	■
AUGUST	■
SEPTEMBER	
OCTOBER	
NOVEMBER	
DECEMBER	

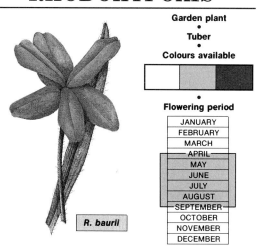

R. baurii

Give this charming little alpine the right conditions and it will bloom continually from late spring to late summer. It is not as delicate as some books claim but it does need a sheltered spot. The place for Rhodohypoxis is in a tiny pocket in the rockery, a sink garden or a pot. The soil or compost must be free from lime and should contain both humus and gritty sand. Top dress around the plants with granite chips and water during the growing season if the weather is dry.

VARIETIES: Choose a variety of **R. baurii** or related species — examples include **'Ruth'** (white), **'Fred Broome'** (pink), **'Pictus'** (pink-flushed white) and **'Tetra Red'** (red). Rhodohypoxis is often bought as a mixture of white, pink and red varieties. The 1 in. (2.5 cm) wide flowers appear on thin stems above the tufts of narrow hairy leaves. The flower form is unusual — there is an outer ring of 3 petals and an inner ring of 3 petals which hide the eye of the bloom. The main enemy of Rhodohypoxis is water-logging in winter — cover the crown with a sheet of glass if you live in a high rainfall area.

SITE & SOIL: Well-drained, gritty soil which is lime-free is necessary. Full sun is essential.

PLANT DETAILS: Planting time: April–May. Planting depth: 2 in. (5 cm). Spacing: 4 in. (10 cm). Height: 2 in. (5 cm).

PROPAGATION: Divide clumps in autumn.

Rhodohypoxis baurii 'Pictus'

ROMULEA Romulea

Garden/Indoor plant
•
Corm
•
Colour available

Flowering period

JANUARY	
FEBRUARY	
MARCH	■
APRIL	■
MAY	■
JUNE	
JULY	
AUGUST	
SEPTEMBER	
OCTOBER	
NOVEMBER	
DECEMBER	

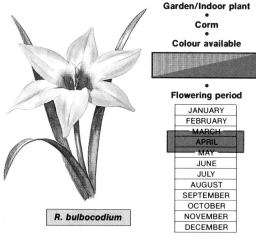

R. bulbocodium

This Crocus-like plant has colourful flowers — the species which is sold for growing outdoors has yellow-throated pale purple blooms. The problem is that it is available from very few bulb suppliers and it is so like a Crocus that the search is not worthwhile. Still, if you like rarities it may be worth the hunt. Romulea is a more demanding plant than Crocus — full sun is essential and it is only moderately hardy. It will also need some protection from heavy spring rain. Protect the crowns with peat or leafmould in winter.

VARIETIES: There are several large-flowering Romuleas with lovely colouring but these are too delicate for growing outdoors. The hardy species in the catalogues is **R. bulbocodium (Crocus bulbocodium)** which has 1 in. (2.5 cm) flowers which open wide when the sun is shining and close up when it is dull. The backs of the petals are veined and streaked with purple and the leaves are long and narrow. The variety **'Clusiana'** has similar colouring but the flowers are larger. Romulea can be grown indoors like Crocus.

SITE & SOIL: Well-drained, sandy soil in full sun is necessary.

PLANT DETAILS: Planting time: September–October. Planting depth: 2 in. (5 cm). Spacing: 3 in. (7.5 cm). Height: 3 in. (7.5 cm).

PROPAGATION: Divide overcrowded clumps in late summer.

Romulea bulbocodium

ROSCOEA Roscoea

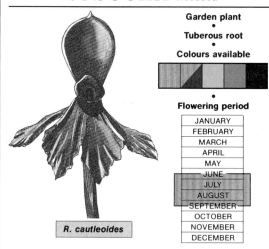

Garden plant

•

Tuberous root

•

Colours available

•

Flowering period

| JANUARY |
| FEBRUARY |
| MARCH |
| APRIL |
| MAY |
| JUNE |
| JULY |
| AUGUST |
| SEPTEMBER |
| OCTOBER |
| NOVEMBER |
| DECEMBER |

R. cautleoides

This plant should be more widely grown in borders and rock gardens. The wide stem-clasping leaves appear in late spring or early summer and are followed by Orchid-like flowers on short stalks in summer. Each tubular flower opens out into a hooded upright petal, 2 narrow side petals and a large downward-pointing lip. Despite its exotic appearance it is not difficult to grow and should quite happily survive over winter if there is a peat or compost mulch above and free-draining soil below.

VARIETIES: R. cautleoides is the most popular Roscoea and also the easiest to grow. Each plant produces about 5 yellow flowers. These blooms appear in early summer — for late summer flowers grow **R. purpurea**. The species is all-purple — for white-centred purple flowers grow the variety **'Procera'**. Another bi-colour is **R. 'Beesianum'** — the inside of the petals is heavily streaked with red veins and blotches. For pink flowers choose **R. alpina** and for near-black ones select **R. scillifolia**.

SITE & SOIL: Well-drained, humus-rich soil in sun or partial shade.

PLANT DETAILS: Planting time: April. Planting depth: 4 in. (10 cm). Spacing: 6 in. (15 cm). Height: 9–12 in. (22.5–30 cm).

PROPAGATION: Divide clumps in late spring when first shoots appear.

Roscoea purpurea 'Procera'

SANDERSONIA Chinese Lantern Lily

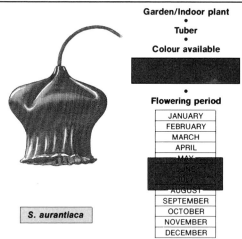

Garden/Indoor plant

•

Tuber

•

Colour available

•

Flowering period

| JANUARY |
| FEBRUARY |
| MARCH |
| APRIL |
| MAY |
| JUNE |
| JULY |
| AUGUST |
| SEPTEMBER |
| OCTOBER |
| NOVEMBER |
| DECEMBER |

S. aurantiaca

This tuber is listed in a few catalogues and if it is illustrated you may well be tempted to order some. The flowers are unique — hanging orange lanterns all summer long. However, do not even think about it unless the soil drains very freely and the site is in full sun. If the location is unsuitable then grow it as a greenhouse plant in the same way as Gloriosa — see page 45 for details. Sandersonia is a climber — the leaves bear tendrils at the tips and some form of support is necessary.

VARIETIES: There is just one species — **S. aurantiaca**. The spring-planted small tubers give rise to thin stems which bear scattered leaves. In summer 1 in. (2.5 cm) long pendent lanterns are borne on stalks in the axils of the upper leaves. In autumn the leaves wither and the stems die down. Indoor plants are left in their pots of dry compost until repotting time in spring, but outdoor plants should be lifted in autumn and the tubers stored in dry peat in a frost-free place until replanting time.

SITE & SOIL: Well-drained soil and a sheltered sunny spot are essential.

PLANT DETAILS: Planting time: April. Planting depth: 2 in. (5 cm). Spacing: 12 in. (30 cm). Height: 24 in. (60 cm).

PROPAGATION: Divide tubers before repotting or replanting in spring.

Sandersonia aurantiaca

SCADOXUS Blood Flower

Garden/Indoor plant
•
True bulb
•
Colour available

Flowering period

JANUARY
FEBRUARY
MARCH
APRIL
MAY
JUNE
JULY
AUGUST
SEPTEMBER
OCTOBER
NOVEMBER
DECEMBER

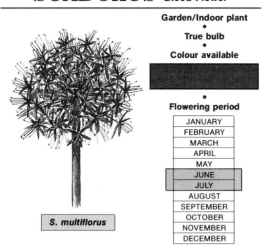

S. multiflorus

The species of Scadoxus described here were once classed as Haemanthus and you will still find them under that name in some catalogues. Like the Haemanthus species the plants described below have a mass of tiny flowers with prominent stamens and large oblong leaves, but the Scadoxus blooms are grouped as large round heads without any showy bracts at the base. They can be grown outdoors in some very mild areas but it is better to treat them as greenhouse or house plants — see Haemanthus for details.

VARIETIES: S. multiflorus is a bold plant which arises from a large bulb. The spherical flower-head on top of the 2 ft (60 cm) stalk bears up to 200 spiky blood-red blooms — this brightly coloured bottle-brush ball measures about 6 in. (15 cm) across. The variety **'Katharinae'** is even taller, reaching up to 3 ft (90 cm) and with red flower-heads as large as 8 in. (20 cm) across. Its wavy-edged leaves are 1–1½ ft (30–45 cm) long. Another striking species is **S. kalbreyeri**.

SITE & SOIL: Use a soilless compost — grow in a brightly lit spot.

PLANT DETAILS: Planting time: March–May. Planting depth: Tip should be just above the surface. Spacing: 1 in an 8 in. (20 cm) pot. Height: 24–36 in. (60–90 cm).

PROPAGATION: Divide and pot up bulblets at repotting time.

Scadoxus multiflorus 'Katharinae'

SCHIZOSTYLIS Kaffir Lily

Garden/Indoor plant
•
Rhizome
•
Colours available

Flowering period

JANUARY
FEBRUARY
MARCH
APRIL
MAY
JUNE
JULY
AUGUST
SEPTEMBER
OCTOBER
NOVEMBER
DECEMBER

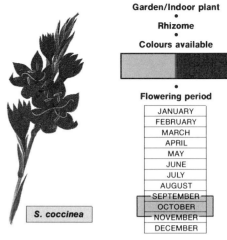

S. coccinea

A bulbous plant which will add colour to the middle of the border at the end of the season. Rising above the grassy foliage are the flowering spikes which look like miniature Gladioli and each of the blooms looks rather like a Crocus. Despite these visual links its common name is Kaffir Lily... although it belongs to the Iris family! Add plenty of organic matter before planting, water in dry weather and dead-head faded blooms. Cut down the stems when the floral display is over and protect the crowns in winter by covering them with peat or leafmould.

VARIETIES: S. coccinea is the only species available. The 1½ in. (4 cm) blooms are pink or red and are recommended as cut flowers. There are numerous varieties listed in the catalogues. **'Major'** is a popular one as the deep red flowers are larger than the species. **'Mrs Hegarty'** is a pink variety which blooms earlier than the others but **'Viscountess Byng'** (pink) does not bloom until November. **'November Cheer'** (pink) is another late-flowering variety and **'Salmon Charm'** is flesh pink.

SITE & SOIL: A well-drained, moisture-retentive soil is necessary — thrives in sun or light shade.

PLANT DETAILS: Planting time: April. Planting depth: 2 in. (5 cm). Spacing: 12 in. (30 cm). Height: 24 in. (60 cm).

PROPAGATION: Divide clumps in spring.

Schizostylis coccinea 'Mrs Hegarty'

SCILLA Bluebell, Squill

Garden/Indoor plant
•
True bulb
•
Colours available
•
Flowering period

JANUARY
FEBRUARY
MARCH
APRIL
MAY
JUNE
JULY
AUGUST
SEPTEMBER
OCTOBER
NOVEMBER
DECEMBER

S. campanulata

S. sibirica

S. peruviana

In recent years the English and Spanish Bluebells have been reclassified as Hyacinthoides or Endymion, but here the Bluebells and the True Squills have been kept together as species of Scilla. The ordinary Bluebells are a common sight in spring in both woodland and gardens. The flowers appear on upright stems above the strap-like leaves — drooping bells in shades of blue or violet. But not all Scillas are the same — there are winter-flowering dwarfs for the rockery and also tall Squills with tight heads of blue stars in early summer. Thus both height and flowering season cover a wide range, and so does flower colour — there are white, pink, purple and mauve as well as the familiar blue ones. Most are easy to grow and can be left in the ground to spread into large clumps. One point to remember is that the bulbs are susceptible to decay when out of the soil and should therefore be planted as soon as possible after purchase.

VARIETIES: The earliest Squills are the dwarf species — height 3 in. (7.5 cm), spacing 3 in. (7.5 cm), flowering period February–March. There are **S. tubergeniana** which has pale blue petals with blue stripes and **S. bifolia** which has deep gentian-blue starry flowers. These dwarfs make a lovely display in late winter, but the favourite early-flowering species is the Siberian or Spring Squill **S. sibirica** — height 6 in. (15 cm), spacing 4 in. (10 cm), flowering period March–April. The violet-blue open bells are borne in loose clusters — there is a white variety **'Alba'** but the best one is the dark blue **'Spring Beauty'**. All of these very early and early Scillas can be planted indoors for blooming in January–March — see the section on Bulbs In The Home for details. The best known species is, of course, the English Bluebell or Wild Hyacinth which has a host of latin names — **S. non-scripta**, **S. nutans**, **Hyacinthoides non-scripta** and **Endymion non-scripta**. The basic details are height 10 in. (25 cm), spacing 4 in. (10 cm), flowering period April–May. Flowering at the same time is the 12–18 in. (30–45 cm) Spanish Bluebell **S. campanulata (Hyacinthoides hispanica)** — blue, pink and white varieties are available. Last to flower is the Cuban Lily **S. peruviana** — height 12 in. (30 cm), spacing 6 in. (15 cm), flowering period May–June.

SITE & SOIL: Any well-drained moist soil will do — thrives in full sun or light shade.

PLANT DETAILS: Planting time: August–September. Planting depth: 2–4 in. (5–10 cm). See above for other details.

PROPAGATION: Divide overcrowded clumps in August–September — replant at once.

Scilla tubergeniana

Scilla non-scripta

Scilla peruviana

SISYRINCHIUM Sisyrinchium

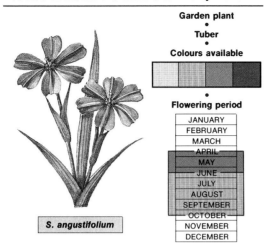

Garden plant
•
Tuber
•
Colours available
•
Flowering period

| JANUARY |
| FEBRUARY |
| MARCH |
| APRIL |
| MAY |
| JUNE |
| JULY |
| AUGUST |
| SEPTEMBER |
| OCTOBER |
| NOVEMBER |
| DECEMBER |

S. angustifolium

Sisyrinchium deserves to be better known. You will find some of the hardy species available as growing plants in larger garden centres and the tubers are offered by a few specialist bulb companies. It is not difficult to grow in a shade-free site and the small species make attractive rockery plants. There is, however, a problem — the plants produce self-sown seedlings very freely so dead-heading may be necessary. The leaves are broad and grassy and the flowers are star- or bell-shaped. These blooms are not long-lived but they appear over a long period.

VARIETIES: S. brachypus grows 6 in. (15 cm) high and bears yellow flowers from June to October. There are 2 species (**S. angustifolium** and **S. bermudianum**) known as Blue-eyed Grass which have the same flowering season as S. brachypus, but produce lavender-coloured flowers and are 1 ft (30 cm) tall. **S. douglasii** is different — it has 1 in. (2.5 cm) pendent purple bells in April–May. **S. striatum** has whorls of creamy flowers on 1½ ft (45 cm) stems in early summer.

SITE & SOIL: Requires well-drained, humus-rich soil in full sun.

PLANT DETAILS: Planting time: September–October. Planting depth: ½ in. (1 cm). Spacing: 4–8 in. (10–20 cm). Height: 6–18 in. (15–45 cm).

PROPAGATION: Divide clumps in autumn or spring — remove and plant up offsets.

Sisyrinchium brachypus 'Californian Skies'

SPARAXIS Harlequin Flower

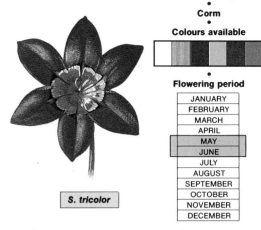

Garden/Indoor plant
•
Corm
•
Colours available
•
Flowering period

| JANUARY |
| FEBRUARY |
| MARCH |
| APRIL |
| MAY |
| JUNE |
| JULY |
| AUGUST |
| SEPTEMBER |
| OCTOBER |
| NOVEMBER |
| DECEMBER |

S. tricolor

In late spring and early summer a Sparaxis mixture will produce a riot of colour. The 2 in. (5 cm) star-shaped blooms are borne on wiry stems above the strap-like leaves. Unfortunately this colourful plant is not for everyone. In the colder parts of the country it must be grown indoors — plant 1 in. (2.5 cm) deep in a compost-filled pot in September. Leave in a cold frame until November before moving into the greenhouse. In milder areas it can be grown in a sheltered spot. Cover with a peat mulch in winter — move this mulch away in April. After flowering there is an unusual routine — lift the corms after the foliage has died down in midsummer and keep them dry until replanting in November.

VARIETIES: S. tricolor is bought as a mixture. Some flowers will be plain — all-orange, all-yellow etc but others will be bi-colours with a distinct black ring separating the petal colour from the bright yellow throat. These Harlequin mixtures are useful in a dull part of the rockery — the flower stems can be cut for indoor display. **S. elegans** (white or orange flowers) is a 6 in. (15 cm) dwarf.

SITE & SOIL: Well-drained soil and full sun are essential.

PLANT DETAILS: Planting time: November. Planting depth: 3 in. (7.5 cm). Spacing: 4 in. (10 cm). Height: 6–18 in. (15–45 cm).

PROPAGATION: Remove cormlets when plants are lifted in summer — replant in November.

Sparaxis tricolor

SPREKELIA Jacobean Lily

Garden/Indoor plant
•
True bulb
•
Colour available

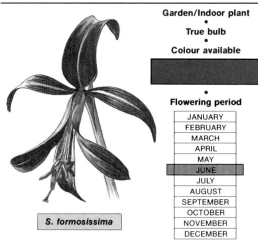

•
Flowering period

JANUARY
FEBRUARY
MARCH
APRIL
MAY
JUNE
JULY
AUGUST
SEPTEMBER
OCTOBER
NOVEMBER
DECEMBER

S. formosissima

This is one of several showy tender bulbs which can be grown outside only if you live in a mild area and have free-draining soil. Choose a sunny, sheltered spot for spring planting. For the less fortunate majority this beauty has to be grown in a greenhouse. Plant in compost in autumn with the neck of the bulb above the surface. Once the flowers have faded and the foliage has withered let the compost dry out. Keep cool until spring and then bring it into growth by watering. Repot every 3 years.

VARIETIES: There is just one species (**S. formosissima**) and there are no varieties from which to make your choice. The 5 in. (12.5 cm) trumpet-shaped green-throated flower looks like an Orchid. The crimson velvety petals are in two groups — the upper 3 are erect and the lower 3 are pendent, forming a flared tube which partially encloses the stamens. The blooms are borne singly at the top of the flower stalk. Lift the bulbs once the foliage has died down and store them in dry peat at about 60°F (16°C) during winter — replant when spring arrives.

SITE & SOIL: Well-drained soil in a sheltered spot is necessary — full sun is essential.

PLANT DETAILS: Planting time: April. Planting depth: 2 in. (5 cm). Spacing: 8 in. (20 cm). Height: 12–18 in. (30–45 cm).

PROPAGATION: Remove bulblets when the bulbs are lifted — plant in spring.

Sprekelia formosissima

STERNBERGIA Autumn Daffodil

Garden plant
•
True bulb
•
Colour available

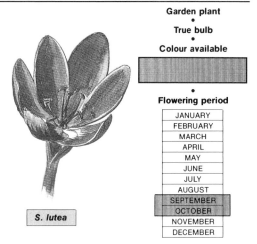

•
Flowering period

JANUARY
FEBRUARY
MARCH
APRIL
MAY
JUNE
JULY
AUGUST
SEPTEMBER
OCTOBER
NOVEMBER
DECEMBER

S. lutea

Despite its name and close relationship to the Daffodil this autumn-flowering plant looks like a Crocus rather than a Narcissus — the leaves are narrow and the flowers have the familiar wineglass shape. These blooms, however, are borne on a short stalk and not an extension of the petal tube, and there are 6 and not 3 stamens. Sternbergia can provide a welcome splash of late colour in the rockery, but its lack of popularity is not really surprising. It needs near perfect drainage, protection from strong winds and warm dry weather in summer if it is to flourish.

VARIETIES: S. lutea is the most widely available and most reliable species. Its leaves appear shortly before the 2 in. (5 cm) high glistening yellow goblets on their 6 in. (15 cm) stems. The variety **'Angustifolia'** is a vigorous form. **S. clusiana** (**S. macrantha**) has larger flowers — the yellow Crocus-like blooms are up to 3 in. (7.5 cm) long. Another difference is that the leaves appear after the flowers and this foliage persists through the winter and spring. The dwarf species is the 3 in. (7.5 cm) **S. sicula**.

SITE & SOIL: Well-drained, chalky soil and full sun are essential.

PLANT DETAILS: Planting time: July–August. Planting depth: 5 in. (12.5 cm). Spacing: 5 in. (12.5 cm). Height: 3–8 in. (7.5–20 cm).

PROPAGATION: Buy new bulbs — Sternbergia hates disturbance.

Sternbergia sicula

TECOPHILAEA Chilean Blue Crocus

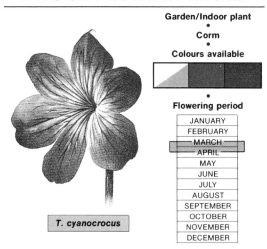

Garden/Indoor plant
•
Corm
•
Colours available

Flowering period

| JANUARY |
| FEBRUARY |
| MARCH |
| APRIL |
| MAY |
| JUNE |
| JULY |
| AUGUST |
| SEPTEMBER |
| OCTOBER |
| NOVEMBER |
| DECEMBER |

T. cyanocrocus

There are several reasons why a bulb may be a rarity. It may be difficult to grow, it may have little visual appeal or it may be very expensive. The Chilean Blue Crocus is extremely uncommon, yet it is not particularly hard to cultivate and it has been described as one of the most eye-catching of all small bulbs. The problem is that it is the most expensive bulb in the few catalogues in which it appears. Tecophilaea can be grown outdoors in free-draining sandy soil in a mild area, but it is better to treat it as an indoor plant and grow it in a frost-free greenhouse.

VARIETIES: The main species is **T. cyanocrocus**. In spring a couple of narrow leaves appear and then several flower stalks each bearing a single funnel-shaped flower which soon opens wide. There is nothing special about the size (1 in. or 2.5 cm across) or the shape — it is the intense blue colour which makes it unique. The variety **'Leichtlinii'** is paler blue with a white throat and **'Violacea'** is deep purple. The corms are dormant during the summer months — keep the compost almost but not entirely dry at this time of the year.

SITE & SOIL: Use a gritty compost — choose a brightly lit spot with some direct sun in summer.

PLANT DETAILS: Planting time: September–October. Planting depth: 2 in. (5 cm). Spacing: 3 in a 5 in. (12.5 cm) pot. Height: 6 in. (15 cm).

PROPAGATION: Remove and plant up offsets when repotting.

Tecophilaea cyanocrocus 'Leichtlinii'

TIGRIDIA Tiger Flower

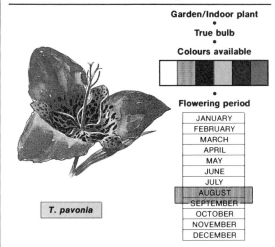

Garden/Indoor plant
•
True bulb
•
Colours available

Flowering period

| JANUARY |
| FEBRUARY |
| MARCH |
| APRIL |
| MAY |
| JUNE |
| JULY |
| AUGUST |
| SEPTEMBER |
| OCTOBER |
| NOVEMBER |
| DECEMBER |

T. pavonia

The flower is a thing of exotic beauty — each one lasts for only a day but a succession appears over several weeks at the end of summer. The upright leaves are pleated and each stem bears several blooms. Unfortunately this bulb is only moderately hardy, so in most districts it is necessary to plant in spring and then lift in October when the leaves have withered. Clean and store the bulbs in dry peat in a frost-free place. For earlier blooms you can start them in compost-filled pots in spring and then plant out in June.

VARIETIES: **T. pavonia** is the only species for growing outdoors. Lift in autumn as described above but you can leave the bulbs in the ground if the site is free-draining and sheltered in a mild region of the country. The flowers measure about 4 in. (10 cm) across. The 3 outer petals are large and single-coloured — the 3 inner petals are small and usually splashed with dark red or purple. The throat is also usually blotched in the same way. This species is sold as a mixture rather than as single-coloured varieties.

SITE & SOIL: A well-drained site in full sun is essential.

PLANT DETAILS: Planting time: Late April. Planting depth: 4 in. (10 cm). Spacing: 6 in. (15 cm). Height: 18 in. (45 cm).

PROPAGATION: Remove offsets when plants are lifted in autumn. Replant in spring.

Tigridia pavonia

TRILLIUM Wood Lily

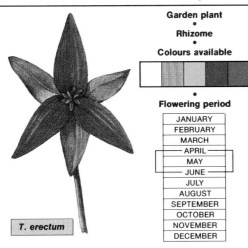

Garden plant
•
Rhizome
•
Colours available

Flowering period

JANUARY	
FEBRUARY	
MARCH	
APRIL	
MAY	
JUNE	
JULY	
AUGUST	
SEPTEMBER	
OCTOBER	
NOVEMBER	
DECEMBER	

T. erectum

An attractive plant, but only in the right situation. Trillium is a woodland flower which needs some leafy shade above and humus-rich soil below. A thick underground rhizome produces several fleshy stems which bear the foliage and flower parts in threes — a whorl of 3 broad leaves and flowers with 3 small sepals and 3 large petals which surround a central group of golden stamens. Leave undisturbed and large clumps will form in time.

VARIETIES: T. grandiflorum (Wake Robin) is the most popular species as well as being the easiest to grow. The 2–3 in. (5–7.5 cm) wide flowers are white at first but slowly turn pink with age. A double-flowering variety (**'Flore Pleno'**) is available. White and pink are not the only colours — **T. cuneatum** is dark red with attractively mottled foliage and **T. erectum** bears wine-coloured blooms. Other species include **T. luteum** (yellow flowers) and **T. undulatum** (purple-streaked white flowers). **T. recurvatum** is a dark red dwarf for the shady rockery.

SITE & SOIL: A well-drained, humus-rich soil is essential — thrives in partial shade.

PLANT DETAILS: Planting time: August–September. Planting depth: 3 in. (7.5 cm). Spacing: 12 in. (30 cm). Height: 6–15 in. (15–37.5 cm).

PROPAGATION: Divide mature clumps in autumn — replant at once.

Trillium grandiflorum

TRITONIA Blazing Star

Garden/Indoor plant
•
Corm
•
Colours available

Flowering period

JANUARY	
FEBRUARY	
MARCH	
APRIL	
MAY	
JUNE	
JULY	
AUGUST	
SEPTEMBER	
OCTOBER	
NOVEMBER	
DECEMBER	

T. crocata

Like its relatives Crocosmia and Ixia, Tritonia produces strap-like leaves and wiry stems bearing starry blooms in bright colours. It is generally regarded as a frost-sensitive plant which can be grown in the garden in mild areas, but should be planted indoors in the rest of the country. There are, however, 2 species available and their ability to withstand winter conditions outdoors differs. T. crocata is best grown as a house or greenhouse plant. T. rosea is hardier and can be grown outdoors if you provide a winter mulch.

VARIETIES: T. crocata has branching flower stems with a double row of blooms. Each flower is a 2 in. (5 cm) open trumpet in white, glowing orange, pink or cream. There are named varieties, such as **'Roseline'** (pink) and **'Isabella'** (yellow-tinged pink), but these are hard to find as most catalogues offer only mixtures in which orange predominates. **T. rosea** is taller, reaching about 2 ft (60 cm), and its flowers have a more distinct funnel shape. They are pink and open only when the sun shines.

SITE & SOIL: A well-drained, sheltered spot is essential.

PLANT DETAILS: Planting time: September. Planting depth: 2 in. (5 cm). Spacing: 6 in. (15 cm). Height: 12–24 in. (30–60 cm).

PROPAGATION: Remove offsets after lifting overcrowded clumps. Replant in autumn.

Tritonia crocata

TROPAEOLUM Perennial Nasturtium

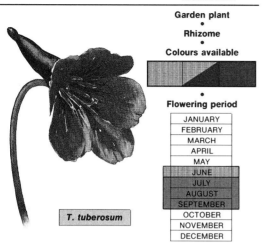

Garden plant
•
Rhizome
•
Colours available
•
Flowering period

JANUARY	
FEBRUARY	
MARCH	
APRIL	
MAY	
JUNE	▓
JULY	▓
AUGUST	▓
SEPTEMBER	▓
OCTOBER	
NOVEMBER	
DECEMBER	

T. tuberosum

The Tropaeolum known to everyone is the Annual Nasturtium grown as a bedding plant — much more unusual is the rhizomatous Perennial Nasturtium grown as a climbing or trailing plant. The foliage is deeply lobed and the blooms have the long spurs associated with all Nasturtiums. Unfortunately these perennial types do not have the grow-anywhere constitution of the hardy annual types — they need a fertile light soil in a sunny spot. Set the rhizome horizontally. Mulch in spring and again in autumn after the withered foliage has been removed.

VARIETIES: T. speciosum (Flame Flower) likes cool and humus-rich soil — it grows up to 15 ft (450 cm) and bears 1½ in. (4 cm) scarlet flowers. **T. tuberosum** is another climber, reaching 6–10 ft (180–300 cm). The flowers are orange-backed yellow and the favourite variety is **'Ken Aslet'. T. polyphyllum** (Wreath Nasturtium) is different — unlike the others which bloom from July to September, this creeper with 3–5 ft (90–150 cm) stems produces its yellow trumpets in June and July amid the silvery leaves. In cold districts lift the rhizomes in October and replant in spring.

SITE & SOIL: Well-drained soil in full sun is required.

PLANT DETAILS: Planting time: April. Planting depth: 1 in. (2.5 cm). Spacing: 12 in. (30 cm). Height: 36–180 in. (90–450 cm).

PROPAGATION: Divide rhizomes in autumn.

Tropaeolum polyphyllum

TULBAGHIA Wild Garlic

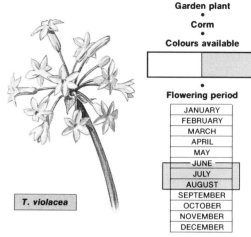

Garden plant
•
Corm
•
Colours available
•
Flowering period

JANUARY	
FEBRUARY	
MARCH	
APRIL	
MAY	
JUNE	
JULY	░
AUGUST	░
SEPTEMBER	
OCTOBER	
NOVEMBER	
DECEMBER	

T. violacea

Another bulb for the collector of rarities. Nearly all of these S. African corms are semi-hardy and can only be safely left outdoors as permanent plants in warm and sheltered situations. The best way to grow them is in containers which are moved under glass from autumn to spring. The evergreen foliage emits an onion-like smell when crushed but the blooms are sweetly fragrant. These flowers appear all summer long and are clustered on top of leafless stalks. Tulbaghia has good drought resistance and the clumps should not be divided for several years.

VARIETIES: T. violacea is the species you are most likely to find in the catalogues. The pale purple tubular flowers are borne in round clusters of 10–20 on top of 2 ft (60 cm) stalks. The variegated variety **'Silver Lace'** is usually chosen rather than the species. Neither of these semi-evergreens is fully hardy and the protection of a winter mulch is essential. The only frost-hardy Tulbaghia is the dwarf **T. natalensis** which grows about 6 in. (15 cm) high. The white and sweet-smelling blooms have yellow centres and appear in midsummer.

SITE & SOIL: Well-drained, light soil in full sun is essential.

PLANT DETAILS: Planting time: April. Planting depth: 1 in. (2.5 cm). Spacing: 8–12 in. (20–30 cm). Height: 6–24 in. (15–60 cm).

PROPAGATION: Remove and plant cormlets when over-crowded clumps are lifted.

Tulbaghia natalensis

TULIPA Tulip

Garden/Indoor plant

•

True bulb

•

Colours available

•

Flowering period

JANUARY
FEBRUARY
MARCH
APRIL
MAY
JUNE
JULY
AUGUST
SEPTEMBER
OCTOBER
NOVEMBER
DECEMBER

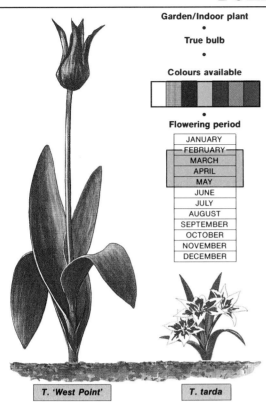

T. 'West Point'   *T. tarda*

There are more Narcissi than Tulips in our gardens and in the countryside in spring, but Tulips are unsurpassed in the bulb world as a source of both subdued and brilliant colours from early to late spring. Hundreds of different varieties are available and the range they cover is remarkable. There are dwarf Species Tulips which open their small flowers on 4 in. (10 cm) stalks in early March and next to them you can have 30 in. (75 cm) Rembrandt Tulips in full bloom in mid May. The colour range is equally extensive with nearly every shade from pure white to near black. The subject of Tulip colour is a fascinating one — most varieties are single- (self-) coloured or simple blends, but there are 'broken' Tulips where second or third colours appear as complex streaks, splashes or feathery lines. This effect is caused by a virus and at one time such bizarre varieties commanded unbelievably high prices, but they are no longer popular. With all Tulips there are shiny petals forming a bell-shaped, bowl-shaped or starry flower on top of a leafless stalk. These blooms are generally borne singly, but in a few cases there may be a flower-head of several blooms. The leaves are generally wide and few in number, but there are a few species with grassy leaves. Tulips will succeed in any reasonable soil which does not become waterlogged. Most Tulips are used either in formal bedding schemes or in containers, but there are other places for them in the garden. The tall varieties can be used as informal colourful clumps in the mixed border and dwarf varieties are useful in the rockery. To make a start, look through the bulb catalogues or the wide selection at your garden centre in autumn. This genus has been split into 15 Divisions, and the Division numbers appear in the rest of this section and in many catalogues. Divisions 1–11 are known as *Garden* Tulips and their ancestry is usually not known — Divisions 12–15 are the *Botanical* Tulips which are either species or hybrids of known species. It is from this Botanical group that you should choose your rockery Tulips — they are generally left in the ground over winter. Choose your bulbs carefully (see the points to look for on page 8) and do not be in a hurry to plant them — November is early enough. Remove dead flower-heads if it is practical. The problem with Garden Tulips is that unlike Narcissi they tend to deteriorate or disappear if not lifted every year and so the usual practice is to lift them when the foliage has turned yellow and then store them in a frost-free place until replanting time in November. Another problem is that Garden Tulips should not be planted in the same bed year after year. Not everybody lifts them — if you plant deeply enough (see below) and lime the soil if it is acid or neutral then you should be able to leave Garden Tulips undisturbed for 2–3 years. It will help if you remove both flowers and foliage when they start to fade. For containers choose one of the low-growing Botanicals such as T. kaufmanniana or T. greigii. These dwarf species can also be used as pot plants for growing indoors, but the most popular house plant Tulips are the Single Earlies and Double Earlies. Read the section on Bulbs In The Home.

SITE & SOIL: Well-drained soil is necessary — thrives best in full sun.

PLANT DETAILS: Planting time: November–December (earlier planting can result in frost damage to the shoot tips). Planting depth: Garden Tulips 6–8 in. (15–20 cm). Botanical Tulips 4 in. (10 cm). Spacing: 4–8 in. (10–20 cm). Height: 4–30 in. (10–75 cm).

PROPAGATION: Remove bulblets at lifting time. Dry, store and replant in late autumn.

FLOWER COLOURS

NORMAL TULIPS
No complex patterning

Self-coloured
(single colour throughout)

Blended
(one colour gradually merged with another)

Bi-coloured
(two distinct colours)

BROKEN TULIPS
Complex patterning caused by a virus

Feathered
(fine lines at edges)

Flamed
(feathered, plus central band)

Streaked
(bands along the petals)

TULIPA continued

Division 1:
SINGLE EARLY TULIPS

Cup-shaped single flowers, smaller than the late-flowering varieties. Flowers early-mid April. Height 9–16 in. (22.5–40 cm).

The blooms are borne on strong stems so they stand up well in rainy and windy weather — recommended for beds, containers and indoors. The flowers open wide in sunny weather. There are numerous popular Single Earlies. **'Apricot Beauty'** is salmon rose tinged with deep orange and **'Bellona'** is a fragrant golden yellow variety. There are several yellow and red bi-colours, including the old favourite **'Keizerskroon'** and the dwarf **'Flair'**. All-red is a popular colour — you can choose from the low-growing **'Brilliant Star'**, the sweet-smelling and long-lasting **'Dr Plesman'** and the bright scarlet **'Charles'**. For orange Tulips choose **'General de Wet'** and for pure white the usual choice is **'Diana'**. There are several interesting colour combinations, including **'Couleur Cardinal'** (purple-backed red) and **'Princess Irene'** (purple-flamed orange).

Tulipa 'Apricot Beauty'

Tulipa 'Bellona'

Tulipa 'Keizerskroon'

Tulipa 'Flair'

Tulipa 'Brilliant Star'

Tulipa 'General de Wet'

Tulipa 'Princess Irene'

TULIPA continued

Division 2:
DOUBLE EARLY TULIPS

Fully double flowers which are long-lasting and good for cutting. Flowers mid April. Height 9–16 in. (22.5–40 cm).

As with the Single Earlies these Tulips have sturdy stems and long-lasting flowers which open wide, but they are generally shorter — the usual height is about 10 in. (25 cm). Despite their compact growth habit the multi-petalled blooms may bend over after heavy rain. Apart from bedding the Double Earlies are a popular choice for containers, window boxes and for forcing indoors. You will have no difficulty in finding the favourite ones at your garden centre or in the catalogues — **'Peach Blossom'** (deep pink), **'Orange Nassau'** (orange-flushed red) and **'Carlton'** (scarlet). There are other reds (**'Electra'**, **'Scarlet Cardinal'**, **'Stockholm'** etc) and whites (**'Snowstorm'**, **'Snow Queen'** and **'Engelenburcht'**). One of the tallest Double Earlies is the yellow **'Monte Carlo'** which reaches 16 in. (40 cm). You will find one or two bi-colours in some of the lists, including **'Willemsoord'** (white-edged red). **'Fringed Beauty'** (yellow-edged red) belongs here and not in Division 7 despite its fringed edge.

Tulipa 'Peach Blossom'

Tulipa 'Orange Nassau'

Tulipa 'Electra'

Tulipa 'Snowstorm'

Tulipa 'Monte Carlo'

Tulipa 'Willemsoord'

Tulipa 'Fringed Beauty'

TULIPA continued

Division 3:
TRIUMPH TULIPS

Single flowers — conical at first and then rounded. Large, but not as big as the Darwin Hybrids. Flowers late April–early May. Height 16–20 in. (40–50 cm).

The Triumphs are listed as Mid-season Tulips in some catalogues. They are grown in beds and borders which will have to be cleared for summer bedding plants and they can be grown in light shade. The stems are sturdy so they are suitable for exposed sites. There are many varieties and new ones continue to appear. The all-reds include **'Cassini'**, **'Paul Richter'** and **'Ajax'**, the all-pinks include **'Peerless Pink'** and **'Don Quixote'**, and for all-yellow there is **'Golden Melody'**. **'New Design'** is pink-edged cream and **'Abu Hassan'** is yellow-edged mahogany. **'Attila'** is all-purple and **'White Virgin'** is all-white, but the showiest Triumphs are bi-colours and there are a number from which to take your pick. For white-edged purple choose **'African Queen'**, **'Dreaming Maid'** or **'Arabian Mystery'** — for red-edged yellow there are **'Kees Nelis'** and **'Los Angeles'**. The red-edged white Triumph is usually **'Garden Party'** — for the reverse (outside white-edged red, inside red) you can grow **'Leen van der Mark'**. For yet another combination there is **'Fidelio'** (orange-edged red).

Tulipa 'Cassini'

Tulipa 'Paul Richter'

Tulipa 'New Design'

Tulipa 'Abu Hassan'

Tulipa 'Dreaming Maid'

Tulipa 'Arabian Mystery'

Tulipa 'Garden Party'

TULIPA continued

Division 4:
DARWIN HYBRID TULIPS

Single flowers — usually rounded but there are various shapes. Very large on tall stems. Flowers late April–early May. Height 24 in. (60 cm).

The Darwin Hybrid blooms are larger and appear earlier than the ordinary Darwins which are now grouped with the Single Lates in Division 5. Some of these Darwin Hybrid blooms measure up to 4 in. (10 cm) or more across — this group have long been popular for massed bedding where a wide area of bright colour is required in a border. Dominating this Division are Apeldoorn and its relatives. **'Apeldoorn'** is red with a yellow base — the inside has a yellow-edged black eye. **'Golden Apeldoorn'** is golden yellow with a black base and **'Apeldoorn Elite'** is yellow-edged scarlet. There are others, such as **'Beauty of Apeldoorn'** (yellow-flushed orange) and **'Striped Apeldoorn'** (yellow-striped red). Apart from the Apeldoorns there are several popular varieties including **'Elizabeth Arden'** (deep salmon pink), **'Gordon Cooper'** (red-edged pink), **'Gudoshnik'** (red-splashed yellow) and the buttercup-yellow **'Yellow Dover'**. Finally there is the Oxford series with **'Oxford'** (purple-flushed red) and **'Golden Oxford'** (yellow).

Tulipa 'Apeldoorn'

Tulipa 'Golden Apeldoorn'

Tulipa 'Apeldoorn Elite'

Tulipa 'Beauty of Apeldoorn'

Tulipa 'Elizabeth Arden'

Tulipa 'Gudoshnik'

Tulipa 'Golden Oxford'

TULIPA continued

Division 5:
SINGLE LATE TULIPS

Square or oval single flowers. Large on tall stems. Flowers early-mid May. Height 24–30 in. (60–75 cm).

This modern Division is made up of the old-fashioned Cottage Tulips and the non-hybrid Darwin Tulips — in some catalogues you will find them listed as May-flowering Tulips. They have been used for generations in beds, borders, around shrubs etc to provide colour after the early varieties have faded. The straight stems are stout and they make good cut flowers. You will find a large selection at the garden centre or in the catalogues in colours ranging from white **'Maureen'** to the near-black **'Queen of the Night'**. Between these extremes you will find **'Golden Harvest'** (yellow), **'Sweet Harmony'** (cream-flushed yellow), **'Esther'** (pink), **'Bleu Aimable'** (mauve), **'Halcro'** (red) and **'Greuze'** (purple). Bi-colours include **'Shirley'** (purple-edged white) and **'Princess Margaret Rose'** (red-edged yellow). There are several old favourites here, including **'Clara Butt'** (salmon pink) and the oldest known named variety **'Zomerschoon'** (cream). **'Georgette'** (orange-edged yellow) and **'Orange Bouquet'** (orange) are unusual — there are 3–5 flowers per stem.

Tulipa 'Maureen'

Tulipa 'Queen of the Night'

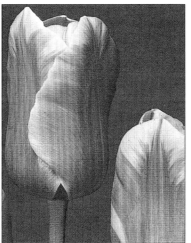

Tulipa 'Sweet Harmony'

Tulipa 'Bleu Aimable'

Tulipa 'Halcro'

Tulipa 'Georgette'

Tulipa 'Orange Bouquet'

TULIPA continued

Division 6:
LILY-FLOWERED TULIPS

Single flowers with long pointed petals reflexed at the tips. Flowers early-mid May. Height 20–24 in. (50–60 cm).

Tulipa 'West Point'

Tulipa 'Ballade'

An elegant flower with a distinctive shape. The Lily-flowered Tulips have strong stems and are used for formal bedding, informal groups in borders, planting in containers and for flower arranging. **'West Point'** is one of the popular varieties — the yellow blooms have a lovely shape. **'Ballerina'** (orange) has an additional feature — it is fragrant. Among the bi-colours are **'Ballade'** (white-edged magenta), **'Marilyn'** (red-banded cream), **'Maytime'** (white-edged reddish violet), **'Aladdin'** (yellow-edged red) and **'Queen of Sheba'** (orange-edged red). For a blended flower there is **'Elegant Lady'** with petals which are cream at the base changing to pink at the top. If you want a tall variety choose **'Red Shine'** (red), **'White Triumphator'** (white) or **'Mariette'** (pink).

Tulipa 'Marilyn'

Tulipa 'Aladdin'

Division 7:
FRINGED TULIPS

Single flowers with petals which are finely fringed at the edges. Flowers early-mid May. Height 18–24 in. (45–60 cm).

These showy plants are usually used as a focal point. The blooms look like Single Late Tulips but at the top there is a mass of hair-like fringes. Examples include **'Blue Heron'** (lilac), **'Burgundy Lace'** (wine red), **'Maja'** (yellow), **'Bellflower'** (pink) and **'Noranda'** (red).

Tulipa 'Burgundy Lace'

Tulipa 'Maja'

TULIPA continued

Division 8:
VIRIDIFLORA TULIPS

Single flowers with petals which are partly green. Flowers early-late May. Height 12–20 in. (30–50 cm).

These stiff-stemmed plants have flowers which have green bands, stripes or blotches — they are grown mainly for cutting. Examples include **'Greenland'** (rose-edged green), **'Spring Green'** (green-striped white), **'Hummingbird'** (green-feathered yellow) and **'Artist'** (salmon and green).

Tulipa 'Greenland'

Tulipa 'Hummingbird'

Division 10:
PARROT TULIPS

Single flowers with deeply frilled and wavy petals. Very large. Flowers mid-late May. Height 20–24 in. (50–60 cm).

These are the most spectacular of all Tulips — the blooms are usually bi-coloured and the cut and twisted petals give an exotic appearance. The fully-open flower can be up to 7–8 in. (17.5–20 cm) across in a few varieties, and they obviously make an eye-catching feature in flower arrangements. Outdoors, however, there can be problems. They are rather too flamboyant for some people and the stems may need support if the site is exposed. The Parrot series of varieties is extensive — there are **'White Parrot'** (white), **'Flaming Parrot'** (red-flamed yellow), **'Blue Parrot'** (violet) and **'Black Parrot'** (purplish black). There are a few other single colours such as **'Texas Gold'** (yellow), but the remainder are bi-coloured. Examples include **'Fantasy'** (green-streaked pink), **'Estella Rijnveld'** (white-flamed red), **'Bird of Paradise'** (yellow-edged red), **'Texas Flame'** (red-flamed yellow) and **'Karel Doorman'** (yellow-edged red).

Tulipa 'Fantasy'

Tulipa 'Estella Rijnveld'

Tulipa 'Texas Flame'

Tulipa 'Karel Doorman'

TULIPA continued

Division 9:
REMBRANDT TULIPS

Single flowers with feathered, flamed or streaked petals. Large. Flowers early-mid May. Height 18–30 in. (45–75 cm).

This Division contains the 'broken' Tulips (see page 85) which were once so valued and are now no longer popular. The bizarre patterns and colours on a white, yellow or red background are due to a virus. Stems require support. Not easy to find — examples include **'Insulinde'** (violet/yellow), **'Cordell Hull'** (red/white) and **'San Marino'** (red/yellow).

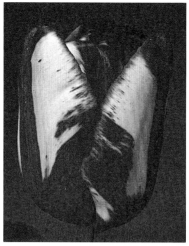

Tulipa 'Cordell Hull'

Tulipa 'San Marino'

Division 11:
DOUBLE LATE TULIPS

Fully double flowers which are large and long-lasting. Flowers mid-late May. Height 16–24 in. (40-60 cm).

The blooms are cup-shaped and filled with petals — they are sometimes listed as Paeony-flowered Tulips. They are eye-catching, but suffer from being too heavy for the stems. To prevent them from toppling over plant the bulbs closely together in a sheltered spot — some support for the group of plants may be needed. Because of their lateness and need for shelter they are much less popular than the Double Earlies and there are fewer varieties on offer, but you should find some at the garden centre or in the catalogue. **'Angelique'** (pale pink) and **'Mount Tacoma'** (white) are offered by several bulb companies, but the brighter bi-colours are harder to locate There are **'Carnaval de Nice'** which is flamed red against a white background and **'Allegretto'** which is yellow-edged red. Others include **'Bonanza'** (yellow-edged red), **'Wirosa'** (white-edged red) and **'Orange Triumph'** (yellow-edged orange).

Tulipa 'Angelique'

Tulipa 'Mount Tacoma'

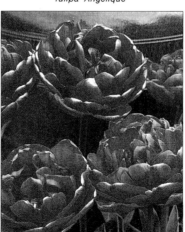

Tulipa 'Bonanza'

Tulipa 'Orange Triumph'

TULIPA continued

Divisions 12-15:
BOTANICAL TULIPS

Species or varieties, plus hybrids of species in which all or some of the original features are present. There is a wide range of flowering periods (March–May), flower shape and height (4–20 in. or 10–50 cm). They can be left in the ground to spread.

The **T. kaufmanniana** hybrids are low-growing (6–10 in. or 15–25 cm) and early-flowering (March). These Water-lily Tulips are a good choice for the rockery, containers, beds and borders, and for naturalising in grass. The flowers open into colourful stars and the greyish leaves are often mottled. Well-known varieties include **'Giuseppe Verdi'** (yellow-edged red), **'Johann Strauss'** (red-striped cream), **'Shakespeare'** (yellow-marked red) and **'Stresa'** (red and yellow).

T. fosteriana hybrids grow to 12–20 in. (30–50 cm) and bloom in April. They are grown for their remarkably wide flowers and bright colours — the foliage is often striped or spotted. The best known one is the bright red **'Madame Lefeber'** (**'Red Emperor'**) — others include **'Hit Parade'** (red and yellow), **'Princeps'** (red), **'Orange Emperor'** (orange) and **'Candela'** (yellow).

T. greigii hybrids are low-growing (8–14 in. or 20–35 cm) and bloom in April–May. The flowers are long-lasting and the leaves are often streaked with brown or purple. The dwarfs such as **'Red Riding Hood'** (black-centred red) and **'Cape Cod'** (yellow-edged apricot) are a good choice for the rockery. Other Greigii hybrids include **'Plaisir'** (red-striped cream), **'Oratorio'** (pink), **'Zampa'** (yellow) and **'Trinket'** (white-edged red).

The Species Tulips are mainly dwarfs with small flowers and are used for permanent planting in rockeries. **T. aucheriana** (pink, April) grows only 4 in. (10 cm) high — **T. batalinii 'Bright Gem'** (yellow, May) is equally small. **T. biflora** (yellow-centred white, March) has about 5 blooms on each stem — other multi-headed species include **T. tarda** (yellow-centred white stars, dwarf, April–May), **T. praestans** (scarlet, April) and **T. turkestanica** (orange-centred white, March–April). **T. clusiana** (pink-streaked white, April) has grass-like foliage. For tiny 4 in. (10 cm) stems which bloom early in March choose **T. pulchella 'Violacea'** (violet) or **'Humilis'** (lavender).

Tulipa 'Shakespeare'

Tulipa 'Stresa'

Tulipa 'Madame Lefeber'

Tulipa 'Red Riding Hood'

Tulipa biflora

Tulipa clusiana

UVULARIA Merrybells

Garden plant
•
Rhizome
•
Colour available

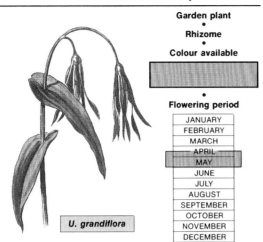

Flowering period

JANUARY	
FEBRUARY	
MARCH	
APRIL	
MAY	
JUNE	
JULY	
AUGUST	
SEPTEMBER	
OCTOBER	
NOVEMBER	
DECEMBER	

U. grandiflora

This woodland plant is not often seen and you will have to hunt through the textbooks to find it, but it is a good choice if you want late spring flowers in a shady patch of acid peaty soil. It is a member of the Lily family, spreading by means of rhizomes. The upright stems bear glossy clasping leaves, and these branching stems bear clusters of pendent bells with narrow and twisted petals. It is an easy plant to grow if the soil conditions are right — Uvularia is hardy in all parts of the country.

VARIETIES: The usual species is **U. grandiflora** and is bought either as a growing plant or as rhizomes for planting. The 1½ ft (45 cm) arching stems bear yellow 2 in. (5 cm) long bells — the lance-shaped leaves clasp the stem and both the flowers and fruit hang from the tips of the stems like bunches of grapes. **U. perfoliata** is similar but both leaves and flowers are rather smaller. The major difference is that with this species the stem appears to pass through the leaves.

SITE & SOIL: Well-drained, humus-rich soil is necessary — thrives in partial shade.

PLANT DETAILS: Planting time: April or October. Planting depth: 1 in. (2.5 cm). Spacing: 9 in. (22.5 cm). Height: 15–18 in. (37.5–45 cm).

PROPAGATION: Divide clumps in summer.

Uvularia grandiflora

VALLOTA Scarborough Lily

Indoor plant
•
True bulb
•
Colours available

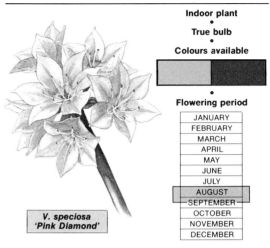

Flowering period

JANUARY	
FEBRUARY	
MARCH	
APRIL	
MAY	
JUNE	
JULY	
AUGUST	
SEPTEMBER	
OCTOBER	
NOVEMBER	
DECEMBER	

V. speciosa 'Pink Diamond'

One of the most attractive of all autumn-flowering indoor bulbs. The only widely available species is the Scarborough Lily or V. speciosa, which can be grown as a house plant or in a frost-free greenhouse. Keep the container well watered during the growing season and place it in a sunny position. After flowering the leaves will start to wither — reduce watering at this stage and stop completely between February and April. Vallota flowers best when overcrowded so do not repot for at least 3 years.

VARIETIES: V. speciosa bulbs are available in early summer. The long leaves appear at the same time as the flowers. These blooms are wide-mouthed trumpets which are about 3 in. (7.5 cm) across — a group of 4–8 are borne on top of each stout flower stalk. The usual colour is scarlet, but you can look for the pink variety **'Pink Diamond'**. In modern textbooks this well-known species has been reclassified as **Cyrtanthus purpureus**, which is perhaps unfortunate as the Cyrtanthus species in the catalogues bear narrow tubular flowers on short stalks.

SITE & SOIL: Use a soilless compost — choose a spot which receives some sun.

PLANT DETAILS: Planting time: June. Planting depth: Tip should be above the surface. Spacing: 1 in a 5 in. (12.5 cm) pot. Height: 18 in. (45 cm).

PROPAGATION: Separate bulblets and pot up at repotting time.

Vallota speciosa

VELTHEIMIA Forest Lily

Indoor plant
•
True bulb
•
Colour available

Flowering period

| JANUARY |
| FEBRUARY |
| MARCH |
| APRIL |
| MAY |
| JUNE |
| JULY |
| AUGUST |
| SEPTEMBER |
| OCTOBER |
| NOVEMBER |
| DECEMBER |

V. bracteata

This South African bulb is not hardy and should therefore be grown on the windowsill or in a frost-free greenhouse. It is easy to recognise — the flower-head looks like a miniature Red Hot Poker. After planting in autumn water moderately until the shoots appear. Water freely once active growth has started and feed regularly with a liquid fertilizer. Stop watering and feeding once the leaves have yellowed after flowering — keep the compost dry until September.

VARIETIES: The species you are most likely to find is **V. bracteata**. The wavy-edged 1 ft (30 cm) long leaves form a rosette at the base and in late winter or early spring the spotted flower stalk appears from the centre of this rosette. At the top of this stalk there are about 60 small and tubular pink and green flowers. This 4 in. (10 cm) flower-head lasts for about a month. Some people water the compost sparingly during spring and summer to keep the leaves alive — with the deciduous **V. capensis** you must keep the compost dry until the autumn. Repot every 2–3 years.

SITE & SOIL: Use a soilless compost — choose a brightly lit spot.

PLANT DETAILS: Planting time: September. Planting depth: Tip should be level with the surface. Spacing: 1 in a 5 in. (12.5 cm) pot. Height: 18 in. (45 cm).

PROPAGATION: Separate bulblets and pot up at repotting time.

Veltheimia capensis

WATSONIA Bugle Lily

Garden/Indoor plant
•
Corm
•
Colours available

Flowering period

| JANUARY |
| FEBRUARY |
| MARCH |
| APRIL |
| MAY |
| JUNE |
| JULY |
| AUGUST |
| SEPTEMBER |
| OCTOBER |
| NOVEMBER |
| DECEMBER |

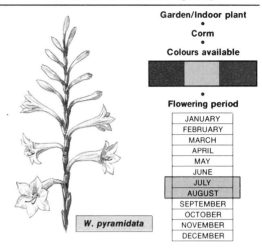

W. pyramidata

An uncommon plant which is related to Gladiolus and should be treated in the same way — plant it in the spring and lift in the autumn. Allow the corms to dry in a warm room before storing in a frost-free place. The leaves are sword-like as with Gladioli, but the flowers are different. They are star-faced tubes borne on either side of the flower stem. There are a number of species in the specialist catalogues, ranging in height from 1½–6 ft (45–180 cm), but you are only likely to find 2 or 3 types and they grow 3–5 ft (90–150 cm) high.

VARIETIES: W. beatricis (W. pillansii) is an evergreen when grown as a greenhouse plant or in a sheltered spot in a mild area — in other districts grow it as a summer bedding plant as described above. It bears dense spikes of orange or red flowers on 3 ft (90 cm) stems. **W. pyramidata (W. rosea)** is a more tender plant and should always be lifted in autumn when grown outdoors. It is also taller (5 ft or 150 cm) and the flowers are pink. The stems require staking. There are also several named hybrids, but there are very few suppliers.

SITE & SOIL: Any well-drained soil will do — full sun is necessary.

PLANT DETAILS: Planting time: April–May. Planting depth: 4 in. (10 cm). Spacing: 12 in. (30 cm). Height: 36–60 in. (90–150 cm).

PROPAGATION: Remove and store cormlets at lifting time. Plant in spring.

Watsonia beatricis

ZANTEDESCHIA Arum Lily

Garden/Indoor plant
•
Rhizome
•
Colours available

Flowering period

| JANUARY |
| FEBRUARY |
| MARCH |
| APRIL |
| MAY |
| JUNE |
| JULY |
| AUGUST |
| SEPTEMBER |
| OCTOBER |
| NOVEMBER |
| DECEMBER |

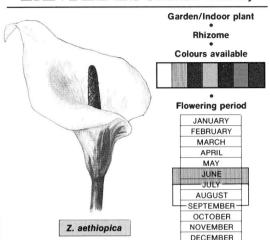

Z. aethiopica

Zantedeschia (Arum Lily in Britain, Calla Lily in the U.S) is one of the beauties of the greenhouse world. The upturned trumpets are 6–9 in. (15–22.5 cm) long and are borne on upright stalks above the arrow-shaped leaves. The rhizome is planted 3 in. (7.5 cm) deep in a compost-filled 6 in. (15 cm) pot in autumn or winter for early summer flowers. Water sparingly at first and then liberally when growth starts. Reduce water after flowering — start into growth again by more liberal watering in autumn.

VARIETIES: There are several species, including **Z. elliottiana** (yellow) and **Z. rehmannii** (pink), plus many hybrids in various colours for growing indoors. The most popular one, however, can be grown outdoors, as described below. **Z. aethiopica** (White Arum Lily) will survive the winter in nearly all areas if the crown is 6 in. below the surface. Choose the variety **'Crowborough'**. It is usually grown in boggy ground around a pond and the blooms are truly eye-catching. Cover the crowns with a peat mulch in winter.

SITE & SOIL: Moist, humus-rich soil is essential. Thrives best in full sun.

PLANT DETAILS: Planting time: April. Planting depth: 6 in. (15 cm). Spacing: 18 in. (45 cm). Height: 24–36 in. (60–90 cm).

PROPAGATION: Divide clumps in late summer.

Zantedeschia rehmannii

ZEPHYRANTHES Zephyr Lily

Garden/Indoor plant
•
True bulb
•
Colours available

Flowering period

| JANUARY |
| FEBRUARY |
| MARCH |
| APRIL |
| MAY |
| JUNE |
| JULY |
| AUGUST |
| SEPTEMBER |
| OCTOBER |
| NOVEMBER |
| DECEMBER |

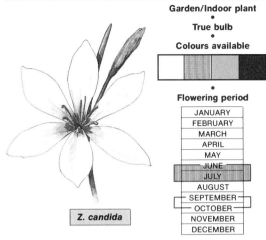

Z. candida

There are several species of this dainty and compact plant which produce large Crocus-like blooms which open out into white or coloured stars. All but one (see below) are too frost-sensitive to be grown outdoors and so are cultivated as conservatory or house plants. Plant 6 bulbs 2 in. (5 cm) deep in a 5 in. (12.5 cm) pot in early spring. Stop watering when the foliage withers — start into growth again in spring by moistening the compost. Repot only when the plants are pot-bound. The blooming period indoors is June–July.

VARIETIES: For indoor flowering you can choose from **Z. flavissima** (yellow), **Z. grandiflora** (deep pink), **Z. rosea** (pink) or **Z. citrina** (yellow). For growing outdoors pick **Z. candida**. The flower stalks appear in large numbers in autumn above the needle-like foliage — each stalk bears at its tip a single 2 in. (5 cm) wide pink-backed white bloom. It is not invasive and so is a good choice for a sheltered pocket in a sunny rockery. Cover with a peat or leafmould mulch in winter. For planting details see below.

SITE & SOIL: Free-draining, sandy soil is essential — thrives best in full sun.

PLANT DETAILS: Planting time: April. Planting depth: 2 in. (5 cm). Spacing: 4 in. (10 cm). Height: 6–12 in. (15–30 cm).

PROPAGATION: Divide overcrowded clumps in the spring — remove and plant up offsets.

Zephyranthes rosea

CHAPTER 3

GROWING BULBS

In general the planting and aftercare of hardy bulbs are straightforward — unlike seeds the planting material is easy to handle and unlike shrubs there are no large holes to dig. There is no thinning, pruning, routine spraying etc, but there is still more to bulb growing than merely scooping out a hole and dropping in the planting material. First, make sure that the type you have chosen is right for your situation and that the time is suitable for planting — always check in the A–Z guide before you begin. Next, choose sound stock and ensure that the soil will not be waterlogged in winter. Follow the rules laid down for planting and then follow the various aftercare techniques described on the next few pages. Some of these routines for individual bulbs may seem a little odd, such as having to withhold watering during dry spells in summer for a few types, but all the rules have a purpose. The basic purpose of proper aftercare is to ensure that the display in future years will be at least as good as this year's show.

PLANTING

It is necessary to use some form of tool to make a hole for the bulb. The depth of this hole varies greatly from type to type — it may be as little as ½ in. (1 cm) or as much as 10 in. (25 cm). There is no 'right' tool for every job — the 3 basic pieces of equipment are illustrated below.

As a general rule bulbs should be planted as soon as possible after purchase, but the big four (Tulip, Hyacinth, Crocus and Narcissus) will come to no harm if stored in a cool, dry place before planting. However, they must go into the ground while they are still firm and without prominent sprouts. Bulbs with roots and without a protective tunic can be stored in moist peat for a little time but planting should not be long delayed.

On the next page the technique for planting a bulb with a trowel in a bed or border is illustrated. These days this planting is just as likely to take place in a tub, window box or other container, and many bulbs are planted indoors in compost or even plain water. In addition they may be planted under turf — all these variants are dealt with in Chapter 4.

Trowel

The trowel is the most popular planting tool and is the best one to use if you have just a few bulbs to plant and/or if the bulbs have widely differing diameters. To make the job easier you can buy a trowel with measurements marked down the length of the blade. A dibber is sometimes used for planting small bulbs but the compaction in heavy soil can lead to problems.

Bulb Planter

The hand-held bulb planter is often recommended where a large number of bulbs are to be planted. It is pushed into the soil and then removed with a core of earth within — an easy job in sandy soil but it is hard work in clayey ground. The long-handled model pushed in with the foot is easier to use. The problem with bulb planters is that all holes are the same diameter and depth.

Spade

The spade is the best tool to use when a large area is to be planted with bulbs. Remove the soil to the required depth, loosen the surface at the bottom of the trench, place the bulbs in position and then replace the earth. Firm gently and then rake lightly to prevent surface capping when it rains. The spade is also the best tool for naturalising bulbs in grass — see pages 101 and 108.

Standard planting

STEP 6:
MARK THE SPOT
Compared with shrubs, roses etc bulbs have the disadvantage of leaving no above-ground indication of their presence after planting. It is therefore sometimes necessary to put in a label to remind you that there are bulbs below a bare patch of earth

STEP 4:
PUT IN THE BULB
Push the bulb down to the base of the hole and twist gently. Make sure the bulb is the right way up — see the Bulb Types section on pages 4–5 if in doubt

STEP 5:
REPLACE THE SOIL
Put the earth back and press it down gently. Use the dug-out soil for this job, but it is a good idea to mix it with peat, coarse sand, well-rotted compost or leafmould if the ground is heavy. Rake over the surface if a large area has been planted and water in if the weather is dry

STEP 3:
PREPARE THE BASE OF THE HOLE
It is vital that there should not be an air space between the bottom of the bulb and the soil at the base of the hole. If the soil is heavy it is useful to put in a shallow layer of grit or moist peat — this cushion layer should not be too deep

STEP 2:
DIG THE HOLE
The hole should be about twice the diameter of the bulb. The depth of the hole will depend upon the variety you are planting — check in the A–Z guide. The bulb can be slightly deeper than the recommended distance if your soil is sandy — in heavy soil the bulb can be set slightly closer to the surface. As a general rule, the common large bulbs such as Tulip, Narcissus and Hyacinth will need to be covered by twice their own height with soil or compost — most small bulbs are covered to about their own height. The bottom of the hole should be reasonably flat and the sides reasonably vertical — avoid making 'ice cream cone' holes

STEP 1:
PREPARE THE SOIL
Nearly all bulbs require free-draining soil. Dig about a week before the planting date if the soil is compacted — adding coarse sand or grit will help if the ground is heavy. Never incorporate fresh manure. Rake a handful of Bone Meal per sq.m into the surface before planting. Free drainage is equally or even more important when planting up containers — make sure that the drainage holes are large enough and not blocked

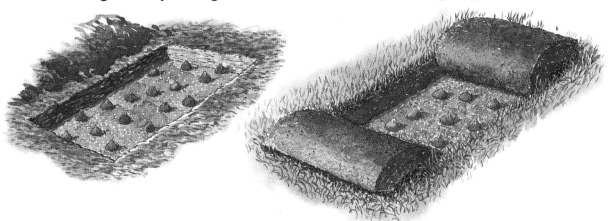

Large-area planting

Naturalising in grass

FEEDING

There are no universal rules for the feeding of bulbs — the best way to feed them depends on both the type and the situation in which they are grown.

Perhaps there is just one general rule. If the ground is not particularly fertile it is useful to work a fertilizer into the soil before planting. This feed must be a slow-acting one such as Bone Meal.

If you are planting bulbs for a single season display and plan to discard them once the show is over then no further feeding is necessary. If on the other hand the bulbs are to stay in the ground from one season to the next or if they are to be lifted for planting after the dormant period then extra feeding may be necessary. The critical time is between the onset of flowering and the time when all the leaves are brown. At this stage feeding with a phosphate-rich liquid fertilizer may help, but some genera show little response.

Bulbs in containers generally require more regular feeding than garden-grown ones once the food reserves in the compost have been exhausted. Use a liquid fertilizer or slow release feed.

WATERING

There should not be any need to water spring-flowering bulbs up to the flowering stage, but it is essential to keep the leaves growing as long as possible after flowering and this may mean watering in late spring until the foliage turns yellow or brown. Summer- and autumn-flowering bulbs such as Dahlias and Gladioli do need watering during periods of drought. Water thoroughly to reach the deep-seated roots — a daily sprinkle may well do more harm than good.

A few additional points. There is no need to water the ground above dormant bulbs — in a few cases it may be positively harmful. With evergreens, however, there is a year-round requirement for moisture at the roots. Do not use a strong jet when watering long-stalked bulbs as there is a danger of bending or even breaking the stems. With outdoor container- and indoor pot-grown bulbs the growing plants will have to be watched carefully for signs of water shortage. The basic requirement is to keep the compost moist but not waterlogged.

STAKING

Stakes, wires and other means of support are never things of beauty and can be distinctly ugly when carelessly used. Still, they are necessary for weak-stemmed plants such as Achimenes, tall varieties on exposed sites such as some Tulips, for large-headed flowers like some Decorative and Semi-Cactus Dahlias and finally for climbers like Gloriosa. The golden rule is never to leave staking until the stems have collapsed.

AFTER FLOWERING

Proper aftercare is a key part of the annual bulb cycle — on it depends the quality of next season's display. The removal of spent blooms is recommended where such a task is practical — obviously it is out of the question for large areas.

The dead flowers should be removed with either a knife, secateurs or scissors — don't tug them. Remove only the blooms — leave the stalks.

Never remove the leaves at this stage. The leaves produce food reserves for the bulb and so must be retained until they are yellow or brown and withered. Do not tie long leaves into a knot.

These yellowing leaves can be unsightly, and there are several ways of tackling the problem. In a mixed border surround the bulbs with plants which will be in leaf or flower when the bulb leaves turn yellow. Sometimes a bedded area is needed for other plants — here the bulbs should be lifted after flowering and heeled in out of sight until the foliage has turned brown.

WINTER PROTECTION

Some bulbous plants can be overwintered in the garden with no problems at all — Crocus, Narcissus and Snowdrops are examples. At the other end of the scale are the half hardy and tender varieties which cannot be left in the ground during the winter months. Some of them like Gladioli and Begonias are lifted and then stored for planting later — others are grown as house or conservatory plants.

Between these two groups are the rather tender bulbs which will survive outdoors if given some protection in winter. This protection consists of a 3 in. (7.5 cm) thick mulch of peat, bracken, straw, shredded bark or leafmould. It is essential that this mulch is neither airtight nor watertight. Put down the mulch when the first frost occurs and move it away when the danger of late frosts has passed.

The bulb is protected from penetrating frosts and also from starting into premature growth if there is a warm spell in winter or early spring.

STORAGE

Numerous bulbs in the A–Z section require a period of dry and cool storage when they are dormant. The usual procedure is to lift the bulbs carefully and then allow them to dry for about a week. Discard any diseased or damaged ones and then remove soil.

Bulbs with a protective scaly or fibrous cover (tunic) are stored in boxes, open-mesh bags etc. Other bulbs do not have a tunic — these are put in a box and are then covered with peat or sand.

In the A–Z section it is recommended that some indoor bulbs are left in their pots without water during the dormant period and are brought to life by watering at the recommended time.

INCREASING YOUR STOCK

There are a number of ways of increasing your stock of bulbous plants, but only one or two will be right for the plants in your home or garden. Some bulbs spread steadily over a period of years, and the easiest method of propagation is to lift the clump, divide it and then replant at the appropriate time. True bulbs and corms often form offsets around them and these bulblets or cormlets can be removed for planting. Large offsets from the bulbs (e.g Narcissi) will flower in the season after planting, but the tiny cormlets or cormels taken from the base of Gladioli corms may take 3 years before they reach flowering size. Rhizomes, tubers and tuberous roots can be propagated by cutting the parent storage organ or organs into sections, making sure that each section is capable of developing into a flowering plant.

The underground part of a bulbous plant is not the only source of propagation material. Some Lilies produce tiny bulbs (bulbils) in the axils of their leaves and these can be detached for planting and growing on in moist compost. Sowing seeds may sound like an attractive proposition, but there are drawbacks. You will have to wait 3–7 years for flowers to appear and named cultivars may not reproduce true to type. Lastly, some bulb seeds are notoriously difficult to germinate.

There are several additional techniques for specific plants — stem cuttings for Dahlias and Begonias, scoring for Hyacinth bulbs and scaling for Lilies as described on these two pages. For most gardeners, however, there are just two methods for increasing stock — buying new bulbs at the start of the planting season and the division of clumps of bulbs and corms so that large offsets can be used as extra planting material.

SOWING SEEDS

Despite the difficulties described above many keen gardeners raise bulbs from seed for one or more reasons. Some rare species are only available as seed, it is a cheap way to produce a large number of plants, interesting hybrids are sometimes obtained and there is the joy of starting from scratch. Whatever the reason it is necessary to begin with fresh seed and sow it as soon as possible — follow the rules in The Garden Expert. Sow in trays or pots and transplant as soon as the seedlings are large enough to handle. The young plants should be grown on in the garden or indoors depending on their hardiness. Some winter-growing types need a cold spell before they will germinate. Place the seed tray after sowing in the autumn in the refrigerator for 3 weeks and then treat in the normal way.

TAKING CUTTINGS

Taking cuttings is an excellent way of propagating tubers and tuberous roots because the rooted cuttings will bloom in the first season. The two popular subjects are Begonias and Dahlias and the plants are generally used for summer bedding. The tubers are planted in moist compost in spring under glass — protect from strong light until the shoots appear. When these shoots are 2–3 in. (5–7.5 cm) high they should be severed with a sharp and clean knife and their ends dipped in a hormone rooting powder. Plant them in pots filled with soilless compost and water in gently — cover the pot with a polyethylene bag and secure with a rubber band. Stand the pot in a bright spot away from direct sunlight. Once rooted the plants should be potted on — harden off if they are to be planted outdoors.

DIVIDING UNDERGROUND ORGANS

True Bulbs

Most true bulbs produce offsets from their basal plate after one or more seasons in the soil. If these offsets are large they are often referred to as daughter bulbs — small ones are called bulblets. Some bulbs spread steadily into crowded clumps — to increase your stock lift at the time recommended in the A–Z guide, divide up and then replant the separated small clumps. Alternatively you can separate all the bulbs and their offsets for storage or immediate planting. Large Tulip offsets will flower the year after planting but small ones will take 2–3 years to reach flowering size. Generally it is best to use offsets which have separated naturally but large daughter bulbs can with care be broken away from the basal plate. Lilies can be propagated by scaling (see page 56) and Hyacinths can be induced to produce offsets by scoring — 2 cuts are made at right angles at the base before planting.

Scoring

Dividing

Corms

Most corms, like true bulbs, produce offsets. At the end of the season the old corm dies and above it are the new corm with tiny corms (cormlets or cormels) around the edge. Divide clumps as with true bulbs or lift and remove cormels for planting and growing on to reach flowering size in 2–3 years.

Tubers

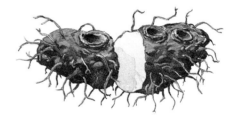

Tubers generally grow larger with time but they do not form offsets nor do they break up naturally into separate plants. In order to increase your stock dig up the tubers and cut them into 2 or more pieces with a sharp knife. Make sure that each piece has at least one growing point — replant immediately.

Rhizomes

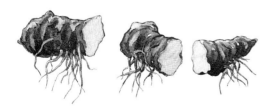

To propagate rhizomes lift them after flowering and cut up into sections. Each section must have at least one growing point and discard all old and exhausted sections. Replant at the recommended depth (see A–Z guide) and make sure that there is as little delay as possible between lifting and replanting.

Tuberous Roots

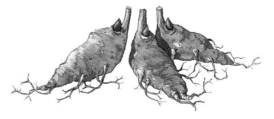

Do not attempt to divide tuberous roots until the growing points ('eyes') at the crown have started to swell. At this stage each of the tuberous roots should be cut with a sharp knife so that at the top of each one there is a piece of old stem and at least one eye. Leave to dry for a day or two before planting.

CHAPTER 4

USING BULBS

The basic role of bulbs in the garden and in the home must be known to everyone. The main show is in the early part of the year, beginning with the windowsill bowls filled with Narcissi, Crocuses and Hyacinths which bloom in January and ending with the late Tulips in the garden in May. Begonias, Lilies and Gladioli brighten up the summer plot and in late summer and autumn the Dahlias provide a blaze of colour.

It has already been stressed in earlier chapters that we can fill in the gaps in this calendar and add a great deal more variety by widening the list of bulbs we buy. There is no need to make this point again, nor is it necessary to extol their beauty — the photographs in the A–Z section make it apparent.

It is however worthwhile in this chapter to mention the two drawbacks from which bulbs suffer. The first one is that there is usually only a short flowering period, lasting for weeks rather than months. Secondly there is often a long dormant period which is preceded by the yellowing of the foliage.

There are a number of ways of using bulbs, and most of them are designed to cope with these drawbacks. Bulbs grown for seasonal bedding are lifted when the display is over and the ground is then used for other plants — where the bed or border is required for immediate planting the lifted bulbs are moved to another part of the garden so the foliage can continue to grow after flowering. If bulbs are to stay in the ground permanently then the usual practice is to grow them among other plants which will have green leaves and perhaps flowers when the bulb foliage is unsightly or absent.

These techniques for avoiding the sight of dying foliage in the height of the season or the presence of bare earth for much of the year do nothing to overcome the short flowering period. There are a couple of ways in which you can extend the time a particular genus will be in bloom. Some types, especially the popular ones, have early, mid-season and late varieties, so by choosing carefully you can have the genus in bloom for months. A Tulip bed can be in bloom from March to May — a Crocus patch in the border can be in flower from February to April. For a single species it is of course much more difficult to extend the flowering period, although planting some at normal depth and others at a deeper level can add weeks to the display.

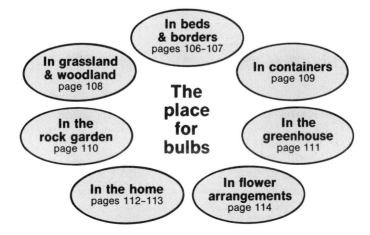

In beds & borders
pages 106–107

In grassland & woodland
page 108

In containers
page 109

The place for bulbs

In the rock garden
page 110

In the greenhouse
page 111

In the home
pages 112–113

In flower arrangements
page 114

BULBS IN BEDS & BORDERS

The traditional way of using bulbs is to plant them in beds and borders. You can make your choice from all of the outdoor plants listed in the A–Z guide, provided your site and soil are suitable, and so what to grow is a difficult decision.

To make things easier your first step should be to pick one of the three basic planting patterns. They are Bedding out, Permanent planting and Filling in. Having made your choice the selection of suitable bulbs becomes a simpler task. There is a fourth planting pattern which is often seen but should be avoided — Pepper pot planting whereby groups of a few bulbs are scattered all over the garden.

BEDDING OUT is the planting pattern beloved by the Victorians, public parks and many gardens, both large and small, throughout the country. The two essential features of bedding out are that most or all of the bed or border is planted up with bulbs and the display is temporary — the bulbs are removed when flowers and leaves have withered so that the space can be used for other plants.

Devoting a bed or border entirely to bulbs is not usual but the effect can be stunning. The simplest approach is the blanket bed in which the whole area is filled with just one variety. Its critics regard the effect as too dull and that may be true for a small front garden, but using a brilliantly-coloured Hyacinth, bi-coloured Tulip or unusual Narcissus in a large irregularly-shaped drift can look dramatic.

For most purposes, however, gardeners choose several different bulbs of varying heights — more colourful, of course, but it will look distinctly bitty if you choose too many different varieties. For maximum effect the classic planting scheme shown below is used — the dot plant (Canna, Lily etc) can be omitted if the bed is small. Just a couple of rules — the types you choose should bloom at around the same time because dying foliage is not hidden, and make sure that the varieties need approximately the same growing conditions.

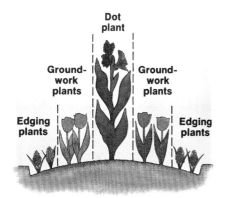

There are two ways of setting out the bulbs at planting time. Formal bedding is the style chosen by most people when filling a small bed with bulbs — the divisions between the different types are clearly defined and the bulbs are put in at regular distances. This method is frowned upon by many purists from the design point of view, but it also has its drawbacks from the practical point of view. The visual effect can be distinctly poor if growth is uneven or if some of the bulbs fail, so it is necessary to make sure that the soil is consistent throughout the planting site and that there is no difference in illumination over the site during the day. It is also a good idea to grow a few extra bulbs in an out-of-the-way spot which you can use to fill in any gaps which may develop.

Informal planting is easier — the bulbs are planted at irregular distances and geometric shapes are avoided. There is no particular virtue in keeping solely to bulbs when bedding out — spring-flowering bulbous plants with bedding plants such as Pansies, Polyanthus, Wallflowers, Double Daisies, Forget-me-nots etc is the plan adopted by millions.

PERMANENT PLANTING has the obvious advantage of removing the need for annual lifting — here the bulbs are grown as an important part of a mixed bed or border. The shrub border is an excellent home. In herbaceous borders the rapid spread of the clumps of perennials means that lifting every few years is generally essential, and so there is inevitable disturbance of the bulbs between them.

Choose bulbs for permanent planting which will add to and do not compete with the basic scheme. Choose bold subjects such as Crown Imperials, Lilies, Foxtail Lilies, tall Narcissi etc where low-growing shrubs are nearby, and use low-growing subjects such as Erythronium, Corydalis, Scilla and Snake's-head Fritillary at the front of the border or under shrubs which are bare at the base. Always plant the bulbs in informal groups — never in straight lines. These groups may spread and so lifting and dividing may be necessary after a time. Check in the A–Z guide as some bulbous types respond badly to transplanting.

It was stated at the start of this section that permanent planting has the distinct advantage over bedding out because there is no need for annual planting and lifting. There is an additional important advantage — the surrounding plants help to hide the withered foliage of the bulbs when they come to the end of their growing season. The ground will be bare during the dormant period — a label will help you to avoid the area when planting nearby.

FILLING IN is the term for planting seasonal bulbs in a bed or border which is dominated by other subjects. Pocket planting involves leaving a few gaps in a border so that spring-, summer- or autumn-flowering bulbs can be planted each year.

Bedding out, Permanent planting and Filling in are the basic planting patterns for adorning our beds and borders with bulbs. Growing in containers may have suddenly increased in popularity, but bulbs in the open ground will still continue to brighten up every garden-lined street in the country.

BED

A bed is a planted area designed to be viewed from all sides. A *flower bed* is made up of non-woody flowering plants — there may be bulbs and nothing else but it is more usual these days to have hardy perennials and bedding plants as well as bulbs. Planting may be formal or informal. In an *island bed* the hardy perennials and/or shrubs are dominant and bedding plants and bulbs are grown in pockets between them.

BORDER

A border is a planted area designed to be viewed from one, two or three sides but not from all angles. A *flower border* is occasionally devoted solely to bulbs but it is much more likely to contain a mixture of hardy perennials, bedding plants and bulbs. In an *herbaceous border* the hardy perennials are dominant and in a *mixed border* there is a selection drawn from shrubs, roses, conifers, hardy perennials, bulbs and annuals.

NATURALISING BULBS

'Naturalising' means growing bulbs in a way and situation that make them look like wild flowers in grassland or growing under trees. To achieve this effect is not quite as easy as it sounds. First of all only a number of bulbous plants are small enough not to look out of place, vigorous enough to compete with turf, hardy enough to stand up to our winters and prolific enough to spread rapidly over a period of years. Next, the grass must be managed in such a way as not to harm the bulbs and the woodland must be open enough to enable the bulbous plants to develop and flower properly.

Setting bulbs in grassland is by far the more popular form of naturalising, and there is one basic consideration you must take into account if you want to use bulbs in this way. It is essential to wait at least 6 weeks after the flowers have faded before cutting the grass. The reason is that the leaves must be left to produce the food for the developing bulbs below ground — the bulbs which will provide next year's show. These remarks concern the spring-flowering bulbs which are the most popular type of planting material — with autumn-flowering bulbs you must stop cutting the grass at the beginning of September to let the shoots develop.

Obviously the traditional closely-cut lawn is not a suitable site for naturalising bulbs — choose instead a semi-wild area at the back of the lawn, an area of grass in a wild flower garden or a circle of uncut grass around a tree.

To naturalise bulbs in grassland the first step is to choose your bulbs. A single species or a mixture of types can be used — it is up to you but the purists consider that just one type of bulb is the better choice. The next job is to cut the grass and then planting can begin. A bulb planter can be used, but the turf-lifting method described on page 100 and illustrated on page 101 is generally much more satisfactory. Whichever method is used it is vital to avoid a geometric planting pattern — the classic technique is to drop a handful of bulbs on the ground and plant them where they fall. As a general rule the tips of small bulbs should be about 2 in. (5 cm) below the surface and larger ones about 4 in. (10 cm) deep. The grass can be fed each April if necessary, but do not use a fertilizer/weedkiller mixture.

Do not think that naturalising bulbs in woodland is only for the large garden — a clump or drift or two under a single tree can look quite charming. Some of the bulbs used can tolerate shade but most grow and flower before the leaves are fully open on the trees in spring.

●

NATURALISING IN GRASSLAND SELECTION: Camassia • Colchicum • Erythronium • Fritillaria • Galanthus • Leucojum • Muscari • Narcissus • Ornithogalum • Scilla

NATURALISING IN WOODLAND SELECTION: Allium • Anemone • Arisaema • Arum • Brimeura • Chionodoxa • Crocus • Cyclamen • Endymion • Eranthis • Erythronium • Fritillaria • Galanthus • Ipheion • Leucojum • Lilium • Muscari • Narcissus • Ornithogalum • Scilla • Trillium • Tulipa

BULBS IN CONTAINERS

One of the most outstanding features of the container boom during recent years is that about half the bulbs we buy are planted in containers rather than in the open garden.

As in the garden spring is the major season for bulbs in containers. Tulips, Hyacinths, Muscari, Crocuses and Narcissi are prime sources of colour in March and April, and even earlier there are Galanthus, Eranthis, Iris reticulata, Cyclamen coum, Anemone blanda and Chionodoxa.

Spring should not be the end of the container bulb year. Summer pots can be brightened up with Gladiolus, Lily, Begonia, Agapanthus etc and for later flowers you can grow Nerine, autumn-flowering Crocus, Colchicum and Cyclamen.

With careful planning and several containers you can have bulbs in flower nearly all year round. Small varieties which may be invisible in a bed become things of beauty when brought closer to eye level. In addition many bulbous plants do better in containers than in the bed or border because they are grown in compost with adequate drainage.

Despite these advantages bulbs are not ideal container plants as there are three drawbacks. As noted at the start of this chapter the flowering period of the average bulb is shorter than that of the average bedding plant. Secondly, there are the non-decorative times when there is bare compost before the shoots appear and then the dying leaves after flowering. Finally, bulbs grown in containers rarely put on enough leaf growth to produce worthwhile bulbs for a second year's display. Several different systems have been evolved for growing bulbs in containers — some are designed to overcome one or more of the difficulties so do consider each one before deciding what to grow and how to plant.

SINGLE-TYPE PLANTING: This method simply ignores the problems. The container is filled with bulbs and the floral display is enjoyed, after which they are lifted and either thrown away or planted in another part of the garden until the leaves have withered. After lifting, the container is filled with other plants to provide a different show. Large and showy bulbs such as Agapanthus are sometimes grown as single specimens in pots and are kept from year to year.

LAYER PLANTING: This is similar in principle to single-type planting, but here two or more types with different flowering seasons are planted in layers so as to extend the display time.

IN-POT PLANTING: The purpose of this method is to avoid having a bare container for months before the bulbs emerge. With this technique bedding plants are grown and then cleared before pots of bulbs in bud are inserted in the compost. After flowering the pots are removed and replaced with other plants.

PART PLANTING: All the techniques so far have treated bulbs as the sole residents of the container. Part planting relies on the presence of other plants to disguise the pre-flowering and the dying-down stages. For example a Tulip/Hyacinth/Polyanthus/Ivy/Conifer display for spring from which all but the Ivy and Conifer are removed after the flowers have gone.

●

CONTAINER SELECTION: Agapanthus • Anemone • Begonia • Chionodoxa • Colchicum • Crocosmia • Crocus • Cyclamen • Eranthis • Erythronium • Fritillaria • Galanthus • Gladiolus • Hyacinthus • Ipheion • Iris • Leucojum • Lilium • Muscari • Narcissus • Nerine • Puschkinia • Schizostylis • Scilla • Sisyrinchium • Sternbergia • Tigridia • Tulipa

STEP 1:
BEGIN PLANTING
Prepare the container, put it in place and add the drainage and optional peat layer as shown on page 101. Now add soilless potting compost, pressing down gently with your hands. Stop adding compost when the correct height is reached — which is when the bulbs placed on the layer will be covered with the recommended height of compost, measured from the tip of the bulb to the top of the growing medium. Buy bulbs which are large, firm and healthy — place them on the compost with little space (approximately 1 in. or 2.5 cm) between them

STEP 2:
FINISH PLANTING
Sift compost between the bulbs and then add more of the planting medium so that a 1–2 in. (2.5–5 cm) watering space is left at the top of the container. There are two alternative techniques. In layer planting the addition of this compost stops at an earlier stage so that a layer of smaller bulbs can be added (for example Crocuses over Narcissi) in order to extend the display. Another variant is part planting — here the trees, shrubs and/or bedding plants are put in first and the bulbs are then planted with a trowel to the correct depth in the compost. Whichever technique you use the compost should be kept moist and the bulbs should be lifted when the display is over for later planting in the garden

BULBS IN THE ROCKERY

Rockeries are popular for all sorts of reasons. The basic appeal is that the sloping site with its outcrop of stones is a feature in itself — a reconstruction of a mountain scene in one's own garden. Whether the basic structure is attractive depends on the skill of the person who made it — a well-constructed rockery with weathered rocks in layers can give a truly natural appearance, but a mound dotted with chunks of Westmorland Stone has little charm. This rockery or rock garden (the two terms are interchangeable) can be extensive for alpine enthusiasts to show off their skill or it may be just a few square feet to add interest to a small garden.

In all cases it is the presence of rockery plants which brings the thing to life. Clumps and drifts of flowers add colour at various times of the year, and in the well-stocked rockery you will find true alpines, low-growing perennials, dwarf shrubs and sometimes bedding plants. To this list must be added bulbs, because dwarf bulbous plants are a vital part of rockery planting. If the rock garden is a large one then mid-sized or even tall bulbs can be used as well as these dwarfs.

The well-made rockery offers an excellent home for bulbs. Its raised and sloping construction is free-draining and its gritty soil is an additional feature which helps to ensure that the bulbs will never be waterlogged. There is also a variety of environments to suit all needs — sunny spots, shady areas, and pockets which can be filled with acid compost or peaty soil if the particular species has such requirements. The advantages of a rockery do not end there — small beauties are brought closer to eye level and the surrounding plants offer protection and perhaps support.

The favourite choices are bulbs which flower in late autumn, winter, early spring and mid spring. This is the time when many bulbs are at the height of their flowering season but nearly all other rockery plants are not. With some low-growing genera such as Crocus, Snowdrop, Eranthis etc you can choose any species or variety, but with more varied genera such as Tulip, Narcissus, Iris and Allium you must take care to pick varieties and species which will be in keeping with their surroundings, and that means looking for dwarfs. Unless you are really keen it is generally a good idea to pick hardy bulbs which can be left to spread rather than half hardy ones which will have to be lifted at the end of the season. Plant in the usual way (see pages 100–101), but small bulbs can be pushed with your finger to the required depth between established permanent plants.

You may be lucky enough to possess an attractive rockery, in which case you should try to increase the range of bulbs you grow in order to replace some of the overused Aubrietia, Arabis, Allysum saxatile, Cerastium etc. If you do not have a rockery then think carefully before trying to build one. It will take a lot of time, money and effort, so you should think of a raised bed made with real or reconstituted stone as an easier alternative.

●

ROCKERY SELECTION: Allium • Anemone • Brimeura • Bulbocodium • Chionodoxa • Colchicum • Convallaria • Corydalis • Crocus • Cyclamen • Eranthis • Erythronium • Fritillaria • Galanthus • Hyacinthella • Ipheion • Iris (Reticulata Group) • Leucojum • Merendera • Muscari • Narcissus • Ornithogalum • Oxalis • Puschkinia • Rhodohypoxis • Scilla • Trillium • Tulipa

BULBS IN THE GREENHOUSE

The title of this page conjures up a picture of tropical beauties which could not be expected to grow in this country without the warmth provided by a heated greenhouse or conservatory. These tender types are the classic greenhouse bulbs — they cannot tolerate frost and are never placed outdoors in winter. Most are summer- or autumn-flowering and they usually lose their leaves during part of the year. Depending on the variety the bulb may be left in the pot during this dormant period or it is removed from the container and stored in peat. Do not guess what to do — look in the A–Z guide for advice.

One or two, such as Eucharis, require a minimum temperature of 65°F (18°C) and so do best under stove house conditions, but many more will flourish in a cool greenhouse or conservatory provided that the temperature does not fall below 45°F (7°C) during the growing season of the plant. The list of these cool house plants includes Acidanthera, Amaryllis, Chlidanthus, Freesia, Habranthus, Homeria, Lachenalia, Nerine, Pancratium, Sparaxis, Tritonia, Veltheimia and Zephyranthes.

About an equal number prefer rather warmer conditions during their growing season — this requirement for a minimum temperature of 55°F (13°C) means that some form of heat will be required in the house during most of the year. The list here is Achimenes, Babiana, Canna, Clivia, Crinum, Eucomis, Gloriosa, Haemanthus, Hippeastrum, Hymenocallis, Ornithogalum, Polianthes, Sandersonia, Sprekelia, Vallota and Zantedeschia.

All of this makes it sound as if the unheated greenhouse is not a suitable place for bulbs, but this is certainly not the case. All the hardy spring bulbs can be grown here, and so can those which will only overwinter outdoors in mild and/or dry areas. Examples include Brodiaea, Homeria, Ixia, Romulea and Tigridia. An unheated greenhouse is also a good place to grow bulbs such as Hyacinthella which need to be kept dry during their summer dormant period. So do use your unheated greenhouse for more than Tomatoes and storing empty pots — here stately Lilies and giant tuberous Begonias can be grown away from the wind and rain outdoors.

BULBS IN THE HOME

Bulbs are an important part of the house plant scene, and many species and varieties can be used to decorate rooms at various times of the year. There are several ways in which bulbs are employed for this purpose, and the most obvious one is the forcing of spring-flowering bulbs to provide flowers in bowls or pots before their garden counterparts are in bloom. Forcing involves keeping the planted up bulbs both cold and dark until the roots have developed and spread in the compost, and then moving the container to a well-lit and warmer spot indoors as soon as the shoots are an inch or two high. There is also the straightforward non-forcing approach whereby pots of a wide range of bulbs grown in the garden can be brought indoors when they are in bud or flower so as to provide their display in kitchen, living room or hall. So far we have covered only the use of hardy types, but there is also a range of tender bulbous plants which is used to beautify our homes — these are the indoor bulbs.

GARDEN BULBS — THE FORCING TECHNIQUE The types usually chosen are the early-blooming large bulbs — Hyacinth is the most reliable and Tulip is generally the least satisfactory. Narcissi are also very popular and Crocus is the favourite smaller bulb, but there are many others from which to choose including Muscari, Eranthis, Iris reticulata, Ornithogalum and Puschkinia.

If a large number of varieties are available do make sure that you choose one which is recommended for indoor cultivation, and select bulbs which are good-sized, disease-free and firm. Both pots with drainage holes and bulb bowls without them are widely used as containers — it is advisable to choose pots with holes at the base if forcing is to take place in the open garden.

Bulb fibre is sometimes used as the growing medium, but it is better to use a peat-based compost if you intend to save the bulbs for garden use after they have flowered. Place a layer of moist compost in the bottom of the bowl or pot and set the bulbs on it — a 6 in. (15 cm) pot will hold 3 Hyacinths, 6 Narcissi, 6 Tulips or 12 Crocuses. The bulbs should be close together but they should not touch each other nor touch the sides of the container. Never force the bulbs down into the compost.

Fill up with more compost, pressing it firmly but not too tightly around the bulbs. When finished the tips should be just above the surface and there should be about ½ in. (1 cm) between the top of the compost and the rim of the container. Water if necessary so that the growing medium is damp but not soggy.

The bulbs now need a cold but frost-free period in the dark. A temperature of 40°F (4°C) is ideal, and the traditional technique is to 'plunge' the container in a shallow trench in the garden or to set it in a cold frame and then cover with a 4 in. (10 cm) layer of ashes, peat or sand. An alternative technique is to place the container in a black plastic bag and keep it in a shed, cellar or garage. This cold dark period will last for 8–14 weeks, depending on the variety and the conditions. Check occasionally to make sure that the compost is still moist and that above-ground growth has not yet started — remember that any warmth at this stage will lead to failure.

When the shoots are about 1–2 in. (2.5–5 cm) high it is time to move the container into a room indoors. This room should be cool — 50°F (10°C) is ideal. Place in a shady spot at first and then move near to the window after a few days. The leaves will now develop and in a couple of weeks the flower buds will appear. When these buds begin to colour the bowl or pot should be moved to the chosen site for flowering. This spot should be bright but not sunny, free from draughts, away from a radiator or heater and not too warm — 60°–65°F (15°–18°C) is ideal. Keep the compost moist at all times. Turn the bowl occasionally so that growth will be even, and provide some support for tall-growing types.

After flowering cut off the dead blooms but not the flower stalks. The next step depends on whether you intend to keep the bulbs for future use. If you do, then it is necessary to continue watering until the leaves have withered. Remove the bulbs and allow to dry, then remove the dead foliage and store the bulbs in a cool dry place. These bulbs will not provide a second display indoors — plant outdoors in autumn.

GARDEN BULBS — THE NON-FORCING TECHNIQUE Any garden bulb which is suitable for growing in a container outdoors can be planted in a pot with adequate drainage, using a suitable soilless compost, for indoor display. The tips should be completely covered and the pots then placed in the garden. When the plants are fully grown and the flower buds are present bring the pot indoors. This indoor site should be bright without direct sun and it should not be too warm. The next step depends on the type of bulb you have grown. After flowering the container can be returned to the garden if annual repotting is not recommended (see the A–Z guide) or the plants can be treated in the same way as forced bulbs, as described above.

INDOOR BULBS A large number of half hardy bulbs can be grown as house plants. Some of these bulbous plants keep their leaves all year round (Clivia, Eucharis, Vallota etc) and so are generally regarded as 'Flowering House Plants' rather than 'Bulbs'. Most indoor bulbs however, such as the popular Hippeastrum, lose their leaves during the dormant period. The routine here is to leave them in the pot when the foliage dies down, and the compost is kept almost dry until growth starts again. With a few such as Tuberous Begonia and Canna the usual technique is to lift the bulbs when the leaves have withered and store them in peat until potting time comes round again.

BULBS AT CHRISTMAS

It is not difficult to grow Hyacinths, Narcissi and Tulips for blooming on Christmas Day, but it is not a matter of planting the bulbs earlier than the recommended time. The essential step is to buy bulbs which have been specially treated — look for the word 'prepared' on the label or catalogue entry. These bulbs are more expensive than ordinary garden types and they must be planted as soon as possible after purchase. September is the usual time for planting, and the forcing technique should be followed. Bring the pots indoors when the shoots are 1 in. (2.5 cm) high — this should be no later than the first day of December. After flowering the bulbs can be stored for planting outdoors in autumn.

BULBS IN WATER

Hyacinths are sometimes grown in water instead of compost. The lower section of a 'hyacinth glass' is filled with water and the bulb is then placed in the upper section with its base just touching the water. Follow the forcing technique using a black plastic bag as described on page 112. Some small bulbs, especially non-hardy ones such as Tazetta Narcissi, are sometimes grown in glass bowls partly filled with pebbles. Lay each bulb on a shallow layer of small stones and then add more pebbles until half the bulb is covered. Add water so that the base of each bulb is wet. Keep at about 50°F (10°C) and in a shady spot until the leaves start to grow — then move to a warmer, brightly-lit spot. Throw the bulbs away after flowering.

BULBS AS CUT FLOWERS

The blooms of bulbous plants are a favourite source of material for the flower arranger. Narcissi and Tulips, of course, for spring display and then the Lilies, Gladioli and Freesias of summer and Dahlias at the end of the season.

Gather the flowers from your garden if you can as they are likely to last longer than shop-bought ones, but you will have to rely on the florist for out-of-season blooms and the types you cannot grow for yourself. If your need for cut flowers is modest or if your garden is small then collecting a few from the bed or border is the standard source. If you are a keen flower arranger, however, it is better to grow your bulbs for cutting in rows in an out-of-the-way spot or in the vegetable garden. At cutting time go out into the garden in the morning or evening with a bucket half-filled with tepid water. Choose flowers at the Open Stage — for single-flowered stems this is when the bud is showing colour and beginning to open and for multi-flowered stems a few flowers should be open and buds should be showing colour. Make a clean, sloping cut, remove lower leaves if present and get the stems into the bucket as quickly as possible.

Before making your arrangement it is necessary to condition the stems. They should be immersed in tepid water in a bucket — stand this container in a cool and dark place for 2–8 hours. For most plants deep immersion is recommended, but spring-flowering bulbs are an exception. Tulips, Narcissi etc should be conditioned in shallow water.

Some types need pre-treatment before this conditioning is carried out. The bottom of Dahlia flower stalks should be singed before immersion — hold a flame (cigarette lighter, match or candle) to the cut end until it is blackened. Tulips, Hyacinths and Narcissi also need special treatment before conditioning. Cut away the white part of the stem as this zone cannot take up water efficiently — a sloping cut on the green part of the stem is required for maximum vase-life. Some spring-flowering bulbs have sap which shortens the life of other flowers — let the stems drain by standing them in their own bucket of water overnight before conditioning.

Placing the blooms in a vase or jug of water is the age-old way of creating displays, but these days it is more usual to use 'mechanics' to keep the stalks in place in the container. The most popular type is floral foam — the other two are the pinholder and chicken wire. See The Flower Arranging Expert for details. Floral foam is suitable for many bulbous plants but Tulips and Narcissi find water uptake difficult from foam and are better in water to which a cut flower preservative has been added.

●

CUT FLOWER SELECTION: Agapanthus • Allium • Alstroemeria • Amaryllis • Anemone • Canna • Convallaria • Crocosmia • Crocus • Cyclamen • Dahlia • Eremurus • Freesia • Fritillaria imperialis • Gladiolus • Hippeastrum • Hyacinthus • Iris • Lilium • Muscari • Narcissus • Nerine • Ornithogalum • Polianthes • Ranunculus • Scilla • Sparaxis • Tulipa • Vallota • Zantedeschia

CHAPTER 5

FLOWERS ALL YEAR ROUND

When we think of bulbs in the garden the immediate impression is one of Snowdrops and Crocuses in late winter or early spring and then the Narcissi in April and Tulips in May. But the outdoor bulb season is much more extended and by careful selection you can have flowers all year round. For each month there is a list below of bulbs which can be expected to be in full flower, but do remember that not all will be suitable for your conditions. It is also necessary to remember that in your garden some of the varieties may come into bloom earlier and can continue for several weeks later than the times shown in the chart.

JANUARY

Crocus
Cyclamen coum
Eranthis
Galanthus

FEBRUARY

Anemone blanda
Arisarum proboscideum
Bulbocodium vernum
Chionodoxa
Crocus
Cyclamen coum
Eranthis
Galanthus
Iris
Leucojum vernum
Narcissus
Scilla bifolia
Scilla tubergeniana
Tulipa

MARCH

Anemone apennina
Anemone blanda
Anemone coronaria (Sept planting)
Arisarum proboscideum
Bulbocodium vernum
Chionodoxa
Crocus
Cyclamen coum
Eranthis
Galanthus
Hermodactylus tuberosus
Hyacinthus multiflora
Iris
Leucojum vernum
Merendera trigyna
Muscari azureum
Narcissus
Puschkinia scilloides
Romulea bulbocodium
Scilla bifolia
Scilla sibirica
Scilla tubergeniana
Tulipa

APRIL

Anemone apennina
Anemone blanda
Anemone coronaria (Sept planting)
Anemone nemorosa
Arisarum proboscideum
Arum
Asarum
Bulbocodium vernum
Chionodoxa
Convallaria majalis
Corydalis
Crocus
Cyclamen repandum
Erythronium
Fritillaria
Hermodactylus tuberosus
Hyacinthella
Hyacinthus orientalis
Ipheion
Iris
Leucojum aestivum
Muscari armeniacum
Narcissus
Ornithogalum
Pleione bulbocodioides
Puschkinia scilloides
Rhodohypoxis baurii
Romulea bulbocodium
Scilla campanulata
Scilla non-scripta
Scilla sibirica

Sisyrinchium douglasii
Trillium
Tulipa
Uvularia

MAY

Allium
Anthericum
Arisaema
Arum
Asarum
Asphodelus
Babiana
Brimeura amethystina
Brodiaea
Camassia cusickii
Camassia leichtlinii
Convallaria majalis
Corydalis
Erythronium
Fritillaria
Gladiolus Species
Hyacinthella
Hyacinthus orientalis
Ipheion
Iris
Ixiolirion
Leucojum aestivum
Moraea
Muscari ambrosiacum
Muscari comosum
Muscari macrocarpum
Narcissus
Nectaroscordum siculum
Notholirion
Ornithogalum
Pleione bulbocodioides
Rhodohypoxis baurii
Romulea bulbocodium
Sandersonia aurantiaca
Scilla campanulata
Scilla non-scripta
Scilla peruviana
Sisyrinchium douglasii
Sparaxis
Trillium
Tritonia rosea
Tulipa
Uvularia

JUNE

Allium
Alstroemeria
Anemone coronaria (Mar planting)
Anthericum
Arisaema
Arum
Asarum
Asphodelus
Babiana
Begonia
Belamcanda chinensis
Brimeura amethystina
Brodiaea
Camassia quamash
Chlidanthus fragrans
Dracunculus vulgaris
Eremurus
Gladiolus Species
Habranthus tubispathus
Iris
Ixiolirion
Lilium
Moraea
Nectaroscordum siculum
Nomocharis
Notholirion
Oxalis
Paradisea liliastrum
Ranunculus asiaticus
Rhodohypoxis baurii
Roscoea
Sandersonia aurantiaca
Scilla peruviana
Sisyrinchium brachypus
Sparaxis
Sprekelia formosissima
Trillium
Tritonia rosea
Tropaeolum polyphyllum
Tulbaghia

JULY

Agapanthus
Allium
Alstroemeria
Anemone coronaria (Mar planting)
Anomatheca laxa
Anthericum
Babiana
Begonia
Belamcanda chinensis
Brodiaea
Canna
Cardiocrinum
Chlidanthus fragrans
Crocosmia
Cyclamen purpurascens
Dahlia
Dracunculus vulgaris
Eremurus
Gladiolus
Habranthus robustus
Iris
Lilium
Moraea
Notholirion
Oxalis
Ranunculus asiaticus
Rhodohypoxis baurii
Roscoea

Sandersonia aurantiaca
Sisyrinchium brachypus
Tropaeolum polyphyllum
Tropaeolum speciosum
Tropaeolum tuberosum
Tulbaghia
Watsonia
Zantedeschia aethiopica

AUGUST

Acidanthera bicolor murielae
Agapanthus
Alstroemeria
Anemone coronaria (Mar planting)
Anomatheca laxa
Begonia
Belamcanda chinensis
Canna
Cardiocrinum
Colchicum
Crinum powellii
Crocosmia
Cyclamen purpurascens
Dahlia
Dierama
Galtonia
Gladiolus
Habranthus robustus
Lilium
Moraea
Ranunculus asiaticus
Rhodohypoxis baurii
Roscoea
Sandersonia aurantiaca
Sisyrinchium brachypus
Tigridia pavonia
Tropaeolum speciosum
Tropaeolum tuberosum
Tulbaghia
Watsonia
Zantedeschia aethiopica

SEPTEMBER

Acidanthera bicolor murielae
Agapanthus
Amaryllis belladonna
Anemone coronaria (Mar planting)
Anomatheca laxa
Begonia
Canna

Colchicum
Crinum powellii
Crocosmia
Crocus
Cyclamen hederifolium
Cyclamen purpurascens
Dahlia
Dierama
Galtonia
Gladiolus
Habranthus robustus
Leucojum autumnale
Lilium
Merendera montana
Rhodohypoxis baurii
Roscoea
Schizostylis coccinea
Sisyrinchium brachypus
Sternbergia
Tigridia pavonia
Tropaeolum speciosum
Tropaeolum tuberosum
Zantedeschia aethiopica
Zephyranthes candida

OCTOBER

Amaryllis belladonna
Canna
Colchicum
Crocus
Cyclamen hederifolium
Dahlia
Dierama
Lilium
Schizostylis coccinea
Sisyrinchium brachypus
Sternbergia
Zephyranthes candida

NOVEMBER

Colchicum
Crocus
Cyclamen hederifolium
Dahlia
Schizostylis coccinea

DECEMBER

Crocus
Cyclamen coum

CHAPTER 6

BULB TROUBLES

Pests and diseases on the stems and flowers of bulbous plants are not usually a serious problem, but they can occur as with the other plants in the garden or greenhouse. The spring-flowering bulbs are the most fortunate ones as their flowering season ends before aphids, leaf-eating caterpillars etc become a nuisance in the garden. The underground parts of bulbs, however, are at risk at any time — there are numerous soil diseases and pests as well as animals searching for food.

So pests and diseases can be a problem, but you are likely to see very few of them. When things go wrong the cause is usually a cultural or environmental fault rather than a specific pest or disease.

There are two golden rules — try to prevent trouble before it starts and deal with any problem promptly as soon as it is seen. Make sure that the bulbs you plant are firm and healthy, the soil is free-draining and the guidance in the A–Z entry is followed. If something goes wrong in the garden check through the following pages for the cause. In the greenhouse there are additional pests such as red spider mite and whitefly — check in The Greenhouse Expert.

PESTS

SWIFT MOTH

These soil-living caterpillars attack Gladiolus corms, some rhizomes and all types of true bulbs. Unlike cutworms they move backwards when disturbed. Rake in a soil insecticide before planting if it is a problem — keep under control by regular hoeing

BULB APHID

Colonies of greenfly may develop on Tulip and Lily bulbs and on Crocus and Gladiolus corms where they shelter under the tunic. Young growth is severely affected when infested bulbs are planted. Chemical treatment is not necessary — rub off aphids before planting

MICE, SQUIRRELS & BIRDS

Mice and squirrels can be wintertime pests — newly-planted bulbs are dug up and eaten. The effect on formal planting schemes can be disastrous as blank spaces are the result. There is no easy answer. Traps for mice and various barriers for squirrels are sometimes recommended but the most satisfactory way of protecting the bulbs is to cover the planted area with plastic netting and peg down the sides. This is not practical, of course, if the bulb bed or border is extensive. Birds are much more selective in their choice of bulbs. The main victims are Crocus flowers, especially the yellow-flowering varieties. Control is difficult as netting is unsightly — bird repellents are not reliable

THRIPS

Thrips (thunderflies) swarm over leaves and flowers in a hot summer. The usual symptom is silvery flecking of flowers and leaves. Gladioli are particularly susceptible and the flowers may be ruined by a bad attack. Spray the plants with an insecticide as soon as trouble is seen

CUTWORM

These green, grey or brown soil-living caterpillars grow up to 2 in. (5 cm) long and can damage most bulbous plants. Roots are eaten and holes are gnawed in the bulbs. When sickly plants are removed look for and destroy any cutworms found in the soil. Rake in a soil insecticide next time as a preventative

NARCISSUS FLY

Affected Narcissus and Hyacinth bulbs are soft and rotten. If planted a few narrow leaves but no flowers are produced. The maggots are about ½ in. (1 cm) long. Control is not easy — always discard soft bulbs at lifting or planting time and hoe around the plants as the foliage dies down

STEM & BULB EELWORM

Affected bulbs of Narcissus, Tulip, Iris, Hyacinth etc are soft and rotten. Tell-tale dark rings can be seen in a cut bulb. Narcissus leaves are pale, twisted and bear small yellow swellings on the surface. Throw away all soft bulbs. Do not plant bulbous plants on affected land for 3 years

LILY BEETLE

These bright red beetles and their ½ in. (1 cm) long orange grubs should be picked off the leaves when first seen — the foliage and flowers of Lilies, Fritillarias and Convallarias can be seriously damaged by this pest. It can be controlled by spraying with an insecticide such as fenitrothion but this is rarely practical

APHID

Aphids, both greenfly and blackfly, infest many types of garden plant in warm, settled weather but they are not often a serious pest of bulbous plants. A bad attack results in distortion and weakening of young growth, and the foliage is covered with a sticky black deposit. Spray affected plants, if necessary, with a systemic insecticide

SLUG

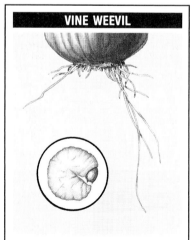

Slugs and snails can be a destructive nuisance, especially in damp soil. Young stems and leaves are eaten above ground and the bulbs below are holed. All types can be attacked — Tulips, Gladioli, Dahlias and Lilies are particularly susceptible. Slugs and snails generally hide under containers and rubbish during the day, so keep the area clean. Use slug pellets with care

EARWIG

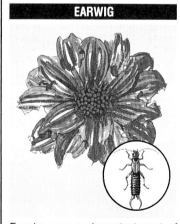

Earwigs are an important pest of Dahlias. At night the petals are eaten, making them ragged and unsightly. During the day the insects hide in the heart of the blooms or beneath dead leaves and other debris on the ground. Always clear away rubbish and shake open flowers if torn petals are seen. Spray plants and soil with an insecticide if necessary

VINE WEEVIL

This insect has become an important pest in recent years — bulbs in pots and other containers are the ones most at risk. The larvae (wrinkled white grubs) in the compost are destructive from autumn to spring. They are about ½ in. (1 cm) long and attack the underground parts of the plant. Pick out and destroy if seen — use a nematode-type insecticide

CAPSID BUG

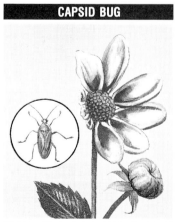

These active, sap-sucking bugs are a serious pest of Dahlias. Small ragged holes are formed in the leaves and the rest of the foliage becomes puckered and distorted. Buds may be killed — if they open the flowers are lop-sided. Chemical control involves spraying with a systemic insecticide at the first sign of attack and repeating at 14-day intervals

DISEASES

TRUE BULB ROTS

Narcissus smoulder causes the bulbs to decay — small fungal growths appear on the tunic. **Basal rot** begins at the base of Narcissus and Lily bulbs — the brown-coloured rot spreads upwards through the inner scales. **Botrytis** results in soft and rotten bulbs — **Grey bulb rot** is a dry rot with grey fluffy mould on the surface. **Tulip fire** is the most serious disease of this bulb — small fungal growths appear on the outer scales. In all cases the procedure is the same — dig up affected plants and never plant soft or mouldy bulbs

Narcissus smoulder   Basal rot   Tulip fire

CORM STORAGE ROTS

Dry rot results in many black spots appearing on the outside — these spots later merge and finally the corm decays. With **Hard rot** the spots are brown and the affected corm becomes shrivelled. The patches of **Scab** are round or oval, brown and shiny. **Core rot** is different from the other diseases — it starts at the centre of Gladiolus corms and then spreads outwards as a wet rot. In all cases the procedure is the same — burn affected corms, remove diseased ones from store and never plant soft or mouldy corms

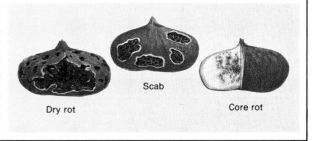

Scab

Dry rot   Core rot

TUBER ROT

Dahlia tubers can be destroyed in store by fungal rots. To prevent this happening, the tubers should be stored upside down after lifting and left to dry. Remove any remaining soil and then store in a frost-free place. Inspect tubers from time to time — cut away any diseased parts at once

TULIP FIRE

Tulip fire is a serious disease of Tulips, resulting in scorched areas on the foliage and spots on the flowers. Young shoots may be covered with a grey, velvety mould. Affected bulbs rot — see above. Do not plant diseased bulbs. Remove badly affected plants — spray the remainder with carbendazim

COLOUR BREAK

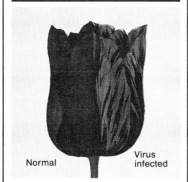

Normal   Virus infected

Petals sometimes possess streaks or patches of an abnormal colour. This colour break is caused by a virus which does not affect the health of the plant. Tulips are the most likely flowers to be affected but it can also occur with Lilies and Dahlias. The result may be attractive but it is undesirable in a single-colour bed. There is no cure

GREY MOULD (Botrytis)

Grey mould is the worst of the bulb diseases and is most likely to strike when the weather is humid. Dahlias, Tulips, Lilies and Anemones are particularly susceptible. Flowers are spotted at first but later rot and become covered with a fluffy mould. Badly diseased buds may fail to open. Pick off diseased leaves and flowers as soon as they are seen

VIRUS

The virus causing colour break does not harm the plant, but there are other viruses which are extremely damaging. Leaves are distorted and the surface is streaked or mottled, flowers are disfigured and growth is reduced or stopped. Watch for it with Lilies — remove and destroy affected plants immediately. Buy healthy bulbs — there is no cure

CULTURAL DISORDERS

NO FLOWERS

There are many reasons why a garden plant may fail to bloom. A severe attack by one of the pests or diseases on the previous pages may be the culprit, or it may be due to too much shade with light-loving varieties. An unusually late frost or growing a rather tender variety on a cold and exposed site may be the cause. Sometimes there is no obvious reason as with 'grassiness' of Narcissi when the bulb produces lots of grass-like foliage but no flowers. The most likely cause of bulbous plants failing to flower is the use of offsets which are below flowering size. To avoid trouble make sure that you buy good-sized bulbs or else you should be prepared to wait a year or two for blooms if you plant small offsets. If a clump of permanent bulbs are blind during the expected time of flowering then lift the clump and divide the bulbs at the recommended planting time

COLD DAMAGE

Hardy bulbs should not be affected by winter's frost and rain provided that the soil is free-draining. A sudden cold snap in spring, however, can damage developing leaves and shoots by destroying chlorophyll. The affected leaf, when it expands, will have lost part of its green colouration. It may be yellow-edged or almost completely white — Narcissus foliage is marked with a white band. Pick off badly affected leaves

CHLOROSIS

Yellow or unusually pale leaves are generally a symptom of a pest, disease or cultural problem rather than being a specific nutrient deficiency as with Rhododendrons, Heathers, etc. Poor drainage, eelworm and attack by underground grubs are common causes — the answer is to correct the underlying problem

INDOOR BULB DISORDERS

Yellow leaves: Draughts are the usual reason. Other possible causes are incorrect watering and keeping the bowl in a spot with insufficient light

Buds fail to open: Water is the problem here. Erratic watering can cause buds to die without opening — so can wetting the buds by watering carelessly

Erratic flowering: The most likely reason is that the bulbs were either different in size or vigour. If the bulbs were evenly matched then the probable cause was failure to turn the bowl occasionally

Long, limp leaves: A clear sign of keeping the bowl in the dark for too long. Another possibility is too little light at flowering time

Stunted growth: The usual reason is that the bowl has not been kept in the dark for the required period — the shoots should be an inch or two high before being exposed to light. Another cause is dry compost

No flowers at all: There are several possible reasons. The trouble may start at planting time by using undersized bulbs. Keeping the bowl too warm or bringing it too quickly into bright sunlight will have this effect. Dry compost will also inhibit flowering

Deformed flowers: A clear symptom of keeping the bowl too warm during the plunging period. At this first stage the temperature should be about 40°F (4°C) — do not keep the pot in a stuffy cupboard or sunny room even if unheated

Rotting flowers: Overwatering is the problem. A bowl without drainage holes kept under cool conditions can easily become waterlogged — take care. Remove excess water by carefully tipping the bowl

CHAPTER 7

GLOSSARY

A

ACID SOIL A soil which contains no free lime and has a *pH* of less than 6.5.

ACUTE Pointed.

ALKALINE SOIL A soil which has a *pH* of more than 7.3. Other terms are chalky and limy soil.

ALPINE A rather vague term used to describe low-growing rockery plants.

ALTERNATE Leaves or buds which arise first on one side of the stem and then on the other. Compare *opposite*.

ANNUAL A plant which flowers and then dies in a single season.

ANTHER The part of the flower which produces *pollen*. It is the upper section of the *stamen*.

AXIL The angle between the upper surface of the leaf stalk and the stem that carries it. An axillary bud arises in this angle.

B

BASAL LEAF A leaf which arises directly from a *bulb*, *corm* etc and not from a stem.

BASAL PLATE The disc of tissue to which the *scales* of a *bulb* are attached.

BASAL ROOTING A root system arising from the *basal plate* of a *bulb* — compare *stem rooting*.

BEARDED A petal bearing a tuft or row of long hairs.

BED A planted area designed to be viewed from all sides.

BEDDING OUT The cover of most or all of a *bed* or *border* with a temporary display.

BELL JAR A large glass jar shaped like a bell, measuring about 18 in. (45 cm) across, used to protect tender plants. Now replaced by the *cloche.*

BERRY A fleshy fruit in which the *seed* or seeds are buried.

BI-COLOURED A flower bearing two distinctly different colours.

BIENNIAL A plant which completes its life cycle in two growing seasons.

BLEEDING The abundant loss of sap from severed plant tissues.

BLENDED A flower which has one colour gradually merged with another.

BLIND Term applied to a mature bulb which produces normal foliage but fails to flower.

BLOOM Two meanings — either a fine powdery coating or a flower.

BORDER A planted area designed to be viewed from one, two or three sides but not from all angles.

BRACT A modified leaf at the base of a flower. A cluster of small bracts is a bracteole.

BUD A flower bud is the unopened bloom. A growth bud or eye is a condensed shoot.

BULB A *bulbous plant* with a storage organ composed of fleshy *scales* held together by the *basal plate*.

BULBIL A small *bulb* produced on the stem of a *bulbous plant*.

BULBLET A small *offset* produced below ground by a *bulb*.

BULBOUS PLANT A somewhat vague term for plants which produce fleshy *storage organs* at their base. Included here are *bulbs, corms, tubers* etc.

C

CALLUS The scar tissue which forms at the base of a cutting.

CALYX The ring of *sepals* which protect the unopened flower bud.

CAMPANULATE Bell-shaped.

CHANNELED LEAF A leaf with a distinct V-shaped groove along its length.

CHLOROPHYLL The green pigment found in leaves which is capable of using light-energy to transform carbon dioxide and water into carbohydrates by the process known as photosynthesis.

CHLOROSIS An abnormal yellowing or blanching of the leaves due to lack of *chlorophyll.*

CLOCHE A structure of glass or plastic sheets used to protect plants in the open. See *bell jar.*

CLONE A group of identical plants produced by *vegetative reproduction* from a single parent plant.

COMPOST Two meanings — either decomposed vegetable or animal matter for incorporation in the soil or a potting/cutting/seed sowing mixture made from *peat* ('soilless compost') or sterilized soil ('loam compost') plus other materials such as sand, chalk and fertilizers.

COMPOUND FLOWER A flower composed of *florets*.

COMPOUND LEAF A leaf composed of two or more *leaflets*.

CORDATE Heart-shaped.

CORM A *bulbous plant* which is bulb-like but is composed of solid tissue, not *scales*. It withers at the end of the season and is replaced by a new corm above.

CORMEL See *cormlet*.

CORMLET A small *offset* produced at the base of a *corm*.

COROLLA The ring of *petals* inside the *calyx* of the flower.

CORONA The tube- or cup-like centre of certain flowers, e.g Narcissus.

CROCK A piece of broken flower pot used at the bottom of a container to improve drainage.

CROSS The offspring arising from cross-pollination.

CROWN The bottom part of a *herbaceous* plant from which the roots grow downwards and the shoots arise.

CULTIVAR Short for 'cultivated variety' — it is a *variety* which originated in cultivation and not in the wild. Strictly speaking, virtually all modern varieties are cultivars, but the more familiar term 'variety' is used for them in this book.

CUP A *corona* which is broader than it is long.

D

DEAD-HEADING The removal of faded flowers.

DECIDUOUS A plant which loses its leaves at the end of the growing season.

DIBBER A blunt-ended wooden stick used to make holes in the soil for planting small bulbs.

DORMANCY The time when a bulb has stopped growing due to natural conditions such as low temperature, day length etc.

DOT PLANT A bulb grown singly or in a small group at the centre of a bedding scheme where it is large enough and bold enough to act as a focal point.

DOUBLE A flower with many more than the normal number of *petals*. When the whole of the bloom appears to be composed of petals it is called 'fully double' —a 'semi-double' flower is the half-way point between a *single* bloom and a fully double one.

E

EDGING PLANT A low-growing bulb planted at the rim of the bed or border.

EVERGREEN A plant which retains its leaves in a living state during the winter.

EYE Two meanings — a dormant growth bud or the centre of a single or semi-double bloom where the colour of this area is distinctly different from the rest of the flower.

F

FALL One of the outer petals of an Iris.

FAMILY A group of related *genera*.

FEATHERED A petal on which there are feather-like markings on a ground colour which is distinctly different.

FERTILISATION The application of *pollen* to the *stigma* to induce the production of *seed*.

FERTILIZER A material which provides appreciable quantities of one or more major plant nutrients without adding significantly to the *humus* content of the soil.

FILAMENT The supporting column of the *anther*. It is the lower part of the *stamen*.

FLAKED A flower with petals bearing broad stripes running inwards from the edges.

FLAMED A *feathered* petal which bears a distinct central band.

FLORET The individual flowers of a *compound flower* or dense flower-head.

FLOWER The reproductive organ of the plant.

FORCING The inducement of flowering before its natural time.

FORMAL BEDDING A *bed* or *border* in which the plants are arranged in a geometrical pattern.

FUNGICIDE A substance used to control infectious diseases caused by fungi — e.g mildew, damping off and rust.

G

GENUS (plural **GENERA**) A group of closely-related plants containing one or more *species*.

GERMINATION The emergence of the root and shoot from the *seed*.

GLABROUS Smooth, hairless.

GLAUCOUS Covered with a *bloom*.

GROUND COLOUR The main or background colour of a petal.

GROWING POINT The tip of a stem which is responsible for extension growth.

H

HALF HARDY A plant which will only survive outdoors when the temperature remains above freezing point. The term is not precise — some half hardy plants can be left outdoors in winter in mild regions of the country.

HARDY A plant which will withstand overwintering without protection in this country.

HERBACEOUS A plant which does not form permanent woody stems.

HIRSUTE Covered with stiff or coarse hairs.

HUMUS Term popularly (but not correctly) applied to partly decomposed organic matter in the soil. Actually humus is the jelly-like end-product which coats the soil particles.

HYBRID Plants with parents which are genetically distinct. The parent plants may be different *species*, *cultivars*, *varieties* or occasionally *genera*.

I

IMBRICATE Closely overlapping.

INFLORESCENCE The part of the plant bearing the flowers — the flower-head.

INFORMAL BEDDING A *bed* or *border* in which the plants are arranged in an irregular way without any attempt to create straight lines or geometrical patterns.

INSECTICIDE A chemical used to control insects and other small pests.

INTERNODE The part of the stem between one *node* and another.

J

JOINT See *node*.

L

LANCEOLATE Spear-shaped.

LANKY Spindly growth — a stem with a gaunt and sparse appearance.

LARVA Immature stage of some insects, popularly known as a caterpillar, maggot or grub.

LEACHING The loss of soluble chemicals from the soil due to the downward movement of water.

LEAF BLADE The flat part of the leaf.

LEAF MOULD Peat-like material composed of partially-rotted leaves.

LEAFLET One of the parts of a *compound leaf*.

LEGGY See *lanky*.

LIGHT Movable part of a cold frame.

LINEAR Very narrow with parallel sides.

M

MOUTH The open end of a bell-shaped or tubular flower.

MULCH A layer of bulky *organic* matter placed around the stems.

MULTICOLOURED A flower bearing at least three distinctly different colours.

MULTI-PURPOSE COMPOST A peat-based compost which can be used for seed sowing, potting up plants and for filling hanging baskets and other containers.

N

N : P : K Shorthand for the nitrogen : phosphate : potash content of a *fertilizer*.

NATURALISING Establishing a group of bulbs in grassland or woodland and then letting the bulbs grow and increase without interference.

NECTAR Sweet substance secreted by some flowers to attract insects.

NEUTRAL SOIL A soil which is neither acid nor alkaline — *pH* 6.5–7.3.

NODE The point on the stem at which a leaf or bud arises.

NOSE The tip of a *bulb*.

O

OFFSET Young plant which arises naturally on the parent plant and is easily separated — e.g *bulblet* and *cormlet*.

OPPOSITE Leaves or buds which are borne in pairs along the stem. Compare *alternate*.

ORGANIC A chemical or *fertilizer* which is obtained from a source which is or has been alive.

OVARY The part of the female organ of the flower which contains the *ovules*.

OVULE The part of the female organ of the flower which turns into a *seed* after *fertilisation*.

P

PEAT Plant matter in an arrested state of decay obtained from bogs or heathland.

PEDICEL The stalk of an individual flower.

PEDUNCLE The stalk of an *inflorescence*.

PERENNIAL A plant which will live in the garden or pot for years providing the conditions are suitable.

PERIANTH The outer organs of a flower — the *petals* plus the *sepals*.

PERIANTH SEGMENT See *tepal*.

PERMANENT PLANTING Establishing a group of bulbs in *bed* or *border* and then letting the bulbs grow and increase without disturbance for at least several years.

PETAL One of the divisions of the *corolla* — generally the showy part of the flower.

PETALOID Term applied to organs which assume the form of petals —e.g *stamens* in double flowers.

pH A measure of acidity and alkalinity. Below pH 6.5 is acid, above pH 7.3 is alkaline.

PISTIL The female organ of a flower, consisting of the *stigma*, *style* and *ovary*.

PLUNGING The insertion of a planted-up container into a trench in winter and then covering with *peat* or sand.

POLLEN The yellow dust produced by the *anthers*. It is the male element which fertilises the *ovule*.

POLLINATION The application of *pollen* to the *stigma* of the flower.

POT BOUND The stage when the roots of a bulbous plant growing in a pot are extensive enough to prevent active growth of the plant. *Potting on* or *repotting* is necessary.

POTTING ON The transfer of a plant from its pot into a larger one.

PROPAGATION The multiplication of plants.

PSEUDOBULB The swollen *storage organ* at the base of the stem of many Orchids.

R

RAISED BED A *bed* with its surface above ground level and enclosed by a retaining wall of stone, brick, wood etc.

REFLEXED A *petal* or *tepal* that is bent back.

REPOTTING The transfer of a bulb from its pot into one of a similar size but with fresh compost.

RHIZOME A *bulbous plant* with a *storage organ* which is a modified stem growing horizontally underground.

ROSETTE Term applied to a *whorl* of leaves arising at the base of a plant.

S

SCALES The fleshy modified leaves which make up a *bulb*.

SEED The reproductive unit of a flowering plant.

SELF-COLOURED A flower which bears a single colour throughout.

SELF-SEED The natural propagation of a plant by the *germination* of its *seeds* around it.

SEMI-DOUBLE A half-way point between a *single* bloom and a *double* one. In most cases there are two rows of petals.

SEPAL One of the divisions of the *calyx*.

SINGLE A flower with no more than the normal number of petals.

SPADIX A fleshy *spike* in which small flowers are embedded.

SPATHE A *bract* surrounding an *inflorescence*.

SPECIES Plants which are genetically similar and which breed true to type from *seed*.

SPIKE An unbranched *inflorescence* which bears stalkless flowers.

STAMEN The male organ of a flower, consisting of the *anther* and *filament*.

STANDARD One of the inner petals of an Iris.

STEM ROOTING A root system arising from the stem of a *bulb* — compare *basal rooting*.

STIGMA The part of the female organ of the flower which catches the *pollen*.

STORAGE ORGAN The basic feature of a *bulbous plant* — the thickened root, stem or miniature plant which stores nutrients and develops both roots and one or more shoots after planting.

STREAKED A flower with coloured bands along the petals.

STYLE The part of the female organ of the flower which connects the *stigma* to the *ovary*.

T

TENDRIL A modified stem or leaf which can wind around a support.

TEPAL The proper name of the 'petal' when the *petals* and *sepals* of the *perianth* are identical. A feature of many bulbs — e.g Crocus, Lily and Tulip.

TRANSPLANTING The movement of a plant from one site to another.

TRUE BULB See *bulb*.

TRUMPET A *corona* which is narrower than it is long.

TRUSS A flower-head or tightly packed *inflorescence*.

TUBER A *bulbous plant* with a *storage organ* which is a swollen underground stem. The buds are scattered over the surface.

TUBEROUS ROOT A *bulbous plant* with a *storage organ* which is a swollen root. The buds are borne at the top of the root.

TUNIC A dry and often papery covering of corms and some bulbs.

V

VARIEGATED Leaves which are spotted, blotched or edged with a colour which is different to the basic one.

VARIETY Strictly speaking, a naturally-occurring variation of a species — see *cultivar*.

VEGETATIVE REPRODUCTION Division, cuttings, grafting and layering as distinct from sexual reproduction by *seeds*.

VIRUS An organism which is too small to be seen through a microscope and which is capable of causing malformation or discoloration of a plant.

W

WHORL Leaves, petals or branches arranged in a ring.

CHAPTER 8
PLANT INDEX

A

page
ACHIMENES ERECTA 13
ACHIMENES GRANDIFLORA 13
ACHIMENES HYBRIDA 13
ACHIMENES HYBRIDA 'AMBROISE VERSCHAFFELT' 13
ACHIMENES HYBRIDA 'CAMEO TRIUMPH' 13
ACHIMENES HYBRIDA 'CATTLEYA' 13
ACHIMENES HYBRIDA 'CLOUDED YELLOW' 13
ACHIMENES HYBRIDA 'FLAMINGO' 13
ACHIMENES HYBRIDA 'MASTER INGRAM' 13
ACHIMENES HYBRIDA 'PAUL ARNOLD' 13
ACHIMENES HYBRIDA 'PEACH BLOSSOM' 13
ACHIMENES HYBRIDA 'PURPLE KING' 13
ACHIMENES HYBRIDA 'SNOW QUEEN' 13
ACHIMENES LONGIFLORA 13
ACIDANTHERA 13
ACIDANTHERA BICOLOR MURIELAE 13
ACIDANTHERA MURIELAE 13
AFRICAN LILY 14
AGAPANTHUS AFRICANUS 14
AGAPANTHUS CAMPANULATUS 14
AGAPANTHUS 'HEADBOURNE HYBRID' 14
AGAPANTHUS ORIENTALIS 14
ALBUCA 14
ALBUCA CANADENSIS 14
ALBUCA HUMILIS 14
ALBUCA NELSONII 14
ALLIUM AFLATUNENSE 15
ALLIUM ALBOPILOSUM 15
ALLIUM BEESIANUM 15
ALLIUM GIGANTEUM 15
ALLIUM KARATAVIENSE 15
ALLIUM MOLY 15
ALLIUM NARCISSIFLORUM 15
ALLIUM OSTROWSKIANUM 15
ALLIUM SICULUM 70
ALLIUM SPHAEROCEPHALON 15
ALLIUM TRIQUETRUM 15
ALSTROEMERIA 9, 16
ALSTROEMERIA AURANTIACA 16
ALSTROEMERIA AURANTIACA 'DOVER ORANGE' 16
ALSTROEMERIA AURANTIACA 'ORANGE KING' 16
ALSTROEMERIA AUREA 16
ALSTROEMERIA 'FREDERIKA' 16
ALSTROEMERIA 'LIGTU HYBRIDS' 16
AMARYLLIS 9, 16, 47
AMARYLLIS BELLADONNA 16
AMARYLLIS BELLADONNA 'HATHOR' 16
AMAZON LILY 39
AMERICAN HYBRID 58
ANEMONE APENNINA 17
ANEMONE BLANDA 17
ANEMONE CORONARIA 17
ANEMONE CORONARIA 'DE CAEN' STRAIN 17
ANEMONE CORONARIA 'ST. BRIGID' STRAIN 17
ANEMONE DE CAEN 'HOLLANDIA' 17
ANEMONE DE CAEN 'MISTER FOKKER' 17
ANEMONE NEMOROSA 17
ANEMONE ST. BRIGID 'THE ADMIRAL' 17
ANEMONE ST. BRIGID 'THE GOVERNOR' 17
ANEMONE-FLOWERED DAHLIA 35
ANOMATHECA 18
ANOMATHECA LAXA 18
ANOMATHECA LAXA 'ALBA' 18
ANOMATHECA VIRIDIS 18
ANTHERICUM LILIAGO 18
ANTHERICUM RAMOSUS 18
ARISAEMA 9, 19
ARISAEMA CANDIDISSIMUM 19
ARISAEMA GRIFFITHII 19
ARISAEMA RINGENS 19
ARISAEMA TRIPHYLLUM 19
ARISARUM 9, 19
ARISARUM PROBOSCIDEUM 19
ARISARUM VULGARE 19
ARUM 9, 20, 37
ARUM CRETICUM 20
ARUM DRACUNCULUS 37
ARUM ITALICUM 'PICTUM' 20
ARUM ITALICUM 'MARMORATUM' 20
ARUM LILY 98
ARUM MACULATUM 20
ASARUM CANADENSE 20
ASARUM CAUDATUM 20
ASARUM EUROPAEUM 20
ASARUM HARTWEGII 20
ASIATIC HYBRID 58
ASPHODEL 21
ASPHODELINE LUTEA 21
page
ASPHODELUS ALBUS 21
ASPHODELUS LUTEA 21
ASPHODELUS RAMOSUS 21
AURELIAN HYBRID 58
AUTUMN CROCUS 28
AUTUMN DAFFODIL 81
AUTUMN SNOWFLAKE 55
AUTUMN-FLOWERING CROCUS 31

B

BABIANA PLICATA 21
BABIANA RUBRO-CYANEA 21
BABIANA STRICTA 21
BABOON ROOT 21
BACKHOUSE HYBRID 58
BALL DAHLIA 35
BALL-HEADED ALLIUM 15
BASKET BEGONIA 22
BEDDING DAHLIA 34-36
BEDDING HYACINTH 49
BEGONIA BERTINII 22
BEGONIA MULTIFLORA 22
BEGONIA 'NON-STOP' 22
BEGONIA 'NON-STOP YELLOW' 22
BEGONIA PENDULA 22
BEGONIA PENDULA 'CHANSON' 22
BEGONIA PENDULA 'PICOTEE CASCADE' 22
BEGONIA PENDULA 'PINK CASCADE' 22
BEGONIA TUBERHYBRIDA 22
BEGONIA TUBERHYBRIDA 'DIANA WYNYARD' 22
BEGONIA TUBERHYBRIDA 'FAIRY LIGHT' 22
BEGONIA TUBERHYBRIDA 'GUARDSMAN' 22
BEGONIA TUBERHYBRIDA 'MASQUERADE' 22
BEGONIA TUBERHYBRIDA 'ROY HARTLEY' 22
BEGONIA TUBERHYBRIDA 'SUGAR CANDY' 22
BELAMCANDA CHINENSIS 23
BELLADONNA LILY 16
BELLEVALIA ROMANA 49
BELLINGHAM HYBRID 58
BLACKBERRY LILY 23
BLAZING STAR 83
BLETILLA HYACINTHINA 23
BLETILLA OCHRACEA 23
BLETILLA STRIATA 23
BLETILLA STRIATA 'ALBA' 23
BLOOD FLOWER 78
BLOOD LILY 46
BLUEBELL 79
BLUE-EYED GRASS 80
BORDER DAHLIA 34-36
BOTANICAL TULIP 85, 95
BRIMEURA AMETHYSTINA 24
BRIMEURA AMETHYSTINA 'ALBUS' 24
BRODIAEA 24
BRODIAEA GRANDIFLORA 24
BRODIAEA IDA-MAIA 24
BRODIAEA LAXA 24
BRODIAEA TUBERGENII 24
BRODIAEA UNIFLORA 51
BUGLE LILY 97
BULBOCODIUM VERNUM 25
BULLWOOD HYBRID 58
BUTTERCUP 75
BUTTERFLY IRIS 60
BUTTERFLY NARCISSUS 69

C

CACTUS DAHLIA 34, 35
CALLA LILY 98
CAMASSIA CUSICKII 25
CAMASSIA ESCULENTA 25
CAMASSIA LEICHTLINII 25
CAMASSIA LEICHTLINII 'ALBA' 25
CAMASSIA LEICHTLINII 'ELECTRA' 25
CAMASSIA LEICHTLINII 'SEMIPLENA' 25
CAMASSIA QUAMASH 25
CANADA LILY 58
CANDIDUM HYBRID 58
CANNA GENERALIS 26
CANNA GENERALIS 'ASSAULT' 26
CANNA GENERALIS 'DAZZLER' 26
CANNA GENERALIS 'J. B. VAN DER SCHOOT' 26
CANNA GENERALIS 'LUCIFER' 26
CANNA GENERALIS 'ORCHID' 26
CANNA GENERALIS 'PRESIDENT' 26
CANNA GENERALIS 'VERDI' 26
CANNA HYBRIDA 26
CAPE COWSLIP 55
CARDIOCRINUM 26
CARDIOCRINUM CORDATUM 26
CARDIOCRINUM GIGANTEUM 26
CHILEAN BLUE CROCUS 82
CHINCHERINCHEE 72
CHINESE GROUND ORCHID 23
CHINESE LANTERN LILY 77
CHIONODOXA GIGANTEA 27
CHIONODOXA LUCILIAE 27
CHIONODOXA LUCILIAE 'ALBA' 27
CHIONODOXA LUCILIAE 'PINK GIANT' 27
CHIONODOXA SARDENSIS 27
CHLIDANTHUS FRAGRANS 27
CLIVIA MINIATA 28
CLOTH-OF-GOLD CROCUS 31
CLOVER 72
COLCHICUM 9, 28
page
COLCHICUM AUTUMNALE 28
COLCHICUM AUTUMNALE 'ALBUM' 28
COLCHICUM AUTUMNALE 'ROSEUM PLENUM' 28
COLCHICUM 'PRINCESS ASTRID' 28
COLCHICUM SPECIOSUM 28
COLCHICUM SPECIOSUM 'ALBUM' 28
COLCHICUM 'THE GIANT' 28
COLCHICUM 'WATERLILY' 28
COLLERETTE DAHLIA 35
COMMON SNOWDROP 42
CONVALLARIA 9, 29
CONVALLARIA MAJALIS 29
CONVALLARIA MAJALIS 'FONTIN'S GIANT' 29
CONVALLARIA MAJALIS 'HARDWICK HALL' 29
CONVALLARIA MAJALIS 'PROLIFICANS' 29
CONVALLARIA MAJALIS 'ROSEA' 29
CONVALLARIA MAJALIS 'VARIEGATA' 29
CORAL LILY 58
CORN LILY 54
CORYDALIS AMBIGUA 29
CORYDALIS BRACTEATA 29
CORYDALIS CAVA 29
CORYDALIS SOLIDA 29
CORYDALIS SOLIDA 'GEORGE BAKER' 29
COTTAGE TULIP 91
CRINUM POWELLII 30
CRINUM POWELLII 'ALBUM' 30
CROCOSMIA CROCOSMIIFLORA 30
CROCOSMIA 'EMBERGLOW' 30
CROCOSMIA 'EMILY MACKENZIE' 30
CROCOSMIA 'JENNY BLOOM' 30
CROCOSMIA 'LUCIFER' 30
CROCOSMIA MASONORUM 30
CROCOSMIA 'SOLFATARE' 30
CROCUS 31
CROCUS ANCYRENSIS 31
CROCUS ANGUSTIFOLIUS 31, 32
CROCUS BIFLORUS 31
CROCUS 'BLUE PEARL' 31
CROCUS BULBOCODIUM 76
CROCUS 'CREAM BEAUTY' 31
CROCUS 'E. A. BOWLES' 31
CROCUS IMPERATI 'DE JAGER' 31
CROCUS 'JOAN OF ARC' 31, 32
CROCUS 'LADYKILLER' 31, 32
CROCUS LAEVIGATUS 31
CROCUS LONGIFLORUS 31
CROCUS 'MAMMOTH YELLOW' 31, 32
CROCUS NUDIFLORUS 31
CROCUS OCHROLEUCUS 31, 32
CROCUS 'PICKWICK' 31
CROCUS 'PRINCESS BEATRIX' 31
CROCUS 'REMEMBRANCE' 31, 32
CROCUS SATIVUS 31, 32
CROCUS SIEBERI 31
CROCUS SIEBERI 'BOWLES WHITE' 31
CROCUS SIEBERI 'TRICOLOR' 31, 32
CROCUS 'SNOWBUNTING' 31
CROCUS SPECIOSUS 31, 32
CROCUS TOMMASINIANUS 31
CROCUS 'VANGUARD' 31
CROCUS VERNUS 31
CROWN IMPERIAL 41
CUBAN LILY 79
CUCKOO PINT 20
CYCLAMEN 33
CYCLAMEN COUM 33
CYCLAMEN COUM 'ROSEUM' 33
CYCLAMEN EUROPAEUM 33
CYCLAMEN HEDERIFOLIUM 33
CYCLAMEN HEDERIFOLIUM 'MOIRA REID' 33
CYCLAMEN NEAPOLITANUM 33
CYCLAMEN PERSICUM 33
CYCLAMEN PURPURASCENS 33
CYCLAMEN REPANDUM 33
CYCLAMINEUS NARCISSUS 62, 67
CYNTHELLA HYACINTH 49-50
CYRTANTHUS PURPUREUS 96

D

DAFFODIL 62-69
DAHLIA 34-36
DAHLIA 'ANDRIES WONDER' 35
DAHLIA 'ATHALIE' 34, 35
DAHLIA 'BAMBINO' 35
DAHLIA 'BISHOP OF LLANDAFF' 35, 36
DAHLIA 'CHERIDA' 35, 36
DAHLIA 'CLAIRE DE LUNE' 35
DAHLIA COCCINEA 35
DAHLIA 'COMET' 35, 36
DAHLIA 'DAVID HOWARD' 35
DAHLIA 'DORIS DAY' 35, 36
DAHLIA 'GERRIE HOEK' 35, 36
DAHLIA 'GIRAFFE' 35
DAHLIA 'GOLDEN CROWN' 35
DAHLIA 'HOUSE OF ORANGE' 35, 36
DAHLIA 'IRISH VISIT' 35
DAHLIA 'JESCOT JULIE' 35
DAHLIA 'JOCONDO' 35
DAHLIA 'LA GIOCONDA' 35
DAHLIA 'LITTLE JOHN' 34, 35
DAHLIA 'LUCY' 35
DAHLIA MERKII 35
DAHLIA 'MOOR PLACE' 35
DAHLIA 'MURILLO' 35
DAHLIA 'NOREEN' 35
DAHLIA 'PARK PRINCESS' 35

page

DAHLIA 'RED RIDING HOOD' 35
DAHLIA 'SCARLET BEAUTY' 35
DAHLIA 'SNEEZY' 35
DAHLIA 'STOLZE VON BERLIN' 35
DAHLIA 'SYMBOL' 35, 36
DAHLIA 'VERA HIGGINS' 35
DAHLIA 'VICKY CRUTCHFIELD' 35
DAHLIA 'WILLO'S VIOLET' 35, 36
DAHLIA 'WOOTTON CUPID' 35
DAHLIA 'YELLOW HAMMER' 35, 36
DAISY-FLOWERED ANEMONE 17
DARWIN TULIP 91
DARWIN HYBRID TULIP 90
DECORATIVE DAHLIA 34, 35
DELICATE LILY 27
DICHELOSTEMMA 24
DIERAMA DRACOMONTANUM 37
DIERAMA PENDULUM 37
DIERAMA PULCHERRIMUM 37
DIERAMA PULCHERRIMUM 'ALBUM' 37
DIERAMA PULCHERRIMUM 'BLACKBIRD' 37
DIERAMA PULCHERRIMUM 'HERON' 37
DIERAMA PULCHERRIMUM 'MAJOR' 37
DIERAMA PULCHERRIMUM 'MOONLIGHT' 37
DIERAMA PULCHERRIMUM 'NIGRA' 37
DIERAMA PUMILUM 37
DIETES VEGETA 60
DOG'S-TOOTH VIOLET 39
DOUBLE EARLY TULIP 85, 88
DOUBLE LATE TULIP 94
DOUBLE NARCISSUS 66
DRACUNCULUS 9, 37
DRACUNCULUS VULGARIS 37
DRAGON ARUM 37
DUTCH HYACINTH 49-50
DUTCH IRIS 52

E

EASTER LILY 56, 58
ENDYMION NON-SCRIPTA 79
ENGLISH BLUEBELL 79
ENGLISH IRIS 52
ERANTHIS CILICICA 38
ERANTHIS HYEMALIS 38
ERANTHIS TUBERGENII 38
EREMURUS BUNGEI 38
EREMURUS HIMALAICUS 38
EREMURUS ROBUSTUS 38
EREMURUS 'RUITER' 38
EREMURUS 'SHELFORD' 38
EREMURUS STENOPHYLLUS 38
ERYTHRONIUM 39
ERYTHRONIUM AMERICANUM 39
ERYTHRONIUM DENS-CANIS 39
ERYTHRONIUM 'PAGODA' 39
ERYTHRONIUM 'WHITE BEAUTY' 39
EUCHARIS AMAZONICA 39
EUCHARIS GRANDIFLORA 39
EUCOMIS BICOLOR 40
EUCOMIS COMOSA 40
EUCOMIS PUNCTATA 40

F

FIESTA HYBRID 58
FLAME FLOWER 84
FLORIST ANEMONE 17
FLORIST CYCLAMEN 33
FLOWERING ONION 15
FOREST LILY 97
FOXTAIL LILY 38
FREESIA 40
FREESIA HYBRIDA 40
FREESIA HYBRIDA 'AURORA' 40
FREESIA HYBRIDA 'BALLERINA' 40
FREESIA HYBRIDA 'MARIE LOUISE' 40
FREESIA HYBRIDA 'OBERON' 40
FREESIA HYBRIDA 'RED LION' 40
FREESIA HYBRIDA 'ROYAL BLUE' 40
FREESIA HYBRIDA 'WINTERGOLD' 40
FRENCH BUTTERCUP 75
FRINGED TULIP 92
FRITILLARIA ACMOPETALA 41
FRITILLARIA GRAYANA 41
FRITILLARIA IMPERIALIS 41
FRITILLARIA IMPERIALIS 'AURORA' 41
FRITILLARIA IMPERIALIS 'MAXIMA LUTEA' 41
FRITILLARIA IMPERIALIS 'RUBRA' 41
FRITILLARIA MELEAGRIS 41
FRITILLARIA MELEAGRIS 'ALBA' 41
FRITILLARIA MELEAGRIS 'APHRODITE' 41
FRITILLARIA MICHAILOWSKYI 41
FRITILLARIA PERSICA 41
FRITILLARIA PLURIFLORA 41
FRITILLARY 41
FUMARIA BULBOSA 29

G

GALANTHUS 9, 42
GALANTHUS 'ATKINSII' 42
GALANTHUS ELWESII 42
GALANTHUS NIVALIS 42
GALANTHUS NIVALIS 'FLORE PLENO' 42
GALANTHUS NIVALIS 'LUTESCENS' 42
GALANTHUS NIVALIS 'OPHELIA' 42
GALANTHUS NIVALIS 'PUSEY GREEN TIP' 42
GALANTHUS NIVALIS 'VIRIDAPICIS' 42

page

GALANTHUS 'S. ARNOTT' 42
GALTONIA CANDICANS 42
GALTONIA PRINCEPS 42
GALTONIA VIRIDIFLORA 42
GARDEN TULIP 85
GIANT HIMALAYAN LILY 26
GINGER LILY 46
GLADIOLUS 'BO PEEP' 43
GLADIOLUS BYZANTINUS 43, 44
GLADIOLUS CALLIANTHUS 13
GLADIOLUS 'COLUMBINE' 43, 44
GLADIOLUS COLVILLEI 'THE BRIDE' 43, 44
GLADIOLUS 'ESSEX' 43
GLADIOLUS 'FLOWER SONG' 43, 44
GLADIOLUS 'GEORGETTE' 43
GLADIOLUS 'GREENBIRD' 43, 44
GLADIOLUS 'LEONORE' 43
GLADIOLUS 'MELODIE' 43, 44
GLADIOLUS 'PETER PEARS' 43, 44
GLADIOLUS 'ROBIN' 43
GLADIOLUS 'ROYAL DUTCH' 43
GLADIOLUS 'SPIC AND SPAN' 43
GLADIOLUS 'WHITE FRIENDSHIP' 43
GLORIOSA 9, 45
GLORIOSA LUTEA 45
GLORIOSA SUPERBA 45
GLORIOSA SUPERBA 'ROTHSCHILDIANA' 45
GLORY LILY 45
GLORY OF THE SNOW 27
GOLDEN BUNCH CROCUS 31
GOLDEN TURK'S-CAP LILY 58
GOLDEN-RAYED LILY 58
GRAPE HYACINTH 61
GUERNSEY LILY 70

H

HABRANTHUS 45
HABRANTHUS ANDERSONII 45
HABRANTHUS ROBUSTUS 45
HABRANTHUS TUBISPATHUS 45
HAEMANTHUS ALBIFLOS 46
HAEMANTHUS COCCINEUS 46
HARDY CYCLAMEN 33
HARLEQUIN FLOWER 80
HEDYCHIUM COCCINEUM 46
HEDYCHIUM CORONARIUM 46
HEDYCHIUM FLAVESCENS 46
HEDYCHIUM GARDNERIANUM 46
HENRY'S LILY 58
HERMODACTYLUS TUBEROSUS 47
HEXASTYLIS 20
HIPPEASTRUM HYBRIDA 47
HIPPEASTRUM HYBRIDA 'APPLE BLOSSOM' 47
HIPPEASTRUM HYBRIDA 'BELINDA' 47
HIPPEASTRUM HYBRIDA 'BOUQUET' 47
HIPPEASTRUM HYBRIDA 'PICOTEE' 47
HIPPEASTRUM HYBRIDA 'RED LION' 47
HIPPEASTRUM HYBRIDA 'YELLOW PIONEER' 47
HOMERIA 48
HOMERIA BREYNIANA 48
HOMERIA COLLINA 48
HOMERIA FLACCIDA 48
HOMERIA OCHROLEUCA 48
HOOP PETTICOAT 69
HOT WATER PLANT 13
HYACINTH 49-50
HYACINTHELLA 48
HYACINTHELLA ACUTILOBA 48
HYACINTHELLA LEUCOPHAEA 48
HYACINTHELLA PALLENS 48
HYACINTHOIDES HISPANICA 79
HYACINTHOIDES NON-SCRIPTA 79
HYACINTHUS 9, 49-50
HYACINTHUS CANDICANS 42
HYACINTHUS ORIENTALIS 49
HYACINTHUS ORIENTALIS ALBULUS 49
HYACINTHUS ORIENTALIS ALBULUS 'BLUE' 50
HYACINTHUS ORIENTALIS ALBULUS 'PALE BLUE' 50
HYACINTHUS ORIENTALIS ALBULUS 'PINK' 50
HYACINTHUS ORIENTALIS 'AMETHYST' 49
HYACINTHUS ORIENTALIS 'AMSTERDAM' 49
HYACINTHUS ORIENTALIS 'ANNE MARIE' 49, 50
HYACINTHUS ORIENTALIS 'BLUE MAGIC' 49
HYACINTHUS ORIENTALIS 'CARNEGIE' 49, 50
HYACINTHUS ORIENTALIS 'CITY OF HAARLEM' 49, 50
HYACINTHUS ORIENTALIS 'DELFT BLUE' 49, 50
HYACINTHUS ORIENTALIS 'JAN BOS' 49, 50
HYACINTHUS ORIENTALIS 'LADY DERBY' 49
HYACINTHUS ORIENTALIS 'L'INNOCENCE' 49
HYACINTHUS ORIENTALIS 'LORD BALFOUR' 49, 50
HYACINTHUS ORIENTALIS MULTIFLORA 49
HYACINTHUS ORIENTALIS 'OSTARA' 49
HYACINTHUS ORIENTALIS 'PINK PEARL' 49
HYACINTHUS ORIENTALIS 'VIOLET PEARL' 49
HYMENOCALLIS FESTALIS 51
HYMENOCALLIS 'SULPHUR QUEEN' 51

I

INDIAN SHOT 26
IPHEION 'ROLF FIEDLER' 51

page

IPHEION UNIFLORUM 51
IPHEION UNIFLORUM 'ALBUM' 51
IPHEION UNIFLORUM 'FROYLE MILL' 51
IPHEION UNIFLORUM 'WISLEY BLUE' 51
IRIS 9, 52-53
IRIS BUCHARICA 52
IRIS DANFORDIAE 52, 53
IRIS GRAEBERIANA 52
IRIS HISTRIOIDES 'MAJOR' 52, 53
IRIS 'IDEAL' 52
IRIS LATIFOLIA 52
IRIS 'LEMON QUEEN' 52
IRIS MAGNIFICA 52, 53
IRIS RETICULATA 52
IRIS RETICULATA 'CANTAB' 52, 53
IRIS RETICULATA 'JOYCE' 52, 53
IRIS RETICULATA 'J. S. DIJT' 52, 53
IRIS RETICULATA 'KATHARINE HODGKIN' 52, 53
IRIS RETICULATA 'PAULINE' 52
IRIS 'ROYAL YELLOW' 52
IRIS 'SYMPHONY' 52
IRIS 'WEDGWOOD' 52, 53
IRIS 'WHITE EXCELSIOR' 52, 53
ISMENE FESTALIS 51
IXIA 'ENGLISHTON' 54
IXIA 'HOGARTH' 54
IXIA LILY 54
IXIA 'MABEL' 54
IXIA MACULATA 54
IXIA 'NELSON' 54
IXIA PANICULATA 54
IXIA VIRIDIFLORA 54
IXIOLIRION LEDEBOURII 54
IXIOLIRION MONTANUM 54
IXIOLIRION PALLASII 54
IXIOLIRION TATARICUM 54

J

JACK-IN-THE-PULPIT 19
JACOBEAN LILY 81
JACOB'S ROD 21
JONQUIL 67
JONQUILLA NARCISSUS 67

K

KAFFIR LILY 28, 78

L

LACHENALIA ALOIDES 55
LACHENALIA ALOIDES 'AUREA' 55
LACHENALIA ALOIDES 'LUTEA' 55
LACHENALIA BULBIFERA 55
LACHENALIA PENDULA 55
LACHENALIA TRICOLOR 55
LAPEIROUSIA CRUENTA 18
LAPEIROUSIA LAXA 18
LARGE-CUPPED NARCISSUS 62, 65
LEOPARD LILY 23, 58
LEUCOJUM AESTIVUM 55
LEUCOJUM AESTIVUM 'GRAVETYE GIANT' 55
LEUCOJUM AUTUMNALE 55
LEUCOJUM VERNUM 55
LEUCOJUM VERNUM 'CARPATHICUM' 55
LILIUM 'AFRICAN QUEEN' 58
LILIUM AMABILE 58
LILIUM 'APOLLO' 58
LILIUM 'ARES' 58
LILIUM 'ARTEMIS' 58
LILIUM AURATUM 56, 58, 59
LILIUM 'BLACK DRAGON' 58
LILIUM 'BONFIRE' 58
LILIUM 'BRANDYWINE' 58
LILIUM BULBIFERUM 58
LILIUM CANADENSE 58
LILIUM CANDIDUM 56, 58
LILIUM 'CHERRYWOOD' 58
LILIUM 'CINNABAR' 58, 59
LILIUM 'CITRONELLA' 58
LILIUM 'CONNECTICUT YANKEE' 58
LILIUM 'CORSAGE' 58
LILIUM 'CRIMSON BEAUTY' 56, 58
LILIUM 'DALHANSONII' 56, 58
LILIUM 'DESTINY' 58
LILIUM 'EMPRESS OF CHINA' 58
LILIUM 'ENCHANTMENT' 58
LILIUM GIGANTEUM 26
LILIUM 'GOLDEN SHOWERS' 58
LILIUM 'GOLDEN SPLENDOUR' 58
LILIUM 'GREEN DRAGON' 58
LILIUM HANSONII 56, 58
LILIUM 'HARMONY' 58
LILIUM 'HEART'S DESIRE' 58
LILIUM HENRYI 56, 58
LILIUM 'IMPERIAL SILVER' 58
LILIUM 'JACQUES S DIJT' 58
LILIUM 'JOURNEY'S END' 58
LILIUM 'LIMELIGHT' 56, 58
LILIUM LONGIFLORUM 56, 58
LILIUM 'MARHAN' 58
LILIUM MARTAGON 56, 58
LILIUM 'MRS R O BACKHOUSE' 56, 58, 59
LILIUM 'ORANGE TRIUMPH' 58
LILIUM 'PAPRIKA' 58
LILIUM PARDALINUM 58
LILIUM 'PINK GLORY' 56, 58

page

LILIUM 'PINK PERFECTION' ... 58
LILIUM 'PRELUDE' ... 58
LILIUM PUMILUM ... 56, 58
LILIUM 'RED LION' ... 58
LILIUM REGALE ... 56, 58, 59
LILIUM 'SHUKSAN' ... 58, 59
LILIUM SPECIOSUM ... 56, 58
LILIUM 'STARGAZER' ... 58, 59
LILIUM 'STERLING STAR' ... 58
LILIUM 'SUNBURST' ... 58
LILIUM TESTACEUM ... 58, 59
LILIUM 'THUNDERBOLT' ... 58, 59
LILIUM TIGRINUM ... 58, 59
LILLIPUT DAHLIA ... 34-36
LILY ... 56-59
LILY OF THE VALLEY ... 29
LILY-FLOWERED TULIP ... 92

M

MADONNA LILY ... 58
MARTAGON HYBRID ... 58
MAY-FLOWERING TULIP ... 91
MEADOW SAFFRON ... 28
MERENDERA ... 60
MERENDERA MONTANA ... 60
MERENDERA SOBOLIFERA ... 60
MERENDERA TRIGYNA ... 60
MERRYBELLS ... 96
MID-CENTURY HYBRID ... 56, 58
MID-SEASON TULIP ... 89
MILLA UNIFLORA ... 51
MINIATURE HYACINTH ... 49-50
MONTBRETIA ... 30
MORAEA ARISTATA ... 60
MORAEA IRIDIOIDES ... 60
MORAEA PAVONIA ... 60
MORAEA SPATHULATA ... 60
MORAEA VILLOSA ... 60
MOUSE PLANT ... 19
MULTIFLORA HYACINTH ... 49-50
MUSCARI AMBROSIACUM ... 61
MUSCARI ARMENIACUM ... 61
MUSCARI ARMENIACUM 'BLUE SPIKE' ... 61
MUSCARI ARMENIACUM 'FANTASY CREATION' ... 61
MUSCARI ARMENIACUM 'SAFFIER' ... 61
MUSCARI AZUREUM ... 61
MUSCARI AZUREUM 'ALBUM' ... 61
MUSCARI BOTRYOIDES 'ALBUM' ... 61
MUSCARI COMOSUM 'PLUMOSUM' ... 61
MUSCARI MACROCARPUM ... 61
MUSCARI TUBERGENIANUM ... 61

N

NANKEEN LILY ... 58
NARCISSUS ... 9, 62-69
NARCISSUS 'ACTAEA' ... 68
NARCISSUS 'AFLAME' ... 65
NARCISSUS 'ANGEL' ... 65
NARCISSUS 'ANGEL'S TEARS' ... 66, 69
NARCISSUS 'APRIL LOVE' ... 64
NARCISSUS ASTURIENSIS ... 69
NARCISSUS 'BARRETT BROWNING' ... 65
NARCISSUS 'BEERSHEBA' ... 64
NARCISSUS 'BIRMA' ... 65
NARCISSUS 'BRAVOURE' ... 64
NARCISSUS BULBOCODIUM ... 62, 69
NARCISSUS CANALICULATUS ... 69
NARCISSUS 'CANTABILE' ... 68
NARCISSUS 'CARBINEER' ... 65
NARCISSUS 'CARLTON' ... 65
NARCISSUS 'CHANTERELLE' ... 69
NARCISSUS 'CHEERFULNESS' ... 66
NARCISSUS 'CHINESE SACRED LILY' ... 68
NARCISSUS 'CRAGFORD' ... 68
NARCISSUS CYCLAMINEUS ... 67, 69
NARCISSUS 'DESDEMONA' ... 65
NARCISSUS 'DOUBLE WHITE POETICUS' ... 68
NARCISSUS 'DUTCH MASTER' ... 64
NARCISSUS 'EASTER MOON' ... 65
NARCISSUS 'EDWARD BUXTON' ... 65
NARCISSUS 'EMPRESS OF IRELAND' ... 64
NARCISSUS 'FEBRUARY GOLD' ... 67
NARCISSUS 'FEBRUARY SILVER' ... 67
NARCISSUS 'FLOWER RECORD' ... 65
NARCISSUS 'FORTUNE' ... 65
NARCISSUS 'FOUNDLING' ... 67
NARCISSUS 'FRIGID' ... 65
NARCISSUS 'GARDEN PRINCESS' ... 67
NARCISSUS 'GERANIUM' ... 68
NARCISSUS 'GIGANTIC STAR' ... 65
NARCISSUS 'GOLDEN DUCAT' ... 66
NARCISSUS 'GOLDEN HARVEST' ... 64
NARCISSUS 'GRAND SOLEIL D'OR' ... 68
NARCISSUS 'ICE KING' ... 66
NARCISSUS 'ICE WINGS' ... 66
NARCISSUS 'IRENE COPELAND' ... 66
NARCISSUS 'ITZIM' ... 67
NARCISSUS 'JACK SNIPE' ... 67
NARCISSUS 'JENNY' ... 67
NARCISSUS 'JETFIRE' ... 67
NARCISSUS JONQUILLA ... 67
NARCISSUS 'KENELLIS' ... 69
NARCISSUS 'KING ALFRED' ... 64
NARCISSUS 'LAVENDER LACE' ... 67
NARCISSUS 'LEMON BEAUTY' ... 69
NARCISSUS 'LIBERTY BELLS' ... 66
NARCISSUS 'LILAC CHARM' ... 67

page

NARCISSUS 'LINTIE' ... 67
NARCISSUS 'MAGNET' ... 64
NARCISSUS 'MATADOR' ... 68
NARCISSUS 'MINNOW' ... 62, 68
NARCISSUS 'MOUNT HOOD' ... 64
NARCISSUS 'MRS R O BACKHOUSE' ... 65
NARCISSUS OBVALLARIS ... 69
NARCISSUS 'ORANGERY' ... 69
NARCISSUS 'PAPER WHITE' ... 68
NARCISSUS 'PAPILLON BLANC' ... 69
NARCISSUS 'PEEPING TOM' ... 67
NARCISSUS 'PENCREBAR' ... 66
NARCISSUS 'PHEASANT'S EYE' ... 68, 69
NARCISSUS 'PIPIT' ... 67
NARCISSUS POETICUS RECURVUS ... 69
NARCISSUS 'PROFESSOR EINSTEIN' ... 65
NARCISSUS PSEUDONARCISSUS ... 69
NARCISSUS 'REMBRANDT' ... 64
NARCISSUS 'RIP VAN WINKLE' ... 66
NARCISSUS 'ROSY SUNRISE' ... 65
NARCISSUS 'SALMON TROUT' ... 65
NARCISSUS 'SALOME' ... 65
NARCISSUS 'SEA URCHIN' ... 65
NARCISSUS 'SEMPRE AVANTI' ... 65
NARCISSUS 'SILVER CHIMES' ... 68
NARCISSUS 'SIR WINSTON CHURCHILL' ... 66
NARCISSUS 'SPELLBINDER' ... 64
NARCISSUS 'ST. KEVERNE' ... 65
NARCISSUS 'SUN DISC' ... 67
NARCISSUS 'SUZY' ... 67
NARCISSUS 'TAFFETA' ... 69
NARCISSUS TAZETTA ... 68
NARCISSUS 'TELAMONIUS PLENUS' ... 66
NARCISSUS 'TETE-A-TETE' ... 67
NARCISSUS 'TEXAS' ... 66
NARCISSUS 'THALIA' ... 66
NARCISSUS 'TOPOLINO' ... 64
NARCISSUS 'TREVITHIAN' ... 67
NARCISSUS TRIANDRUS ... 62, 66
NARCISSUS TRIANDRUS ALBUS ... 69
NARCISSUS 'UNSURPASSABLE' ... 64
NARCISSUS 'WATERPERRY' ... 67
NARCISSUS 'WHITE LION' ... 66
NARCISSUS 'WHITE MARVEL' ... 66
NARCISSUS 'W. P. MILNER' ... 64
NARCISSUS 'YELLOW SUN' ... 65
NECTAROSCORDUM DIOSCORIDIS ... 70
NECTAROSCORDUM SICULUM ... 70
NECTAROSCORDUM SICULUM 'BULGARICUS' ... 70
NERINE ... 70
NERINE BOWDENII ... 70
NERINE BOWDENII 'PINK TRIUMPH' ... 70
NERINE FLEXUOSA ... 70
NERINE SARNIENSIS ... 70
NERINE UNDULATA ... 70
NOMOCHARIS ... 71
NOMOCHARIS APERTA ... 71
NOMOCHARIS MAIREI ... 71
NOMOCHARIS PARDANTHINA ... 71
NOMOCHARIS SALUENENSIS ... 71
NOTHOLIRION ... 71
NOTHOLIRION BULBIFERUM ... 71
NOTHOLIRION HYACINTHINUM ... 71
NOTHOLIRION MACROPHYLLUM ... 71
NOTHOLIRION THOMSONIANUM ... 71

O

OLYMPIC HYBRID ... 58
ORANGE LILY ... 58
ORCHID NARCISSUS ... 69
ORIENTAL HYBRID ... 58
ORNITHOGALUM ... 9, 72
ORNITHOGALUM NUTANS ... 72
ORNITHOGALUM THYRSOIDES ... 72
ORNITHOGALUM UMBELLATUM ... 72
OXALIS ADENOPHYLLA ... 72
OXALIS CERNUA ... 72
OXALIS CHRYSANTHA ... 72
OXALIS ENNEAPHYLLA ... 72
OXALIS LACINIATA ... 72
OXALIS TETRAPHYLLA ... 72
OXFORD & CAMBRIDGE MUSCARI ... 61
OXFORD TULIP ... 90

P

PAEONY-FLOWERED BUTTERCUP ... 75
PAEONY-FLOWERED TULIP ... 94
PAINT BRUSH ... 46
PAISLEY HYBRID ... 58
PANCRATIUM MARITIMUM ... 73
PARADISEA LILIASTRUM ... 73
PARADISEA LILIASTRUM 'MAJOR' ... 73
PARDANTHUS CHINENSIS ... 23
PARROT TULIP ... 93
PEACOCK MORAEA ... 60
PERENNIAL NASTURTIUM ... 84
PERSIAN BUTTERCUP ... 75
PERUVIAN LILY ... 16
PINEAPPLE LILY ... 40
PLEIONE BULBOCODIOIDES ... 74
PLEIONE BULBOCODIOIDES 'ORIENTAL GRACE' ... 74
PLEIONE BULBOCODIOIDES 'PITON' ... 74
PLEIONE BULBOCODIOIDES 'SHANTUNG' ... 74
PLEIONE BULBOCODIOIDES 'SNOWCAP' ... 74
PLEIONE FORMOSANA ... 74
POETAZ NARCISSUS ... 68

page

POETICUS NARCISSUS ... 68
POLIANTHES TUBEROSA ... 74
POLIANTHES TUBEROSA 'THE PEARL' ... 74
POMPON DAHLIA ... 35
POPPY-FLOWERED ANEMONE ... 17
PUSCHKINIA LIBANOTICA ... 75
PUSCHKINIA SCILLOIDES ... 75
PUSCHKINIA SCILLOIDES 'ALBA' ... 75

Q

QUAMASH ... 25

R

RANUNCULUS ASIATICUS ... 75
REGAL LILY ... 58
REMBRANDT TULIP ... 85, 94
RHODOHYPOXIS BAURII ... 76
RHODOHYPOXIS BAURII 'FRED BROOME' ... 76
RHODOHYPOXIS BAURII 'PICTUS' ... 76
RHODOHYPOXIS BAURII 'RUTH' ... 76
RHODOHYPOXIS BAURII 'TETRA RED' ... 76
ROCKERY ORCHID ... 74
ROMAN HYACINTH ... 49-50
ROMULEA ... 76
ROMULEA BULBOCODIUM ... 76
ROMULEA BULBOCODIUM 'CLUSIANA' ... 76
ROSCOEA ... 77
ROSCOEA ALPINA ... 77
ROSCOEA 'BEESIANUM' ... 77
ROSCOEA CAUTLEOIDES ... 77
ROSCOEA PURPUREA ... 77
ROSCOEA PURPUREA 'PROCERA' ... 77
ROSCOEA SCILLIFOLIA ... 77

S

SAFFRON CROCUS ... 31
SANDERSONIA AURANTIACA ... 77
SCADOXUS KALBREYERI ... 78
SCADOXUS MULTIFLORUS ... 78
SCADOXUS MULTIFLORUS 'KATHARINAE' ... 78
SCARBOROUGH LILY ... 96
SCHIZOSTYLIS COCCINEA ... 78
SCHIZOSTYLIS COCCINEA 'MAJOR' ... 78
SCHIZOSTYLIS COCCINEA 'MRS HEGARTY' ... 78
SCHIZOSTYLIS COCCINEA 'NOVEMBER CHEER' ... 78
SCHIZOSTYLIS COCCINEA 'SALMON CHARM' ... 78
SCHIZOSTYLIS COCCINEA 'VISCOUNTESS BYNG' ... 78
SCILLA ... 9, 79
SCILLA BIFOLIA ... 79
SCILLA CAMPANULATA ... 79
SCILLA NON-SCRIPTA ... 79
SCILLA NUTANS ... 79
SCILLA PERUVIANA ... 79
SCILLA SIBIRICA ... 79
SCILLA SIBIRICA 'ALBA' ... 79
SCILLA SIBIRICA 'SPRING BEAUTY' ... 79
SCILLA TUBERGENIANA ... 79
SCOTCH CROCUS ... 31
SEA LILY ... 73
SEMI-CACTUS DAHLIA ... 34, 35
SHAMROCK ... 72
SIBERIAN SQUILL ... 79
SINGLE EARLY TULIP ... 85, 87
SINGLE LATE TULIP ... 91
SINGLE-FLOWERED DAHLIA ... 35
SISYRINCHIUM ... 80
SISYRINCHIUM ANGUSTIFOLIUM ... 80
SISYRINCHIUM BERMUDIANUM ... 80
SISYRINCHIUM BRACHYPUS ... 80
SISYRINCHIUM BRACHYPUS 'CALIFORNIAN SKIES' ... 80
SISYRINCHIUM DOUGLASII ... 80
SISYRINCHIUM STRIATUM ... 80
SMALL-CUPPED NARCISSUS ... 65
SNAKE'S HEAD ... 47
SNAKE'S HEAD FRITILLARY ... 41
SNOWDROP ... 42
SNOWFLAKE ... 55
SORREL ... 72
SPANISH BLUEBELL ... 79
SPANISH HYACINTH ... 24
SPANISH IRIS ... 52
SPARAXIS ELEGANS ... 80
SPARAXIS TRICOLOR ... 80
SPECIES TULIP ... 85, 95
SPIDER LILY ... 51
SPLIT-CORONA NARCISSUS ... 69
SPREKELIA FORMOSISSIMA ... 81
SPRING-FLOWERING CROCUS ... 31
SPRING FUMITORY ... 29
SPRING SAFFRON ... 25
SPRING SNOWFLAKE ... 55
SPRING SQUILL ... 79
SPRING STARFLOWER ... 51
SQUILL ... 79
ST. BERNARD'S LILY ... 18, 73
STAR OF BETHLEHEM ... 72
STERNBERGIA CLUSIANA ... 81
STERNBERGIA LUTEA ... 81
STERNBERGIA LUTEA 'ANGUSTIFOLIA' ... 81
STERNBERGIA MACRANTHA ... 81
STERNBERGIA SICULA ... 81
STRIPED SQUILL ... 75

page

SUMMER HYACINTH 42
SUMMER SNOWFLAKE 55
SWAMP LILY 30
SWORD LILY 43

T

TAZETTA NARCISSUS 62, 68, 69
TAZETTA/POETICUS HYBRID 68
TECOPHILAEA CYANOCROCUS 82
TECOPHILAEA CYANOCROCUS
   'LEICHTLINII' 82
TECOPHILAEA CYANOCROCUS
   'VIOLACEA' 82
TENBY DAFFODIL 69
TIGER FLOWER 82
TIGER LILY 58
TIGRIDIA PAVONIA 82
'TOMMY' CROCUS 31
TRIANDRUS NARCISSUS 66
TRILLIUM CUNEATUM 83
TRILLIUM ERECTUM 83
TRILLIUM GRANDIFLORUM 83
TRILLIUM GRANDIFLORUM
   'FLORE PLENO' 83
TRILLIUM LUTEUM 83
TRILLIUM RECURVATUM 83
TRILLIUM UNDULATUM 83
TRISTIGMA UNIFLORUM 51
TRITELEIA 24
TRITELEIA UNIFLORA 51
TRITONIA CROCATA 83
TRITONIA CROCATA 'ISABELLA' 83
TRITONIA CROCATA 'ROSELINE' 83
TRITONIA ROSEA 83
TRIUMPH TULIP 89
TROPAEOLUM POLYPHYLLUM 84
TROPAEOLUM SPECIOSUM 84
TROPAEOLUM TUBEROSUM 84
TROPAEOLUM TUBEROSUM 'KEN ASLET' 84
TROUT LILY 39
TRUMPET DAFFODIL 64, 69
TRUMPET HYBRID 58
TRUMPET NARCISSUS 62
TUBEROSE 74
TUBEROUS BEGONIA 22
TUFTED ALLIUM 15
TULBAGHIA NATALENSIS 84
TULBAGHIA VIOLACEA 84
TULBAGHIA VIOLACEA 'SILVER LACE' 84
TULIP 85–95
TULIPA 9, 85–95
TULIPA 'ABU HASSAN' 89
TULIPA 'AFRICAN QUEEN' 89
TULIPA 'AJAX' 89
TULIPA 'ALADDIN' 92
TULIPA 'ALLEGRETTO' 94
TULIPA 'ANGELIQUE' 94
TULIPA 'APELDOORN' 90
TULIPA 'APELDOORN ELITE' 90
TULIPA 'APRICOT BEAUTY' 87
TULIPA 'ARABIAN MYSTERY' 89
TULIPA 'ARTIST' 93
TULIPA 'ATTILA' 89
TULIPA 'AUCHERIANA' 95
TULIPA 'BALLADE' 92
TULIPA 'BALLERINA' 92
TULIPA BATALINII 'BRIGHT GEM' 95
TULIPA 'BEAUTY OF APELDOORN' 90
TULIPA 'BELLFLOWER' 92
TULIPA 'BELLONA' 87
TULIPA BIFLORA 95
TULIPA 'BIRD OF PARADISE' 93
TULIPA 'BLACK PARROT' 93
TULIPA 'BLEU AIMABLE' 91
TULIPA 'BLUE HERON' 92
TULIPA 'BLUE PARROT' 93
TULIPA 'BONANZA' 94
TULIPA 'BRILLIANT STAR' 87
TULIPA 'BURGUNDY LACE' 92
TULIPA 'CANDELA' 95
TULIPA 'CAPE COD' 95

page

TULIPA 'CARLTON' 88
TULIPA 'CARNAVAL DE NICE' 94
TULIPA 'CASSINI' 89
TULIPA 'CHARLES' 87
TULIPA 'CLARA BUTT' 91
TULIPA CLUSIANA 95
TULIPA 'CORDELL HULL' 94
TULIPA 'COULEUR CARDINAL' 87
TULIPA 'DIANA' 87
TULIPA 'DON QUIXOTE' 89
TULIPA 'DR. PLESMAN' 87
TULIPA 'DREAMING MAID' 89
TULIPA 'ELECTRA' 88
TULIPA 'ELEGANT LADY' 92
TULIPA 'ELIZABETH ARDEN' 90
TULIPA 'ENGELENBURCHT' 88
TULIPA 'ESTELLA RIJNVELD' 93
TULIPA 'ESTHER' 91
TULIPA 'FANTASY' 93
TULIPA 'FIDELIO' 89
TULIPA 'FLAIR' 87
TULIPA 'FLAMING PARROT' 93
TULIPA FOSTERIANA 95
TULIPA 'FRINGED BEAUTY' 88
TULIPA 'GARDEN PARTY' 89
TULIPA 'GENERAL DE WET' 87
TULIPA 'GEORGETTE' 91
TULIPA 'GIUSEPPE VERDI' 95
TULIPA 'GOLDEN APELDOORN' 90
TULIPA 'GOLDEN HARVEST' 91
TULIPA 'GOLDEN MELODY' 89
TULIPA 'GOLDEN OXFORD' 90
TULIPA 'GORDON COOPER' 90
TULIPA 'GREENLAND' 93
TULIPA GREIGII 85, 95
TULIPA 'GREUZE' 91
TULIPA 'GUDOSHNIK' 90
TULIPA 'HALCRO' 91
TULIPA 'HIT PARADE' 95
TULIPA 'HUMMINGBIRD' 93
TULIPA 'INSULINDE' 94
TULIPA 'JOHANN STRAUSS' 95
TULIPA 'KAREL DOORMAN' 93
TULIPA KAUFMANNIANA 85, 95
TULIPA 'KEES NELIS' 89
TULIPA 'KEIZERSKROON' 87
TULIPA 'LEEN VAN DER MARK' 89
TULIPA 'LOS ANGELES' 89
TULIPA 'MADAME LEFEBER' 95
TULIPA 'MAJA' 92
TULIPA 'MARIETTE' 92
TULIPA 'MARILYN' 92
TULIPA 'MAUREEN' 91
TULIPA 'MAYTIME' 92
TULIPA 'MONTE CARLO' 88
TULIPA 'MOUNT TACOMA' 94
TULIPA 'NEW DESIGN' 89
TULIPA 'NORANDA' 92
TULIPA 'ORANGE BOUQUET' 91
TULIPA 'ORANGE EMPEROR' 95
TULIPA 'ORANGE NASSAU' 88
TULIPA 'ORANGE TRIUMPH' 94
TULIPA 'ORATORIO' 95
TULIPA 'OXFORD' 90
TULIPA 'PAUL RICHTER' 89
TULIPA 'PEACH BLOSSOM' 88
TULIPA 'PEERLESS PINK' 89
TULIPA 'PLAISIR' 95
TULIPA 'PRAESTANS' 95
TULIPA 'PRINCEPS' 95
TULIPA 'PRINCESS IRENE' 87
TULIPA 'PRINCESS MARGARET ROSE' 91
TULIPA PULCHELLA 'HUMILIS' 95
TULIPA PULCHELLA 'VIOLACEA' 95
TULIPA 'QUEEN OF SHEBA' 92
TULIPA 'QUEEN OF THE NIGHT' 91
TULIPA 'RED EMPEROR' 95
TULIPA 'RED RIDING HOOD' 95
TULIPA 'RED SHINE' 92
TULIPA 'SAN MARINO' 94
TULIPA 'SCARLET CARDINAL' 88
TULIPA 'SHAKESPEARE' 95
TULIPA 'SHIRLEY' 91

page

TULIPA 'SNOW QUEEN' 88
TULIPA 'SNOWSTORM' 88
TULIPA 'SPRING GREEN' 93
TULIPA 'STOCKHOLM' 88
TULIPA 'STRESA' 95
TULIPA 'STRIPED APELDOORN' 90
TULIPA 'SWEET HARMONY' 91
TULIPA TARDA 85, 95
TULIPA 'TEXAS FLAME' 93
TULIPA 'TEXAS GOLD' 93
TULIPA 'TRINKET' 95
TULIPA TURKESTANICA 95
TULIPA 'WEST POINT' 85, 92
TULIPA 'WHITE PARROT' 93
TULIPA 'WHITE TRIUMPHATOR' 92
TULIPA 'WHITE VIRGIN' 89
TULIPA 'WILLEMSOORD' 88
TULIPA 'WIROSA' 94
TULIPA 'YELLOW DOVER' 90
TULIPA 'ZAMPA' 95
TULIPA 'ZOMERSCHOON' 91
TURBAN BUTTERCUP 75
TURK'S-CAP LILY 58

U

UVULARIA GRANDIFLORA 96
UVULARIA PERFOLIATA 96

V

VALLOTA SPECIOSA 96
VALLOTA SPECIOSA 'PINK DIAMOND' 96
VELTHEIMIA BRACTEATA 97
VELTHEIMIA CAPENSIS 97
VIRIDIFLORA TULIP 93

W

WAKE ROBIN 83
WAND FLOWER 37
WATER-LILY DAHLIA 35
WATER-LILY TULIP 95
WATSONIA BEATRICIS 97
WATSONIA PILLANSII 97
WATSONIA PYRAMIDATA 97
WATSONIA ROSEA 97
WHITE ARUM LILY 98
WHITE ASPHODEL 21
WIDOW IRIS 47
WILD DAFFODIL 69
WILD GARLIC 84
WILD GINGER 20
WILD HYACINTH 79
WILD NARCISSUS 69
WINDFLOWER 17
WINTER ACONITE 38
WOOD ANEMONE 17
WOOD LILY 83
WOOD SORREL 72
WREATH NASTURTIUM 84

Y

YELLOW ASPHODEL 21

Z

ZANTEDESCHIA AETHIOPICA 98
ZANTEDESCHIA AETHIOPICA
   'CROWBOROUGH' 98
ZANTEDESCHIA ELLIOTTIANA 98
ZANTEDESCHIA REHMANNII 98
ZEPHYR LILY 98
ZEPHYRANTHES CANDIDA 98
ZEPHYRANTHES CITRINA 98
ZEPHYRANTHES FLAVISSIMA 98
ZEPHYRANTHES GRANDIFLORA 98
ZEPHYRANTHES ROSEA 98

Acknowledgements

The author wishes to acknowledge the painstaking work of Gill Jackson, Paul Norris, Linda Fensom and Angelina Gibbs. Grateful acknowledgement is also made for the help or photographs received from Pat Brindley, Jacques Amand Ltd, Mary Evans Picture Library, Nigel Francis/The Garden Picture Library, Steven Wooster/The Garden Picture Library, Christel Rosenfeld/The Garden Picture Library, Chris Burrows/The Garden Picture Library, Brian Carter/The Garden Picture Library, David Russell/The Garden Picture Library, Robert Harding Picture Library, Joan Hessayon, Mirror Syndication International, Lady Skelmersdale/Broadleigh Gardens, Harry Smith Horticultural Photographic Collection, Suttons Seeds Ltd and Unwins Seeds Ltd.

John Dye provided both artistry and design work.